A.W. & W.C. Pollard;
in acknowledgement of many
years' kindness,

James Bodrul.

7 Jно. 1896-

THE

QUAKER POETS

OF

GREAT BRITAIN AND IRELAND.

BY

EVELYN NOBLE ARMITAGE,

AUTHOR OF "A DREAM OF THE GIRONDE," "THE PORT IN MAY,"
"THE MESSAGE OF QUAKERISM," ETC., ETC.

LONDON: 5, FARRINGDON AVENUE.
WILLIAM ANDREWS & CO.
—
1896.

TO

Dr. THOMAS HODGKIN.

Not as the distinguished Historian, Critic, and
Scholar, but as the Poet in whose verse I have
found the nearest approach to my ideal of
Quaker Poetry, I dedicate this Book.

EVELYN NOBLE ARMITAGE.

PREFACE.

I DESIRE to express my indebtedness in preparing this volume to Joseph Smith's "Catalogue of Friends' Books and Appendix," to "Nodal's Bibliography of Ackworth," to William Andrews' "North Country Poets" and "Modern Yorkshire Poets," to James Hurnard's and John Harris's Autobiographies, and to many other books and pamphlets too numerous to mention by name. I also wish to express my grateful thanks to all those Friends who have so kindly and generously supplied me with biographical details and poems, and who have spared neither time nor trouble in their efforts to help and advise me.

The great number of good verse-writers in the Society has rendered the task of selection a difficult one, and want of space alone has prevented my including such names as the brothers Wiffen, Mary Sewell, Thomas Letchworth, Paul Moon James, Sarah Ellis, and many others which will at once suggest themselves to the reader.

I have taken every possible precaution with regard to copyright, having in all cases where practicable consulted either the poets, or their publishers, or representatives, before reproducing poems or other matter. Should I, however, have inadvertently infringed any rights, I beg to apologise for the error.

EVELYN NOBLE ARMITAGE.

CONTENTS.

CONTENTS.

QUAKER POETS OF GREAT BRITAIN AND IRELAND.

———►•◄———

BRIEF SKETCH OF THE RISE OF THE SOCIETY OF FRIENDS, AND CHARACTERISTICS OF ITS POETRY.

JAMES ROUTLEDGE in his interesting work, "The Two Counties in their relation to general History," says "that the birth of Quakerism is one of the landmark events in English History, and George Fox one of the master builders of English freedom and nationality, few persons will now be found to gainsay. . . . Never since the days of the early Christians had men and women been so cruelly aspersed. Suffering as great, and even greater, (or at least on a larger scale), there had before been, for the expression of religious opinions; but I do not know any case in the history of bygone times in which men and women, acting on a faith of benevolence and mercy, were at once so basely ill-treated, and so persistently calumniated, both in England and America, and by professed saints as well as by acknowledged sinners. The whippings and torture of pure and gentle women were less hard to bear than the falsehood which pursued those brave women to the grave, and which they knew would follow them, and stigmatise their names long after the grave was closed upon them."

Anyone who has read George Fox's *Journal*, or Sewel's *History of the People called Quakers*, or any of the autobio-

1

graphical memoirs of the early Friends, will recognise the truth of these statements.   But we must remember that George Fox preached to the people of his time an absolutely new religion, the churches had grown into the habit of teaching the spiritual, truths of God as purely material facts : George Fox roughly drew aside the deluding material veil, and showed the spiritual reality ; thus, as of old, taking away the rich livings of those who sold images of the God, and rousing the image makers and image sellers in all the sects against his teaching.

He found a large number of earnest folk indeed, dissatisfied with what Herbert Spencer calls "the current mythology of the day," full of repressed discontent, yearning, and enthusiasm, and amongst these his message spread like flame in dry grass. To these he pointed out the Eternal Light, which had burned on unseen and undreamed of in their souls, and had wakened their sleeping spirits, and set their empty hands blindly groping, and they passed on the blessed tidings to others, until the fire of God crept, sometimes slowly, choked back by men's passions and interests, sometimes by leaps and bounds, over the length and breadth of England.

George Fox* was born in 1624 at Drayton, in Leicestershire. His father was a weaver, and called by his neighbours "Righteous Christer" (his name was Christopher) his mother was Mary Lago, "of the stock of the martyrs."   George Fox was a grave and thoughtful child, noticing all things around him with those large, clear eyes we see in his portraits, and deciding in his child's heart that he would do differently when he became a man, and not give himself to the light and wanton ways of many people he saw around his home.   As he grew up, many of the family's friends advised that he should be made a priest, but he was finally put to learn shoe-making, with a man who dealt also in wool and cattle.

At the age of nineteen, he tells us very quaintly how he

* Fox's Journal.

suddenly came to the parting of the ways, when at a Fair, his cousin and a friend, both religious "professors," as they were called at that time, tried to induce the serious lad to drink too much ale. Taking a groat from his pocket, he laid it on the table, and left them ; but that night he could not sleep ; the spirit of God was calling to him again, as it had called to him since childhood, at certain times and places, warning him to be pure, to be honest, to be true inwardly as well as outwardly ; now it seemed to bid him forsake all, and be a stranger for the love of truth. The youth had not then learned that the commands of God are spiritual laws, and for the spirit ; and that however loathsome a dungeon, however uncongenial a company surrounds the body, the soul may be free, and in the presence of its Father. He therefore took the command literally, and left his parents and friends, wandering about from place to place in great trouble of mind, seeking light from priest after priest, and professor after professor, in vain.

After awhile, he went back to his people in Leicestershire, but we may understand *how* unsympathetic they were, from their advice to him to "get married," or to "join the auxiliary band among the soldiers." One priest to whom he tried to open his troubled soul, advised him to "take tobacco and sing psalms."

After these fruitless attempts to find help and consolation from his relations and teachers, the youth wandered away by himself into the fields, often remaining out all night, sleeping in hollow trees, and having no companion but the Bible. Gradually, the light came to him, and he grew to recognise the spirituality of the Gospel, and although many temptations and doubts still assailed him, and he was often cast into darkness for a time, yet he never again lost the faith that Christ, and Christ only, could speak to his and every man's condition, and that human learning and a humanly-appointed priesthood had nothing in common with the truths of God, which must be directly revealed from the Father of Spirits to the child-spirit in men and women.

Having discovered this great truth, he began to preach to others, and gradually drew around him a company of earnest and devoted men and women, ready to lay down their lives rather than yield to what they believed was treason against God.

The fundamental doctrines of Quakerism which he preached were those of the Inner Light and Immediate Revelation. The Light of God made manifest in Christ was, he taught, set as a seed in every soul, and if followed and watched in the quiet of a pure and peaceful life, would lead each one into communion with God the Spirit, who is also the Father of all spirits, and who would thus immediately (not mediately through church, sacrament, or priest) unite Himself with His obedient child, and lead that child into the knowledge of all truth. From these fundamentals sprang all the peculiar tenets which have distinguished the Society of Friends. The perfect equality of men and women, which, however much of a truism to-day, was a startling doctrine when George Fox preached it ; the anointing of men and women to preach, by Christ himself, with no reference to theological training, or human appointment ; the stern renunciation of all war, fighting, and oath-taking, and the readiness to go to prison or death rather than bear arms, because they believed these things contrary to God's will ; the severe simplicity of dress, language, and manners, because they would be perfectly truthful and pure ; the refusal to pay tithes or church-rates, or to keep holy days and festivals —all these things sprang from their belief in the Inner Light, and the capacity of the soul to receive messages direct from God, if kept perfectly pure and quiet waiting for His Inspiration to enter. The Quaker attitude towards the Scriptures is clearly shown in Margaret Fell's account of the first sermon she heard George Fox preach, when he said :—" The Scriptures were the prophets' words, and Christ's and the apostles' words, and what, as they spoke, they enjoyed and possessed, and had it from the Lord : . . .   then what had any to do with the Scriptures, but as they came to the spirit that gave them forth. You will say, Christ saith this, and the apostles say this ; but what canst thou say?   Art thou a child of light, and hast walked in the light, and what thou speakest, is it inwardly from God ?"

From this view of the Bible and Inspiration, it follows that the Friends never persecuted for religious belief, and they are thus an honourable exception to nearly all sects and saints. They believed so firmly in the absolute necessity of truth in thought, word, and action, that they dared not judge another's spirit, to whom perchance had been revealed a different phase of truth to that their own mind could receive.   It also follows from this view that Friends have no fear of what science, or art, or criticism, or any possible discovery or revelation, may make known.   God reveals Himself through every avenue of nature and life, and although different manifestations may, through man's imperfect sight, *appear* to clash, it is only an *appearance;* truth is God, and cannot be contradictory. Therefore the true Friend, he who has realised, as George Fox realised, the spiritual behind the material, has no fear that the spiritual can be injured or disproved ; he knows that as no dissection of the human body can do away with that mysterious something, whether called soul, or spirit, or life, or merely the effect of physical causes : so no probing of our material surroundings can do away with the Deity, call it God, or Will, or merely Force.   Therefore he can follow Science to its most daring conclusions, yield to art its fairest, wildest dreams, let criticism dissect the flower or the butterfly, and explain all it can, and yet recognise behind all these the God, who, unseen, guides them and inspires them all !

William Penn, Robert Barclay, Thomas Ellwood, and innumerable others of equal learning, probity, and talent,

joined the new prophet, and at one time, during the half
century after George Fox's death, the Society of Friends
numbered such a large proportion of the population that his
dream of the conversion of the whole world to the knowledge
of, and guidance by, the Inner Light in each spirit, seemed
likely to be realised.   Then the tide turned ; the breadth of
view, the wise tolerance, the universal loving idea of brotherhood, and the ardent enthusiasm of its founders, seem for awhile
to have forsaken the Society of Friends, and they, too, lit their
candles and retired into their cellars of orthodoxy and formalism.
Quakerism seemed likely to die out like an exhausted torch ;
but, happily for the world, there is now springing up a new life,
a new hope, within our borders, and the Society has begun to
grow once again in numbers, and, what is of more importance,
in spiritual energy and spiritual faith.   Always occupying an
honourable place among philanthropists, Friends are now
taking the lead in many political questions, and the leaven
wherewith they have been quietly leavening the world is shown
by the tone of opinion on such subjects as war, slavery, opium,
drink, social morality and purity, and all the other burning
questions, not only of this day, but of all days.   The various
editions of the Friends' "Book of Discipline" form probably
the noblest rule of life and conduct ever formulated : on the
highest interests of the spirit, as the smallest details of the body,
this wonderful book suggests right conduct and conversation ;
and all in the tolerant, practical, unsectarian fashion, which is
so strong and noble a characteristic of Quaker teaching.

Having thus briefly glanced at the rise and growth of the
Society of Friends, and seen how beautiful and spiritual were
its doctrines and practice, it is a little disappointing not to
find that, living in such rare ether, the voices of its singers are
no sweeter than others, and the songs they sing, though with
strong characteristics, yet lack that sublimity, that breath of
God, which we should certainly expect to find in them.

Examples of fine poetry, of noble thought, beautiful diction, and divine power, will be found in the following pages, but they are fugitive and scattered ; the stray sunbeams prisoned in a darkened chamber, not the full radiance of a summer noon on the mountain.

The reasons for this are not far to seek, I think, and the chief cause is undoubtedly the imperfection of the human medium : every poet, every artist, every musician, knows well how different is his realised work from his unrealised dream, from his ideal poem, picture, or sonata, and the higher we climb spiritually the more difficult becomes the reproduction in concrete form of our experience, our vision, our revelation. Who could express in cold language the glory and glow of that vision of the Light Within, which comes so vividly yet so inexpressibly to the soul that waits and longs and listens until the darkness parts like a storm-cloud, and the gleam of the guiding-flame shines forth ? What pen could write, what voice could utter, the rapture that floods the patient spirit which, having thrown open all the doors and windows of its being and cleansed each dark corner and niche, waits, pure as the symbolical lily of the vale, and after awhile the King of Glory comes in, the God communes, spirit to spirit, with his worshipping child, and neither heaven nor earth nor hell, nor things present nor things to come, are anywhere, but God is all and Love is everything. . . . Is it possible when the Divine Visitant has passed, and the spirit thrilled to blissful silence, lies low in the Light once more, that it can rise up and indite a poem ?

There is another cause also, and that is the instinctive shrinking of Friends from definitions, from formulating any creed or doctrine : they recognise the great truth that in the defining or formulating a belief, the belief itself is lost, and only its dead body remains. Therefore the early friends *lived* their poetry, and only occasionally wrote it down, and then their unaccustomed exercise made them awkward, and, striving after truth, they missed beauty, and so, as far as poetry went, missed truth too.   Quaint and interesting as it is, the early Quakers' verse is *not* poetry ; but Friends now are *writing* poetry, as well as, I trust, living it, and have discovered that a suggestion, a glimmer, an all-pervading yet invisible spirit, which gives their verse a peculiar and sweet difference, is all they can at present hope to win from words and letters.   But evolution is a universal law, and as spirit and intellect brighten and broaden, symbols for their expression will amplify and enlarge : the Quaker poetry of the future will, I venture to prophesy, be no longer a disappointment and a surprise ; but will be a mirror in which the Light is reflected, a channel for the expression of divine communion, and a golden chain between the angels who sing continually and the men and women whose trembling lips are being touched with the living fire, which will give power of utterance and breath of Inspiration.

Even as it is, Quaker poetry has a subtle charm in its perfect peace and acquiescence with the will of God.   Whittier has touched on the faith of Quakerism with beautiful tenderness and truth, and also with real poetical power, and many of our English and Irish poets included in this volume have done the same in a lesser degree ; but they seem to have recognised that the purely human, with occasional gleams of the Divine, is the fittest subject-matter for poetry, and inasmuch as they have done this, the peculiar aroma of Quakerism has been weakened. The aim of a Quaker poet in the future will be to show the influence of the " Christ in us," of the divine manifesting itself in the human, and the developments that follow this manifestation.   There will no longer be any timidity of expression, but the whole web of many-coloured life will be laid before us with Shakespere's grasp of character and knowledge of motive, but with a clearer judgment and larger vision than even he possessed.   The characteristics of Quaker poetry in the past have been a fear to tread in holy places, a determination *not* to tread, or even look in passing, at evil ones, and a consequently limited view of the world and human passion, whether for good or evil ; a too great restraint, in fact, because of a mistaken feeling of reverence ; but the essentially Quaker doctrine of the Light that lighteth every man would, had it been fully realised, have prevented this.   If the light is there, present, even though invisible, in every soul, why need one fear to drag every feeling, thought, and action of that soul forth, and shed the light upon them ?   An undeveloped germ of the divine lies buried in every spirit, to be developed, if not in this life, then in some following existence : being a portion of God it can never be destroyed, and if God is not afraid to dwell in the distorted and loathsome prison-house of a sinful human soul, why should brother souls be afraid to look and show forth ?

The poet should also be a prophet, and should sing to each and all, " Arise, shine, for thy light has come !" He should bring his beautiful dreams before the people in such wise that they recognise their truth, and so will strive to realise them in their everyday life.   He should show the Light falling on the dark places of the earth and purifying them. All this and much more the future Quaker poet will do, and be; and perhaps he may even now be walking amongst us, seeing what we see, but how differently ; hearing what we hear, but with what added overtones, and writing that " Divine Comedy," and " Paradise Regained " of the future, which shall be the prelude and herald-song of the manifestation of the Sons of God.

JESSIE ADAMS.

THIS talented young writer was born at Ipswich, in 1863, and educated at private schools, partly there, and partly at York, whither her family removed in 1878. In 1889 her father settled with his family near London, first at Tottenham, afterwards at Twickenham, where they still reside.

In 1892, Jessie Adams published (Digby Long & Co.), a clever social satire, called "A good little Book for grown up Boys and Girls," by Squire Tom, Jun. This little volume was received with much appreciative praise, and I hope the writer will give us some more glimpses of what is seen and noted by those innocent, but extremely clear-sighted, child-eyes of Squire Tom, Jun. She has also written much charming verse of a more serious character.

A NEW "PSALM OF A WANDERER."

LIVE they who deem it is unblest to wander,
    And mark my homeless lot with kindly sigh?
With pity I the worldling's portion ponder,
    Whom Fate, however lavish, must deny
The bliss of such a vagrant soul as I.

Who, for *my* portion, take the woods and valleys,
    The fresh, sweet pastures and the pleasant shade,
The countless buds in Spring's celestial chalice,
    The midnight skies with diamond stars inlaid,
The golden harvest-field and leafy glade.

·　　·　　·　　·　　·

JESSIE ADAMS.

In unsubstantial dreams man seeks his pleasure,
   Then mourns the broken idol of his thought;
I ask my Maker but for light and leisure,
   And a pure heart with noble reverence fraught,
The charms of this sweet glowing earth to court.

And every simple joy in mercy given,
   That cheers my wandering youth and makes it blest,
May it accord with this sweet earth and heaven,
   As beautiful and holy as the rest,
So runs my dream, and these my hopes confessed.

FROM "A GOOD LITTLE BOOK FOR THE GROWN-UP BOYS AND GIRLS."

When Jack and Willie shout and stamp,
   Aunt calls them "Naughty Boys;"
But Captain Splinter always makes
   A most tremendous noise.

He laughed so loud, he talked so fast,
   His voice went through my head,
But Mabel laughed, and clapped her hands,
   At every word he said.

If any fun is going on,
   The Captain will be in it,
But no one seems to box his ears
   And say, "Be still this minute."

    .   .   .   .   .   .

I don't know how it is that we
   Can never make a noise,

And laugh and play together gay,
  Like grown up girls and boys.

The Captain's very well, but we
  Can't quite make out his ways,
And was he kind to do the things,
  He did in battle days.

For Dr. Dryer told us once
  That I must never fight,
But when a boy pulled my left ear,
  To turn to him the right.

But Captain Splinter told me how
  He fought against the Blacks,
They stood like nine-pins in a row,
  He sent them on their backs.

He galloped on them afterwards,
  And mashed their bodies flat,
Did no one say, " My little boy,
  It's naughty to do that ? "

    .   .   .   .   .   .

Why is it things are different
  For little boys and girls ;
It isn't as it ought to be
  (That's my idea and Pearl's).

Us children always have, you know,
  To say our prayers at night,
But Mabel says, when she's so tired,
  That she forgets them quite.

    .   .   .   .   .   .

The holidays big people get.
  One every day, I think,

They must forget their tables soon,
   I'd say as soon as wink.

But no one ever dodges them,
   Or asks them nine times eight,
Or makes them write their old mistakes
   Ten times upon a slate.

GULIELMA A. WHEELER BAKER.

THIS gifted woman was born at Edgbaston, Birmingham, in 1831, and after an early education under the wise and tender care of Rachel Barnes, of Waterford, went to Ackworth, and finally to F. Dymond's school at Berkhampstead.

In 1859, she married Morris Baker, of Birmingham, and died in 1886.

Her poems, which were collected and printed for private circulation after her death, by her husband, under the title of "The Consecration of the Temple," are many of them very beautiful, and all of them are full of that tender thoughtfulness and bright culture for which she seems to have been so remarkable.

CONSECRATION OF THE TEMPLE.

1 Kings viii. ; 2 Chron. vi.

THE King bowed low on his brazen throne
Where bright on Moriah's fair summit shone,
In the dazzling light of an eastern sun,
The glorious House of the Holy One ;
And the countless myriads breathless knelt,
Around the cloud where Jehovah dwelt,
  While ascended the monarch's prayer :—

O Lord, God of Israel, who reignest above,
Peerless in justice and perfect in love,
God of my fathers, who walked in Thy ways,
Look on the house I have built for Thy praise ;
And when prayer from this temple is borne toward the sky,

Then hear Thou from Heaven, Thy dwelling-place high,
    And hearing, oh Father, forgive !

If man, to whom evil and weakness belong,
His friend or his neighbour shall wilfully wrong,
Yet repent of his sin toward his brother and Thee,
And hoping for grace to Thy footstool shall flee,
If his prayer from this temple is borne toward the sky,
Then hear Thou from Heaven, Thy dwelling-place high,
    And hearing, oh Father, forgive !

If Israel (whose fountain of power Thou art)
Her dependence forget in the pride of her heart :
And fighting should fall 'neath the enemy's sword ;
Yet humbly repentant should return to her Lord,
If her prayer from this temple be borne toward the sky,
Then hear Thou from Heaven, Thy dwelling-place high,
    And hearing, oh Father, forgive !

If Thy people be chastened with dearth in their land,
Or pestilence spreadeth his withering hand,
Whatever the sickness or sorrow may be,
If they turn from their sin and seek pardon of Thee,
And their prayer from this temple be borne toward the sky,
Then hear Thou from Heaven, Thy dwelling-place high,
    And hearing, oh Father, forgive !

If we sin (and Thou knowest we are but as dust),
And kindle Thine anger eternally just,
The Jew or the Stranger, the bond or the free,
Who e'er may seek blessing and pardon of Thee,
If their prayer from this temple be borne toward the sky,
Then hear Thou from Heaven, Thy dwelling-place high,
    And hearing, oh Father, forgive !

And now, oh Thou God of Salvation, appear!
With the beautiful Ark of Thy Covenant here;
Oh! hallow this temple and make it Thy rest,
Let its priests in the robe of Thy glory be drest,
Let the saints Thou hast saved in Thy fathomless love
Behold Thee descending in light from above,
   And shout—That their joy is in Thee.

So Solomon spoke, and his prayer being ended,
On his offering fire from Heaven descended,
And loud through the temple high glorying rang,
While the people in one mighty utterance sang—
"Oh praise ye Jehovah! eternally praise,
For good are His purposes, great are His ways,
   And His mercy abideth for aye."

Lord! Thou hast seen how that temple decayed,
Not a stone may now trace where Thine altars were laid;
The glories of Moses are faded away,
And our Monarch, Thy Jesus, has taught us to say—
When prayer thro' His Spirit is borne toward the sky,
Then hear Thou from Heaven, Thy dwelling-place high,
   And hearing, oh Father, forgive!

WILLIAM BALL.

WILLIAM BALL was born in January, 1801, at Bridgewater, in Somerset, where his father's family had resided for several generations. He was a delicate child, inheriting from his mother an affection of the heart which darkened his earlier years, and caused him, in a special manner, to be loved and cared for by that mother and his eldest sister, who strove in all ways to smooth the delicate child's path, and protect him from the trials incidental to boyhood and youth. In his twenty-second year he was articled to W. L. White, of Yeovil, who had one of the best practices in the county, and was besides Lieutenant-Colonel of the Somerset Local Militia. While with him William Ball entered freely into society, and his wit, vivacity, and charming manners made him very popular.

In July, 1827, he finally left Yeovil, and in 1828, was admitted as a solicitor. The same year he commenced practice at Bristol, in partnership with a friend of his uncle's, Dr. Gawen Ball, and as his father and unmarried sister had removed there, he again became a member of the home-circle. In 1834, he married Anne Dale, and seems to have been exceptionally fortunate in gaining such a wife. Although possessed of an ample fortune and great personal attractions, together with a charm of manner which rendered her universally popular, she remained perfectly simple and unassuming, and won the hearts of all with whom she came in contact by her kindliness and sympathy. Their marriage was a singularly happy one, and when, in 1861, her long delicacy ended in death, his grief was profound, and life seemed to him a long

2

funeral procession.   After their marriage, William and Anne Ball went to live at Northcote House, Durdham Down, Bristol. In the following year, however, William Ball, having given up the practice of law, they took Ivy Cottage, Rydal, and by a succession of alterations made it into their well-known charming residence, Glen Rothay.   The Wordsworths were their next door neighbours there, Dr. Arnold and his family but a mile distant, Mrs. Fletcher, and her interesting daughter, Lady Richardson, wife of the Arctic explorer, lived within a few miles, and Hartley Coleridge dwelt in Nab Cottage, by Rydal Lake, so that the charms of the beautiful surrounding scenery were heightened by intellectual enjoyment and social pleasures.   After his wife's death, in 1861, William Ball spent much time in travelling, in Scotland and elsewhere, seeking to soothe his ever-present sorrow; at length, in 1871, finding his health much benefited by the air of Tain, in Ross-shire, he bought a small house there, Alderbrae, where he passed much of his time, until July, 1878, when he set out on a short excursion, planned for the gratification of an old servant.   On reaching Aberdeen he went out, according to his usual custom, to take a Turkish bath; while taking the bath he became unconscious, and remained so, with brief intervals of recovery, until the next morning, when he expired.

He published in 1825 "Nugæ Sacræ," in 1827 "The Crowning of Living British Poetesses," in 1828 "Humanity; or, the Cause of the Creatures Advocated," in 1864 "Hymns or Lyrics," and in 1865 "Notices of Kindred and Friends Departed."

The Balls were extremely hospitable, and both at Glen Rothay and Bruce Grove, Tottenham, loved to entertain large parties of Friends and others, and the gracious and graceful hostess and the witty and vivacious host will be lovingly remembered by many who read this.   He felt often a physical need for solitude, probably owing to the heritage of a delicate heart, and in his later years rarely appeared among his guests, excepting at meal times.

From a child he had been both a diligent reader and writer of verse, and his solitary hours were busily occupied with study and composition. Many of his poems are very beautiful, but it is said in the notice of him in the *Annual Monitor*, for 1879, from which much of this sketch is derived, that his "best productions were his humourous ones, thrown off on the spur of the moment to amuse himself and his friends, and bubbling over from beginning to end with genuine wit and drollery. Their quaint verbal conceits, humorous juxtapositions of grave and gay, sly parodies of Quaker phraseology, and a hundred other witty devices, made these *jeux d'esprit* the delight of his intimate friends."

He was recorded a minister in 1846.

FROM "NUGÆ SACRÆ; OR, PSALMS, AND HYMNS, AND SPIRITUAL SONGS."

THERE is a pure and tranquil wave,
That rolls around the throne of love,
Whose waters gladden as they lave
 The peaceful shores above.

While streams, which on that tide depend,
Steal from those heavenly shores away,
And on this desert world descend
 O'er weary lands to stray;
The pilgrim faint, and nigh to sink
Beneath his load of earthly woe,
Refreshed beside their verdant brink,
 Rejoices in their flow.

There, O my soul, do thou repair
And hover o'er the hallowed spring,
To drink the crystal wave, and there
 To lave thy wearied wing!

There droop that wing, when far it flies
From human care, and toil, and strife,
And feed by those still streams, that rise
    Beneath the Tree of Life!

It may be that the breath of love
Some leaves on their pure tide have driven,
Which, passing from the shores above,
    Have floated down from heaven.

So shall thy wounds and woes be healed
By the blest virtue that they bring;
So thy parched lips shall be unsealed
    Thy Saviour's praise to sing!

THOMAS CLARKSON.

A GREAT man falls this day,
Strong to befriend the slave, to break his chain;
By dint of Pity, strong, to brave the array
    Of proud oppression's reign.

He was the hero true
Who clung to Right unmoved—to whom 'twas given
When Wrong prevail'd, the combat to renew;
    Trusting in Truth and Heaven.

The warrior's blazonry
Fills Earth's deluded gaze, while angels frown;
But Clarkson's deeds, of love and peace, to see
    Approving Heavens look down.

Tell not of costly shrines,
Or sculptor's art, chartering his praise to Time,
His record is on high. Be work that shines
    Like His, his meed sublime.

A nation's work of love
Not to consign his matchless deeds to Fame

Alone, but to repeat them and to prove
    Herself worthy his name.

    A name that scatters light
And teaching on his times—proclaims abroad
How one just man may serve and stablish Right
    By faith that works for God!

WILLIAM BARBER THE ELDER, OF GISSING, IN NORFOLK.

THE THIRSTY TRAVELLER IN HIS JOURNEY TOWARDS ZION.

OH! mighty God, great things for me thou hast done,
    Thy love and presence hath my heart o'ercome.
Yea in the feeling life, my heart's refresht,
My soul's rejoyc'd more than can be exprest.
Thy power is great, thy mercy great also,
I' th' sence thereof, my cup doth overflow.
For clearly in the light, it may be seen,
How loving and how gracious thou hast been,
To me poor worm ; who hath been in distress,
And sorrow great my tongue must needs confess :
Yea though the enemy did me sore oppress,
Through strong assaults, and batteries no less.
Then didst thou in thy love, to me appear,
Which did rejoyce my heart, thy seed didst chear,
Thy lovely presence did my soul rejoice,
Exceeding much, when I did hear thy voice.
Which draws me forth, thy goodness to declare :
Thy love and bounty (Lord ; how great they are.)
Oh ! blessed God, great is thy living power ;
Without thy presence who can stand one hour ?
Lord, keep me in thy truth, make me to walk
In thy pure life, and power, not in the talk.
For being in thy fear, kept poor and low,
Living refreshments from my God doth flow.
For when that I i' th' silence pure do sit,
Great's the refreshing, I do feel in it.

And when that any from the life do speak,
Th' immortal seed's refresht, the heart doth break.
Now those that faithful in the truth do stand,
Thou wilt preserve by thy almighty hand.
Yea doubtless those that to the end endure,
The crown of life to wear they will be sure.
And though with trials great we meet with here,
Both inward and without, we need not fear ;
But God his lambs will in his bosom bear.
Yea those that in the living faith do live,
Such to thy name, do living praises give.
All glory unto thee my heart doth sing,
Yea endless glory from thy life doth spring.

From my house at Reveland the 19th of the 10th month, 1663.

BERNARD BARTON.

BERNARD BARTON was born at Carlisle on January 31st, 1784. His quiet plodding, yet intensely independent nature, seems to have come to him from his great grandfather, John Barton, of Ive Gill, a fine simple patriarchal man, who supported himself and his family in plain comfort on the proceeds of his own small estate, the annual rental of which was only estimated at £2 15s.! Yet this small estate not only enabled the family to live, but provided money for charitable purposes, John Barton having been the chief contributor in building the small chapel in the dale. Bernard Barton's father left the Church, and joined the Society of Friends, marrying Mary Done, a Cheshire Quakeress. Three of their children grew up, Bernard and two sisters; one of whom, Maria Hack, wrote several useful children's books. Bernard went to school at Ipswich, and at the age of fourteen was apprenticed to Samuel Jesup, at Halstead, in Essex; here he remained eight years, and in 1806 went to Woodbridge. In 1807, he married Lucy Jesup, his old master's niece, and entered into partnership with his step-brother as a corn and coal merchant. A year after their marriage, his wife died in giving birth to a daughter, the Lucy of his poems, who afterwards married Edward Fitzgerald, and who is still living at Croydon; Edward Verrall Lucas, Bernard Barton's latest biographer, having dedicated his book, "Bernard Barton and his Friends," to her.

After his wife's death he tired of the place, which recalled his lost happiness, and engaged himself as a tutor in the family of Mr. Waterhouse, a Liverpool merchant. Here he became acquainted with the Roscoes and other interesting people, but at the end of a year returned to Woodbridge, and became a clerk in Dykes and Samuel Alexander's Bank. For forty years he worked quietly on as a bank clerk, only leaving his place two days before his death. But his active mind found vent in a long series of poetical productions and a large and varied correspondence. His friendships included nearly all the men of his day eminent in literature and philanthropy. Among his correspondents were Southey, Scott, Wordsworth, Byron, Chas. Lamb, Chas. Lloyd, Allan Cunningham, John Mitford, Airey the Astronomer Royal, Crabbe, and Fitzgerald, and if a poet could be judged by his friends, Bernard Barton would be indeed a king of song, but as it has been said by a friend of his that his talk was far more humourous than his writings, so I think the man must have been far greater than his verse. Possibly the daily monotony of his work in the bank shadowed and chilled the delicate flower of poetry in his soul, but anyone reading E. V. Lucas's word-picture of him, which I cannot forbear quoting, must, I think, feel disappointed with his work :—" At the door our host greets us heartily with a warm handshake, that does not loosen until he has drawn us well within his walls : a man of middle height with a fine open face, eminently genial ; gentle, luminous brown eyes, kindling as he talks ; brown hair, and a rich clear voice of singular pleasant-ness of tone."

Those " luminous brown eyes " must have flashed, one would think, with the humour which was so strong a characteristic of the quiet young Quaker, when Hogg, the Ettrick Shepherd, encouraged by some praiseful verses which Bernard Barton had addressed to him, on reading " The Queen's Wake," asked him, in his letter of thanks, to use his influence with the London managers in getting a tragedy Hogg had written produced there !

Bernard Barton published in 1812 " Metrical Effusions ;" in

1817, "The Triumph of the Orwell;" in 1818, "The Convict's
Appeal" and "Poems by an Amateur;" in 1820, "A Day in
Autumn" and "Poems;" in 1822, "Napoleon and Other
Poems" and "Verses on the Death of Percy Bysshe Shelley;"
in 1823, "A Short Account of Leiston Abbey, with Descriptive
and Illustrative Verses, by Bernard Barton and Others;" in
1824, "Minor Poems," including "Napoleon" and "Poetic
Vigils;" in 1826, "A Missionary's Memorial" and "Devo-
tional Verses;" in 1827, "A Widow's Tale, and Other
Poems;" in 1828, "A New Year's Eve, and Other Poems;"
in 1845, "Household Verses."

Besides these volumes, he wrote a great deal for various
magazines, annuals, etc., and many introductory and valedictory
verses for other people's books and albums.

Bernard Barton is not a great poet, but his verses have the
serene charm of the quiet country in which he lived; a land
of placid streams, and wide green pastures, of cool stretches
of grey distance, and many wild flowers; a land of quaint
old towns, and sleepy villages nestling around their square
church towers; a land of peace and plenty to the outward eye,
bounded and glorified by the sea, whose music beats a
ceaseless refrain to the quiet lives of the Woodbridge poet and
his daughter, in the poetry which pulsed an ever-active tide
through what might otherwise have been the stagnant existence
of a banker's clerk.

Bernard Barton died at his Suffolk home, February 19th,
1849, aged sixty-five, and was buried in the Friends' burial
ground at Woodbridge.

STANZAS ADDRESSED TO PERCY BYSSHE SHELLEY.

FORESTS, and lakes, the majesty of mountains,
   The dazzling glaciers, and the musical sound
Of waves and winds, or softer gush of fountains :
   In sights and sounds like these thy soul has found

Sublime delight ; but can the visible bound
   Of this small globe be the sole nurse and mother
Of knowledge and of feeling ?   Look around !
   Mark how one being differs from another;
Yet the world's book is spread before each human brother

Was this world, then, the parent and the nurse
   Of him whose mental eye outlived the sight
Of all its beauties ?   Him who sang the curse
   Of that forbidden fruit, which did invite
Our first progenitors, whom that foul sprite,
   In serpent form, seduced from innocence.
By specious promises, that wrong and right,
   Evil and good, when they had gathered thence,
Should be distinctly seen, as by diviner sense ?

They plucked, and paid the awful penalty
   Of disobedience : yet man will not learn
To be content with knowledge that is free
   To all.   There are, whose soaring spirits spurn
At humble lore, and, still insatiate, turn
   From living fountains to forbidden springs ;
Whence having proudly quaffed, their bosoms burn
   With visions of unutterable things,
Which restless fancy's spell in shadowy glory brings.

Delicious the delirious bliss, while new ;
   Unreal phantoms of wise, good, and fair,
Hover around, in every vivid hue
   Of glowing beauty ; these dissolve in air,
And leave the barren spirit bleak and bare
   As Alpine summits : it remains to try
The hopeless task (of which themselves despair)
   Of bringing back those feelings, now gone by,
By making their own dreams the code of all society.

All fear, none aid them, and few comprehend ;
   And then comes disappointment, and the blight
Of hopes, that might have blessed mankind, but end
    In stoic apathy, or starless night :
And thus hath many a spirit pure and bright,
    Lost that efflulgent and ethereal ray,
Which, had religion nourished it, still might
    Have shone on, peerless, to that perfect day,
When death's veil shall be rent, and darkness dashed away.

Ere it shall prove too late, thy steps retrace :
    The heights thy muse has scaled, can never be
Her loveliest, or her safest dwelling-place.
    In the deep valley of humilty,
The river of immortal life flows free
    For thee—for all.   Oh ! taste its limpid wave,
As it rolls murmuring by, and thou shalt see
    Nothing in death the Christian dares not brave,
Whom faith in God has given a world beyond the grave !

DRAB BONNETS.

THEY may cant of costumes, and of brilliant head-dresses,
    A la Grecque—à la Françoise—or what else they will ;
They may talk of tiaras, that glitter on tresses
    Enwreathed by the Graces, and braided with skill :
Yet to my partial glance, I confess the drab bonnet
    Is the loveliest of any, - -and most when it bears
Not only the bright gloss of neatness upon it—
    But, beneath,—the expression Benevolence wears !
Then let fashion exult in her vapid vagaries,
    From her fascinations my favourite is free :
Be folly's the head-gear that momently varies,
    But a Bonnet of drab is the sweetest to me.

Though stately the ostrich-plume, gracefully throwing

Its feathery flashes of light on the eye ;
Though tasty and trim the straw-bonnet, when glowing
  With its ribbons so glossy of various dye :—
Yet still I must own, although none may seem duller
  Than a simple drab bonnet to many a gaze—
It is, and it will be, the favourite colour,
  Around which my fancy delightedly plays :—
And it well suits my muse with a garland to wreathe it,
  And echo its praises with gratefullest glee,—
For, knowing the goodness that oft lurks beneath it,
  The Bonnet of drab beats a turban with me.

Full many a rare gem—the poet has chaunted—
  In the depths of the ocean flings round it its sheen ;
And many a floweret, its beauties unvaunted,
  Springs to life, sheds its perfume, aud withers unseen :
And well do I know that our sisterhood numbers,
  Arrayed in the livery that coxcombs reprove,
Forms as fair as e'er rose on a poet's sweet slumbers,
  And faces as lovely as ever taught love.
This I know, and have felt ;—and, thus knowing and feeling,
  A recreant minstrel I surely should be,
If my heart-felt attachment ignobly concealing,
  The Bonnet of drab passed unhonoured by me !

I have basked in the blaze of both beauty and fashion,
  Have seen these united with gifts rich and rare,
And crowned with a heart that could cherish compassion,
  And by sympathy soften what sorrow must bear.
Yet acknowledging this—which I can do sincerely,—
  Far the highest enjoyment this bosom e'er knew,
The glance which it treasures most fondly, most dearly,
  Beamed from under a Bonnet of drab-coloured hue.
'Twas my pleasure,—my pride !—it is past, and has perished,
  Like the track of a ship o'er the dark heaving sea ;

But its loveliness lives, its remembrance is cherished,
And the Bonnet of drab is still beauteous to me!

THE SPIRITUAL LAW.

SAY not the Law Divine
Is hidden from thee, or afar removed ;
That Law within would shine,
If there its glorious light were sought and loved.

Soar not on high,
Nor ask who thence shall bring it down to earth ;
That vaulted sky
Hath no such star, didst thou but know its worth.

Nor launch thy bark
In search thereof upon a shoreless sea,
Which has no ark,
No dove to bring this olive-branch to thee.

Then do not roam
In search of that which wandering cannot win
At home, at home,
That word is placed, thy mouth, thy heart within.

O seek it there,
Turn to its teachings with devoted will ;
Watch unto prayer,
And in the power of faith this love fulfil.

A STREAM.

IT flows through flowery meads,
Gladdening the herds that on its margin browse
Its quiet bounty feeds
The alders that o'ershade it with their boughs.

Gently it murmurs by
The village churchyard, with a plaintive tone

Of dirge-like melody,
For worth and beauty modest as its own.

More gaily now it sweeps
By the small school-house, in the sunshine bright,
And o'er the pebbles leaps,
Like happy hearts by holiday made light.

HENRY BINNS.

A YOUNG poet of great promise, was born at Ulverstone, May 14th, 1873, and is the son of Richard and Elizabeth Bryan Binns. He was educated at Christchurch and Hitchin schools, then under the management of Jos. Evans and Isaac Sharp respectively. Henry Binns is thoroughly permeated with the modern spirit in its highest phases, even to the desire, which seems an absolute passion with so many ardent souls since Edward Carpenter set the example, to get back to the land, and labour with the hands as well as the brain. He is engaged in fruit-culture at present, which as it developes, he believes will be of a co-operative character. No training could be better for a young poet. I believe it is almost impossible to labour honestly and earnestly at anything, without having one's nature raised and purified thereby, and I am sure that this is doubly true about labour on the land; the influences of the country, the sweet air, the clear sky, the peaceful growth of the grasses and flowers, the eternally-hopeful song of the often invisible larks, insensibly purify the spirit; and the soul of the poet is peculiarly open to all these blessed influences; it absorbs surrounding sights and sounds, and literally weaves its verses from them, as much as a plant-root absorbs its food from its environment, and transforms that food into a rose or lily. Henry Binns has of course been much influenced by Tennyson and Browning, but far more so by William Morris and Walt Whitman, those large-hearted fiery-tongued leaders of the noblest section of our advancing democracy.

His first published poem appeared in the *British Friend*, in January, 1892, and since then he has frequently published poems in that journal and others, and we may hope before long to have a volume of collected verses bearing his name. At present those interested in the young poet's work, and there are many such, have to hunt through the pages of the *Arbitrator, Co-operative News*, and other magazines and papers.

His verse is full of aspiration and revolt, and is half inarticulate at times, he cannot speak in suitable words the burning, crowding thoughts that rise to his lips; but the aspiration is holy and Godward, the revolt is the strife upward to progress, never the sinking back into the slough of anarchy, and the inarticulateness of his utterance, arises not from lack of ideas, but from imperfect workmanship. The poet learns to sing in an audible voice like all other craftsmen learn their art, although to him, his songs spring from his soul at one breath; he hears them with his spiritual ears, perfect, beautiful, flawless, but has to painfully reproduce them for the world of men, and our poet has not yet learned his craft perfectly, but feels after it, and will find it because he is in earnest, and a genuine poet, not a mere smooth versemaker.

THE SEARCHER
(from The City).

THE artist hath his Paradise to guard,
    The poet in the strife
Hath love's behest to serve, and love's reward,
    And I fulfil my life.

The joy of straining every nerve is mine,
    Of long-enduring strength,
Even the prophet's rapture, fruit divine,
    Foretold, foreseen at length.

Oh beauty hath her roses, diamonds, pearls,
　　Music of mystic bars—
Love hath her heart of hearts, whose flower unfurls,
　　And truth her heaven of stars.

Oh childhood hath its Eden of delight,
　　With peace and dreaming blest ;
Youth hath its consecration, promise bright,
　　And manhood hath its quest,

Its service to accomplish—ease foregone,
　　And all applause hushed down,
Evaded—heard with shame—hard pressing on—
　　Too ardent for a crown.

How should he care for Fame, whom only truth
　　Could call and recompense—
The ever-far ideal of my youth,
　　Desired with thirst intense?

For Fame?   I count my comrades where they stand
　　The laughing stock of years,
The heroes of their scorn, alone,—and grand,—
　　My comrades and compeers.

FOURTH SONNET.

(from Democracy and Song).

THIS is the garden where the flower grew
　　That fills the earth with fragrance—this its home,—
　　An island full of breezes off the foam,
To whom the west-wind bears the ocean's due :
This is the garden where the temperate blue
　　Is tenderly near, and where the burrowing gnome
　　Unearths continual wealth : and where the loam,
Tilled by the frost awakes with vigour new,—

A land of morning, busy with the hum
  Of multitudinous life : a land of streams,
Of meadows and of mountains greatly dumb,
  That blaze as altar-piles i' the slant sunbeams ;
A land of deeds, to whom the messages come,
  Of new emprise, and heaven-directed dreams.

ON SALISBURY PLAIN.

ALL joy is praise, and all desire is prayer ;
And as we pray we grow, and praise is new life ever—
They are the meat and drink of the angel-soul, the Son of
    the wonderful God.

The wonderful God—(list you)—I, who wander from hope
    to dream,
Turn at the touch of fear my eyes to my soul, and
    remember
The meaning of words that grow dim, and of these, "Our
    Father."

The hills and the great free plain and the boisterous wind
    I love,
Grass and clover and larks, and the foam in the blue,
Roses and hearts of roses, and lips and longing of hearts—
All that ever I loved, and that ever was loved, and loved—
All come near at the song of the words, "Our Father ;"
And nothings vanish away when Love says low, "Our
    Father."

For the soul saith, all that is beautiful is true, and cannot
    fail—
And of all earth's beautiful visions Love loveth the Dream
    of God.

JAMES BEALE.

THIS unique portrait painter of the gods, whose few words, and fragments of verse, give us such weirdly beautiful pictures of ideal forms and intangible things, is a son of Joshua and Hannah Beale, of Cork. From his early youth he was devoted to the study of Shakespere and the other Elizabethan dramatists, and has always felt a passionate love for poetry and music. Of late years he has been obliged to give up his studies, to some extent, on account of weak sight. He still resides in Cork. He has the gift of presenting a perfect picture in a few words; each word being the only suitable one for its shade of expression, and fitting into its phrase, like the colours in a mosaic. The majestic and calm beauty of his poems—mere fragments as they are—recall the Greek dramas, and give that sense of supreme satisfaction which it is the aim of all true art to produce, as it then only shows its kinship with the God who inspires it.

DEMETER.

NOT in the pure depths of eternal eyes
Dwells all the mystery, or in thy form—
Girdled and gleaming like a summer storm—
But in thy tones, which evermore arise,
Surging upon a shore of memories,
Mystic, ineffable. O, sigh-swept charm
That comes with sway soft as the circling arm
Of Cypris, in her dream that never dies !
Flower, fruit, and golden grain ; the infinite roll
Of Earth's large murmur ; Spring and joyous bird,
Cycles and climes, all fill thy Goddess soul

With Beauty; the lone Sea is ever heard
Uttering full symphony around thy whole
And pure heart voice, which depths Divine has stirred •

APHRODITE.

COLD Artemis may draw the dim, grey sea
Towards her, and steep all things in barren light
Whereof come shadows.   Foam-born, infinite,
I, Aphrodite, stand on this fair lea
Exultant.   Peerless in beauty, unto me
Shall God-like men build fanes for my delight
In their large awe; yea, on the eternal height
Amidst divine calm, stirs new ecstacy
Among the immortal gods, who evermore
Were dream-drawn throughout cloudland, charioteers
Without a goal; until I brought this lore
Of love from out the infinite surf of tears
Surging for ever.   I laugh around this shore—
And gods yearn, and men sigh through all their years.

ANTIGONE.

THE words are uttered.   Now a pitiless fate
Draws me towards yonder weird and darksome cave
On the dim mountain side; where steps of men—
Of wandering shepherds, homeward to the fold
Guiding their weary flocks at even-tide
Approach not, even the place where I must die;
And thou, O, Hæmon, whom amidst the youth—
The chosen youth of Thebes—I have long loved,
And given my virgin heart, remember me
With calm thoughts of that unforgotten time,
Long hoped for, but now lost, for ever lost.
Yield not thy soul to a passionate despair,
The sunlight, or the eternal roll and change
Of gracious seasons, or the pitying stars

Which light me moving towards perpetual Night,
Or sad Ismene, with her fruitless prayer
For mercy, or the anguish in thy soul
Scare not the awful shadow, which not yet
Has ceased to hover, spreading fatal wings
O'er the doomed race of wretched Œdipus.
Ah me, unhappy! retribution comes
Stalking, a phantom, through deserted halls,
Once beautiful, the stateliest in the land.
Thy home, now cruel Creon : yet my crime
Is not my shame, but thine ; for I behold
Polynices, the beloved on the shore
In the silent land of shadows, and I come.
Lo ! I depart, thro' the dim wavering gates,
The mist-like portals of that Autumn realm
Where mighty Orcus reigns ; and the stern Queen
Persephone, who rules with sceptre pale,
And calm eternal eyes, the gliding shades
That wail around the shores of Acheron,
Calls me, with sweet sad voice, to take my place
In dells divine, and glades of happy rest.

A May Night.

The summer comes ; yet child-eyed lingering May
Folds her wet mantle round her, all too soon ;
Her tears drop at the Cuckoo's faint-toned tune,
Heard like farewell along the fields to-day ;
The young leaves droop ; the snow-white fragrant spray
Glimmering, half-shadowed, bends beneath the moon
In voiceless yearning for the face of June,
Song, and all floral hues in soft array.
Lo, in this Night of leaves, the sleeping mere
Awakes not ; yet one timid sound is heard :
A Kingfisher's bright wing has gently stirred

The star-lit waters, more in joy than fear—
A Naiad turned her dreaming face—the bird
Left all to Silence and a listening ear.

HOPE.

Look forth to-day, O, Spring, this hour is thine :
Now, the first violet raises its pure head
To listen for the onward, joyous tread--
The thrilling touch that stirs the stately pine
From clasping root to tasselled top—as wine
Stirs weary hearts, or calm faith changes dread
And doubt, by barren fables lately fed—
To that embracing dawn of truth divine.
Lo, how the crimson cloud-valves open wide !
And Spring comes forth with waving, sunny hair,
With eyes all youth, and laugh so softly rare,
Moving like Eve in Eden yet a bride—
While the glad waters of Euphrates' tide
Murmured a morning song thro' all the air.

MARY ELIZABETH BECK.

M ARY ELIZABETH BECK, better known by her initials "M. E. B.," is the author of "Turning Points in the Lives of Eminent Christians" (Hodder and Stoughton); "Heavenly Relationships" (Nisbet); "Bible Readings on Bible Women" (E. Hicks and Partridge); "Collateral Testimonies to Quaker Principles" (E. Hicks); "Fresh Diggings in an Old Mine" (R. T. Society), etc., etc. She has also contributed much, both in prose and verse, to "Chambers' Edinburgh Journal," "Sunday at Home," "Lippincott," etc. Permission has been given by her publishers to insert the following poem, which was placed by Wemyss Reid at the end of his life of W. E. Forster, by the express desire of the latter's widow.

The Two Funerals.

WILLIAM FORSTER	and	W. E. FORSTER.
(*Obit.* 27 i., 1854.)		(*Obit.* 5 iv., 1886.)

In Tennessee, across the wide Atlantic,
  There rests the clay
Of one who bore the image of his Master—
  Long passed away.

A lonely grave, with few to stand beside it,
  To shed a tear,
Although to the oppressed of many a nation
  His name was dear.

Beneath that massive form a heart was bleeding
  For all earth's woe,
Till the strained tension burst the clay-built dwelling,
  And laid it low.

But angels, hovering o'er, on snow white pinions,
    Their loved to greet,
Bore the freed soul with joyful hallelujahs
    To Christ's own feet.

    .   .   .   .   .

In England's stately, world-renowned Walhalla,
    A mournful train
Of great and noble meet, while—slowly—slowly—
    A dirge-like strain—

A funeral anthem in the grand old Abbey,
    Far-off, yet near,
Floats on the air—Hush! stand all ye uncovered,—
    Room for the bier!

Silence—deep silence—for the dead is coming
    In deathly state.
Ah! what is *life?* Before that kingly sceptre
    Earth's proudest wait.

Yet speak those floral wreaths of resurrection—
    Not born to die—
The mortal perishes, but the immortal
    Mounts up on high.

The fixed heroic aim, the will unswerving,
    True to the line,
Not earth-born, but a glorious emanation
    Of the divine.

These cannot pass away, and still thou livest
    Among thy peers,
Thy name a banner-cry to all the noble,
    Through coming years.

"Dust unto dust."   Mid nature's lonely wildness
    A kindred band
Around a simple grave in his own Wharfedale
    In silence stand.

Make way—make way, and let the long procession
    Pass on—pass on—
One of yourselves, ye toiling sons of England,
    To rest has gone.

One of yourselves, your ever-honoured Master ;
    Yet more—your *Friend ;*
Yes, mourn ye may, ye will not find his fellow
    Till time shall end.

But lift your thoughts above this narrow casket,
    He is not there—
Of all Eternity's untold resources
    The chosen heir !

And meet it is with tears that praise should mingle ;
    On bended knee,
Hearts bowed with anguish raise their grateful tribute,
    O Lord, to Thee ;

Calling, from Time's brief span, Thy servant higher,
    To endless days,
Where, sire with son, in wider fields of service,
    Blend work with praise.

LOUISA BIGG.

LOUISA BIGG was born at Banbury, her people, who had been Friends for several generations, were connected with Bernard Barton, and the associations of her home greatly tended to strengthen that love of literature and art, which seemed hereditary in her family. At an early age the legends of Greece and Rome exercised a strong fascination over the imaginative mind of the future writer, and when she was sent to a school conducted by Emma Ravis and Caroline Smith, both of them poets, and fell under their strong personal influence, the child's bent became the woman's aim. Her first published volume was a slender book, entitled "Urban Grandier and Other Poems," which contains some fine poetry, and this was followed in 1878 by "Pansies and Asphodels," (Chapman and Hall). The Russian legends contained in the latter volume were freely translated into German by B. Schulze Smidt, and brought out in a quaintly illustrated volume by Perthes of Gotha in 1885.

In 1889 appeared "Gods of Men," a study of the chief religions of the world, and in 1891 "Prince Nushizad and Other Poems," from which I have quoted two short poems. Louisa Bigg has also published various prose tales and sketches. She resigned her membership in the Society of Friends some years ago, although still continuing to feel warm sympathy with its chief aims and beliefs, and cherishing close friendship with many of its members.

PROLOGUE.

FROM " GODS OF MEN."

ON every land some quickening sunbeams shine,
All creatures see the sun, God's mighty sign.
O Thou, immutable, creative Word,
Whose name we know not—Father, Saviour, Lord !
I love to think that every distant clime,
All peoples born within the bounds of time,
Have caught some glimpses of the eternal day,
Some light divine to guide them on their way.
In spite of bigot's creed and pious hate,
I love to think that none can shut the gate
Upon Thy love, as none can raise a wall
To keep Thy sun from shining on us all.

PRESENT AND FUTURE.

MEN blow their brazen trumpets loud
In presence of the gaping crowd,
With noisy voices, shrill and high,
They shout—'Tis I, 'tis I, 'tis I !
I have the nostrum that shall cure
The ills that mortals must endure—
I have of heaven's gate the key,
Attend my words and follow me !
I am the wise, the eloquent,
To guide the nations was I sent !

And all the while, in some still nook
Is making, page by page, the Book,
The Light, by whose enduring rays
Our age shall shine in coming days.

Where does the Century's master write?
Is it in some chill garret's height,
Or in a mansion rich or fair,
With spacious room and marble stair?

Is he despised, unknown, obscure,
Who writes the word that shall endure,
Or is he famous, rich and great,
A prince and ruler in the state?
We cannot tell, he may have sat
Beside thy fire in common chat;
We cannot tell, it may be I
To-day, unknowing, passed him by.

FAME.

HE poured his heart in song, but in the wide
Unheeding world no other voice replied.
Still he sang on, and all the world defied.

His gifted soul, for happiness athirst,
Strove through the bands of circumstance to burst:
He fell—men mocked and called his name accurst.

Wounded and sick, beside the world's highway,
Untended and alone the poet lay;
Men passed him by, unknowing, day by day.

He died.   Then one from out the mud and mire,
Picked up a verse alive with heaven's own fire,
"Behold," he cried, "the man of our desire."

Then the crowd stopped and listened, "Good," it said,
"Sound forth his praise, with laurel crown his head,
"What living man can match this poet dead?"

ROBERT BIRD.

ROBERT BIRD was born at Govan on the Clyde in May
1854. His parents were natives of Linlithgow and
were thoroughly Scotch ; indeed, our poet always declares that
he inherits from his mother, his knowledge of, and affection
for, the sweet Doric, in which he writes so forcibly. She spoke
it with epigrammatic humour and ease, and with a fascinating
softness seldom heard now, and taught it to her son as a
native language.

Robert Bird was educated at Glasgow College, where he
took honours in Scotch Law, and a prize in the English
Literature Class for a poem on "The Glasgow Statue to
Burns," which was afterwards printed in the *Glasgow Weekly
Herald*. In 1878, he passed as a procurator before the
Sheriff Courts of Scotland, and immediately thereafter began
practice in Glasgow.

Although a very successful lawyer, he has, from his boyhood,
been a writer of verse ; while yet in his teens he contributed
frequent poems to the *Glasgow Weekly News*. He is a
member of the "Glasgow Ballad Club," formed in 1876 for the
study of ballads, and ballad literature, and for friendly criticism
of the verses contributed by members   He is also a member
of the "Ruskin" Society, Vice-Chairman of Council of the
Scottish Society of Literature and Art, and Vice-President of
the Glasgow Peace Society. Robert Bird has had several
selections of his poems printed for private circulation, but his
'Law Lyrics" was first published in 1885, and "The Falls of
Clyde and Other Poems" in 1888. From J. H. Edward's
Modern Scottish Poets (from which above biographical details

have been taken), we learn that our poet sides in politics with his great co-religionist, John Bright, and in sociology with John Ruskin : the lover of liberty, and the lover of beauty ; truly, fit guides for one who·is a lawyer and a poet ! It does not come within the scope of my present volume to consider the prose work of poets, but *The Carpenter of Nazareth*, *A Child's Religion*, and *Joseph the Dreamer* are so exceptional in character, and fascinating in treatment, that I cannot resist this brief mention of them ; more especially as they show, in quite as large measure as his verse, their author's possession of some of the highest characteristics of the true poet, viz., a vivid and sustained imagination, and the faculty of seeing things from quite other points of view than his own. This faculty is shown very clearly and sweetly in his *Fairy Pieces for Children*, one of which we quote, to give an idea of the lightness of touch with which he treats these fanciful themes ; truly, in his own words, Robert Bird has "found the key of Dreamland's door," and has left it ajar for us to peep behind. He is equally at home in the land of reality, and is a very Quaker of the Quakers in his hatred for shams, and abuses, and wrongs ; and it is most refreshing, in these days of apologetics for crime and criminals, to read his outspoken denunciations of whatever appears to him false or unjust, whether in law, custom, or conduct. He denounces these things with that humour, so essentially Scotch, which says the most biting or mirth-provoking things without a smile, and with a perfection of technique which adds double force to its sentiment. Any notice of his poetry which left unremarked his great love for, and joy in Nature, would be very incomplete. His descriptions of scenery carry one into the open air at once, and we seem to be wandering with the poet as we read, by the banks of the Clyde, or among "the trees about the old house."

Like a warm dreepin' roast
  Is the table o' fees.

Man! it gangs wi' a clack!
  Like a mill makin' flour;
Three-and-fourpence a crack!
  Six-and-eightpence an hour;
Half-a-crown for a wink,
  And a shillin' a sneeze,
Come like stour o' sma ink
  Frae the table o' fees.

I could hand ye my stule,
  Ruler, inkhorn, and dask;
I could hand ye my quill,
  Or whate'er ye might ask;
And could yet wi' my tongue—
  Whilk nae man can appease—
Fill a cask tae the bung
  Frae the table o' fees.

ON OATHS.

THERE is a little thing
  Which magistrates administer,
Said with the hand upraised,
  In their peculiar way;
The great Judicial oath,
  With smiling face or sinister,
Told like a parrot rhyme
  For witnesses to say.

But surely it is plain,
  Amid the law's verbosity,
That if a man would lie,
  Or falsify his soul,

'Tis not in swearing oaths,
　Or any such monstrosity,
To bind him to the truth,
　Or keep his conscience whole.

'Tis not the oath he fears,—
　'Twould take an act of surgery,
To get into some heads
　Its weight and meaning due,—
'Tis not the power of awe,
　But 'tis the dread of perjury,
That tooths the legal vice,
　And turns the legal screw.

To ears both quick and slow,
　To willing tongues and stuttering,
The judge supplies the words
　He recollects so well,
While some rush on before,
　So glibly are they uttering
The sacredest of things,
　That sages fear to tell.

And shepherds tell their flocks
　Of curses and profanity,
Of wicked words in streets
　That wicked people say,
While in a court they'd find
　A text for all humanity,
Of how a sacred name
　Is cheapened every day.

FROM "THE FALLS OF THE CLYDE."

CORRA LYNN.

WITH backward look he sees the mighty flood,
'Tween walls of rock, heave down its hill of white,

Down, down, torn by the jagged stone, cut by
The sharpened ledge, it spreads from Fall to Fall,
In doubling sheets and heavenly, waving fleece,
To mingle in its downward rolling smoke,
With leaping clouds, white-peaked, and whirl-wind toss't,
Up-driven from the sounding gulf below.
From that dread gulf a steam of vapour mounts,
In shining column, slowly up the Fall,
And spreads a wind-blown rain-cloud o'er the foam,
Dispersing ever in the thin, blue air.
And rising, too, from that abyss of snow,
There glows and wanes the vision of heaven's arch
Of dewy orange, of wedded blue and rose,
Like angel's wing upcleaving from the foam,
Expanding bright, to rest with texture fine,
A rosy pinion on the waterfall,
An orange on the flood, and arching, spread
Its iris hues athwart the bushy cliffs,
Through whose transparency the grey rocks weep,
The mantling brushwood shines, until it fades
From the green fringe of trees that top the crags,
Lost in the cloud-flecked sky, of brilliant blue—
Oh! sight most welcome to the wearied eye,
Of constant, tender colour; promise sweet,
That e'en in smoke of hoarsely-battling floods,
One flash of heaven can instantly reveal
A bow, celestial and magnificent,
Of peace triumphant o'er the war of Falls,
Enriched with every hue that heaven can yield,
Harmonious-blended, and in shape complete—
And thus the triumph of a peaceful mind
Bridges the passions of a warring world!

ELIAS BOCKETT.

ELIAS BOCKETT was born in 1695, and was the son of John Bockett of London, author of "A Diurnal Speculum," and many other quaint and curious works. He lived in George Yard, Lombard Street, and carried on business as a distiller. Most of his works were published anonymously, and are extremely rare and curious. The chief of them are as follows :—"Aminadab's Courtship, or the Quaker's Wedding," a poem; "A Character" (of William Gibson), in verse; "A Character Defended;" "Arguments for Exposing False Teachers;" "The Counter Plot and *Something Else*;" "The Yea and Nay Stock-Jobbers;" "A Poem to the Memory of Aquila Rose;" "A rod for the Author of the Little Switch;" "Punchinello's Sermon;" "Geneva," a poem; "Blunt to Walpole," a familiar epistle in behalf of the British Distillery.

Elias Bockett died of a fever in 1735, aged forty years, and was buried in the Friends' Burial Ground, Bunhill Fields.

TO THE MEMORY OF AQUILA ROSE.

DAMON, MARINO.

DAMON.

MARINO! welcome from the western shore,
Welcome to *Britain*! to thy friend once more:
Why silent thus? Why this dejected air?
The melancholy cause let *Damon* hear.
By some fair tyrant has my friend been crost?
Or was his cargo in a tempest lost?
Or to what more disastrous accident,
Must I impute these signs of discontent?

MARINO.

Impute 'em to a loss that human pow'r
Can ne'er retrieve .   .   .   .   *Amintas* is no more!

DAMON.

Forbid it Heav'n .   .   .   .

MARINO.

.   .   .   .   Yes 'tis a fatal truth .   .   .   .
Cold in the earth, lies the lamented youth.

DAMON.

Then died the man, the muse so oft inspir'd ;
Belov'd so justly, and so much admir'd ;
In whom, with wit, sincerity was join'd,
A pleasant, generous, and a faithful friend.

MARINO.

Merit, like his, cou'd ne'er be long unknown,
His native *Britain* saw it not alone ;
Where'er he came distinguish'd it appear'd,
At ev'ry port *Amintas* was rever'd,
Scarce was our *Philadelphia* in his view,
Before his fame o'er all the province flew ;
His virtues, Pennsylvania soon confest
They shone conspicuous, tho' by fate opprest ;
Fate, even there, frown'd on the bard awhile,
But smooth'd her brow, at length, and cast a flatt'ring
      smile.
To him the blooming Myra yields her charms,
And faints with pleasure, folded in his arms.
A scene of affluence then attracts his view,
And he the prospect boldly does pursue ;
But ere he reaches it .   .   .   .   invidious death,
At once deprives him of his hopes and breath.

.   .   .   .

So when the heavens appear serene and gay,
Some gallant ship, now prosperous on the sea,
With colours flying and expanded sails,
Born tow'rds her port by kind, auspicious gales ;
From pirates late escap'd and storms blown o'er,
Strikes on a rock and sinks in sight of shore.

DAMON.

If through the cloud of envious fortune's frown,
The genius of *Amintas* radiant shone,
With what advantage had his worth been seen
Amidst her smiles, propitiously serene ?
So does the glorious parent of the day,
Not his full lustre thro' thick fogs display ;
But those dispers'd, the lucïd orb of light
Shoots beams around, insuperably bright.

MARINO.

'Tis fortune's common pastime to dispense
To fools her favour, scorn to men of sense ;
Desert neglected with delight she sees,
And sots in gilded chariots loll at ease.
This once *Amintas* knew . . . .   but now no more
Can feel th' effects of her capricious pow'r.
He's gone—the debt to Nature when he paid,
Around him swift the fatal news was spread,
And all that knew him living, mourn'd him dead.
In moving lays, our bards his worth rehearse,
(For *Pennsylvania* has her sons of verse,)
Lively they paint the beauties of his mind
With freedom, just, and without flatt'ry kind.

.   .   .   .

But who can calm the lovely *Myra's* grief,
Too mighty, ev'n for verse to give relief:

On *Schuykill* banks disconsolate she mourns,
Her wonted pleasure there to sorrow turns.
"Whither (she cries) dear partner of my bed,
"Ah! whither art thou from thy *Myra* fled?
"With thee my gay, my smiling hours are flown!
"My joy! my happiness! my all is gone!
"Thy soft expressions I no more shall hear,
"No more thy pleasing voice delight my ear;
"My longing eyes no more be fixed on thine,
"Nor thy fond arms around thy *Myra* twine.
"In thee was my felicity complete,
"In thee, the husband and the lover met   .   .   .   .
"But Heav'n has snatch'd thee from me, and in vain
"I Heav'n invoke, to give thee back again."
Thus mourns the widowed fair in sorrow drown'd
And her complaints the ambient hills resound.

DAMON.

We must resign to Nature what she gave,
But fame, immortal, triumphs o'er the grave;
To distant ages virtue will survive,
Nor wit from death a period can receive.
When tombs, and what we leave with them in trust,
Appear one undistinguish'd heap of dust,
Preserv'd to late posterity by fame,
Amintas' works shall eternize his name.
.   .   .   But see my friend! the skies begin to low'r,
And clouds condens'd foretell a sudden show'r   .   .
Octavio yonder lives—there we may find
A timely shelter and reception kind.

HANNAH BOWDEN.

HANNAH BOWDEN was the daughter of John and Hannah Marsh, of Croydon, both well-known ministers in the Society of Friends. She was born in 1822. Her sister Priscilla married George Pitt, of Mitcham, the author of an exceedingly clever and interesting volume of travels. Hannah Marsh became a teacher in a school at Worcester, presided over by Lucy Westcombe, assisted by her sister Anna Louisa, who was a very dear friend of Hannah Marsh's. Here she remained until the school was given up in 1856. The following year she married J. Bowden, but died when her child was born in 1859. In 1860, some of her many fugitive pieces were collected by her sister Priscilla, and published under the title of, "Poetical Remains of Hannah Bowden." The next year another edition was called for, as the book had attracted a good deal of attention and interest.

Many of the pieces in this book are very beautiful, full of music and fervour; and although occasionally marred by conventional references to "wreaths" and "lyres," and the other poetical properties of our grandmothers, they show a real poetical faculty and sense of harmony, and one and all are full of the deeply religious spirit, tinged with sadness, which the shadow of an early death seems frequently to cast over its victims.

"For so He Giveth His Beloved Sleep."

Sleep, my beloved, sleep—
   The stormy winds are high—
The gathered lightnings sweep
   In splendour through the sky,—-

Yet fear thou not the tempest's voice of dread,
While keeps my love its vigil round thy bed.

Rest, my beloved, rest—
 The ocean waves beat loud—
Each billows foaming crest
 Involves thee like a shroud,—
Yet shrink not, Christian, from the raging main—
I bind the waters in their crystal chain.

Peace, my beloved, peace—
 Do anxious thoughts appal?
At my command they cease—
 My word dispels them all.
Dark though the visions o'er thy slumber hung,
Rouse not, nor start, my arms are round thee flung.

Sleep, my beloved, sleep—
 The brazen voice of war,
From vale and mountain-steep,
 Is thundered forth afar,—
That awful trump the nations quake to hear,
Falls but in distant murmurs on *thine* ear.

Hush! my beloved, hush!
 The tumult threatens near—
Thou hear'st the gathering rush—
 Thou see'st the blanch of fear,—
Yet quail not *thou*, though empires round thee fall—
They sink or rise, responsive to *my* call.

Soft! my beloved, soft!
 Through sickness and through pain
Thou hear'st glad notes aloft—-
 The rich angelic strain.
Do not I smooth thy couch, and hush thy dreams,
And cool thy parched lips from celestial streams?

Sleep, my beloved, sleep,
    Beneath the quiet sod
Is still repose, and deep,
    Till sounds the trump of God.
For *thee* no terror hath the awful grave—
Strong is mine arm to rescue—strong to save.

    Wake, my beloved, wake,
        At the right hand of Love !
    Thine, for thy Saviour's sake,
        The crown prepared above.
Wake, my beloved one, to the eternal morning—
Robed in the vesture of the saints' adorning !

LULLABY.

SLEEP, my child ! the moonlight sleepeth
    On the ocean billow ;
'Tis thy mother's eye that keepeth
    Watch beside thy pillow.
Darling, sleep ! the waves are sleeping
    'Neath the moonbeam's smile ;
And thy mother's heart is keeping
    Watch o'er thee the while.

Sleep, my bright one ! zephyr slumbers
    'Midst the forest leaves,
Where all night her plaintive numbers
    Philomela weaves.
On the hills the lonely echoes
    Softly sink to rest ;
In the groves the solemn shadows—
    Thou upon my breast.

Sleep, my babe ! The lily sleepeth
    On the lakes calm bosom—
Drowsy sense of slumber creepeth

O'er each bud and blossom.
On the hills green slope reclining,
    Sleeps the mist afar—
Gem-like through the darkness shining
    Smiles the vesper star.

Lo! the clouds that skirt the mountain,
    Fold their pinions free ;
Silence broods o'er fell and fountain—
    Silent love o'er thee.
E'en the stormy winds are sleeping
    In their caverns deep—
Watch and ward mamma is keeping,—
    Sleep then, darling, sleep!

DR. JOHN LE GAY BRERETON.

THIS many-sided quaker doctor and poet, was born at Bawtry, Yorkshire, October 28th, 1827, and was the son of a prominent physician of that town. He was at Ackworth from 1837 to 1841, and afterwards studied at Edinburgh and St. Andrews, took his M.D. in 1851, and practiced at Bradford for eight years, and in 1859 settled in Sydney. Here he soon distinguished himself by assisting in bringing about radical reforms in the lunatic asylums of the Colony. For many years he carried on a large practice in Sydney, and became a medical authority in the first rank; so much influence did he exercise, that having, on scientific grounds, an objection to vaccination, neither the Government nor the medical profession were able to carry a compulsory law in its favour. In his latter years he joined the Swedenborgians, and did much to establish and increase the New Church in Sydney.

His biographer says, " He cared much for the spirit of love and truth, but nothing for the empty bottles of mere ritual. I never met a man who realized so thoroughly the existence and reality of the spiritual world." He once mounted, the same authority tell us, the free-thought platform in response to an invitation to lecture on Swedenborg. He wrote "Genesis and the Beatitudes," and "One Teacher one Law," in defence of christianity; but his chief literary work was poetical, and as a poet he will continue to take high rank. He published in 1857, "Travels of Prince Legion," in 1865, "Poems," in 1883, "The Goal of Time," "One Teacher one Law," and "Beyond and other Poems," in 1887, "Genesis and the Beatitudes," and "The Triumph of Love."

He married in 1857 Miss Mary Tongue, and it was on account of her delicate health that they settled in Australia. He died on the 28th October, 1886, and was buried at St. Ann's Rhyde, one of the loveliest spots on the Paramatta river, not far from his own home. John Le Gay Brereton is described as having been singularly handsome in his youth, and full of life and vivacity; he was warm hearted, impulsive, and generous, and much beloved by those who knew him well.

His poetry is a good reflex of his nature; tender, musical, half sad, half playful, with a deeper note always underlying its graceful beauty, it never loses count of the spiritual realities behind the phenomena it describes with the pen of a poet and the soul of a mystic.

An Autumn Wreath.

The white frost's on the hill, love,
    The white mist on the lea;
The yellow leaves are falling
    From each still and drooping tree,—
Through the silent mist, love,
    That creepeth o'er the lea.

And hark! the night-wind waketh,
    It moaneth sad and low,
For the summer that must die, love,
    Though it linger never so;
The longest, happiest Summer
    That ever we shall know.

O sweetly came the Spring, love,
    And tenderly she moved
O'er every dewy meadow,
    Through every tangled wood,
And by the freshening burnie,
    Each slender blade and bud.

And tender was the plant, love,
  That in our bosom grew ;
One chilly blast had killed it ;—
  Oh ! little then we knew
How great a tree we reared, love,
  To shelter me and you.

And still we nursed and knew not
  What meant the little shoot ;
We wondered at the blossom
  And dreamed not of the fruit ;
And as aye the branches rose, love,
  Still wider spread the root.

Still grew the stately branches,
  And waved them to and fro
In every Summer breeze, love,
  That through the land did blow,
The longest, happiest Summer,
  That ever we shall know.

Lo all the pleasant woods, love,
  Are growing old and sere,
But Summer from our hearts, love,
  Shall never disappear,
The long and happy Summer
  Of Love's immortal year.

To my Wife, Mary.

As I lay on my sick-bed, Mary,
  With a weight upon my heart,
And a fire within my head,
  The thought came,—we must part.
And men will say, " He's dead," Mary,
  " He has played his little part,
And another will stand in his stead,
  In council and in mart."

Though many a joy and woe, Mary,
  Our memories intertwine,
Though sweet the interflow,
  'Twixt hearts like thine and mine,
The pleasures of long ago, Mary,
  The sorrows of lang-syne,
And the present all aglow,
  With light and love divine ;

And though I had always yearned, Mary,
  And strained my childish eyes,
For a glimpse of some undiscerned,
  And beautiful Paradise ;
And though since then I've learned, Mary,
  With a spirit calm and wise,
That the hopes which in me burned,
  Are splendid realities ;

And though I stood so near, Mary,
  I heard the waters roar,
And heard, beyond, the cheer,
  Of those who had gone before,
The friends we hold most dear, Mary,
  The spirits we most adore ;
O many a bard and seer,
  And hero heart of yore.

And though God I still did own, Mary,
  Was wiser far than we,
I answered with a groan,
  O sad, if this should be !
For what were Heaven, alone, Mary,
  And who would care for thee ;
Till then I had not known,
  How dear thou wert to me.

SPIRIT VOYAGING.
A SONG OF HASCHISH.

THE soft wind bloweth, the blithe stream floweth,
    To Paradisal airs :
Where are we going? there's no knowing,
    And who amongst us cares?
Then row! brothers row! for merrily, ho!
The wild birds sing and the soft winds blow.

The soul that is wary, the land of the fairy,
    Never, never may find ;
But the stream grows dark, and the black woods stark,
    And shrill the icy wind,
Then row! brothers row! for brighter grow,
The woods and the flowery banks as we go.

O, fragrant the showers of leaves and of flowers,
    That greet us passing along!
While under the wave, each starry cave
    Sends up its fairy song ;
And! brothers, lo! more rosily glow,
The sky above, and the plain below.

ELIZABETH NAISH CAPPER.

ELIZABETH NAISH CAPPER was born in 1818, at a farm near Devizes, and has resided for most of her life in Bristol, where she is still living. She has written for many papers and magazines, and a volume of her pieces was collected and published in 1882, under the title of "Voices of the Twilight and other Poems." (Samuel Harris & Co., London). The first edition of this was quickly sold out, and as another has not yet been issued, the book is now difficult to get. I have quoted from it the universally popular "Pilgrim of Earth who art journeying to Heaven," which has been printed in numberless collections of sacred poetry. Elizabeth N. Capper writes with ease and grace, and all her poems are full of a deeply religious spirit.

DISCOURAGED BECAUSE OF THE WAY.

PILGRIM of earth who art journeying to Heaven,
    Heir of eternal life, child of the day,
Cared for, watched over, beloved and forgiven,
    Art thou discouraged because of the way?

Cared for, watched over, though often thou seemest,
    Justly forsaken nor counted a child ;
Loved and forgiven, though rightly thou deemest
    Thyself all unlovely, impure and defiled.

Weary and thirsty, no water-brook near thee,
    Press on, nor faint at the length of the way ;
The God of thy life will assuredly hear thee ;
    He will provide thee with strength for the day.

Break through the brambles and briars that obstruct thee,
　　Dread not the gloom and the darkness of night ;
Lean on the hand that will safely conduct thee ;
　　Trust to His eye to whom darkness is light.

Be trustful, be steadfast ; whatever betide thee,
　　Only one thing do thou ask of the Lord ;
Grace to go forward wherever He guide thee,
　　Simply believing the truth of His word.

Still on thy spirit deep anguish is pressing,
　　Not for the yoke that His wisdom bestows :
A heavier burden thy soul is distressing ;
　　A heart that is slow in His love to repose.

Earthliness, coldness, unthankful behaviour,—
　　Ah ! thou may'st sorrow, but do not despair ;—
Even this grief thou may'st bring to thy Saviour,—
　　Cast upon Him e'en this burden and care.

Bring all thy hardness, His power can subdue it,
　　How full is the promise, the blessing how free !
" Whatsoever, ye ask in My name, I will do it,"
　　" Abide in My love and be joyful in Me."

JANE CREWDSON.

JANE FOX was the second daughter of George Fox, of Perranarworthal, and was born at that place in October, 1808. She married at Exeter, in October, 1836, Thomas Dillworth Crewdson, a Manchester manufacturer. She contributed several hymns to Lovell Squire's "Selection of Scriptural Poetry," in 1848; and, in 1851, published a small volume of her own, entitled, "Aunt Jane's Verses for Children;" this was reprinted in 1855 and 1871; in 1860, she issued "Lays of the Reformation, and other Lyrics." Her last book, "A Little While, and other Poems," was not published until 1864, a year after her death, which took place at her residence in Manchester in September, 1863.

The Little While.

Oh, for the peace that floweth as a river,
    Making life's desert places bloom and smile!
Oh, for the faith to grasp Heaven's bright "for ever,"
    Amid the shadows of Earth's "little while!"

"A little while" for patient vigil-keeping,
    To face the stern, to wrestle with the strong;
"A little while" to sow the seed with weeping,
    Then bind the sheaves and sing the harvest song!

"A little while" to wear the robe of sadness.
    To toil, with weary steps, thro' miry ways;
Then to pour forth the fragrant oil of gladness,
    And clasp the girdle round the robe of praise!

" A little while " 'mid shadow and illusion,
  To strive, by faith, Love's mysteries to spell ;
Then read each dark enigma's bright solution,
  Whilst meekly owning "*He* doth all things well !"

" A little while " the earthen pitcher taking
  To wayside brooks, from far-off fountains fed,
Where the cool lip, its thirst for ever slaking,
  May taste the fulness of the Fountain-head !

" A little while " to keep the oil from failing,
  " A little while " faith's flickering lamp to trim,
And then, the Bridegroom's coming footsteps hailing,
  To haste to meet Him with the bridal hymn !

And *He*, who is Himself the Gift and Giver,
  The future glory, and the present smile,
With the bright promise of the glad " for ever "
  Will light the shadows of the " little while !"

IN EVERYTHING GIVE THANKS.

O Thou whose bounty fills my cup
  With every blessing meet,
I give Thee thanks for *every* drop—
  The bitter and the sweet !

I praise Thee for the desert road,
  And for the river-side ;
For all Thy goodness hath bestowed,
  And all Thy grace denied !

I thank Thee, both for smile and frown,
  And for the gain and loss ;
I praise Thee for the future crown,
  And for the present cross !

I thank Thee for the wing of love
  Which stirred my worldly nest;
And for the stormy cloud, that drove
  The flutterer to Thy breast!

I bless Thee for the glad increase,
  And for the waning joy;
And for this strange, this settled peace,
  Which nothing can destroy!

ELFRIDA MARY CROWLEY.

THIS gifted young poet was born at Croydon, in April, 1863. She was all her life a great sufferer from asthma, and travelled much in Egypt and the Riviera; spending her, winters in these sunny places in search of the phantom health, which, alas, she was fated never to find! She died at her home, Bramley Oaks, Croydon, in June, 1892. Her poems were collected, and printed for private circulation after her death by her family, and show a keen poetic sense and a passionate love of beauty; they were chiefly inspired by her travels in the south. "A Parable," is a very touching and beautiful rendering of her own life, with its long pathway, trodden with such patient feet, and the widening golden rift which was the gateway of death, and "the new life begun."

TRANSFORMATION.

DEAR love, an' thou wert here,
　　Flowers would blossom and birds would sing,—
Brown leaves, shrivelled and sere,
　　At this fall o' the year
Would don the tender green of the spring!
　　Dear love, an' thou wert here.

And the sun would shine
　　Over hill, sea-shore, and valley and plain;
Flooding with light divine
　　This waiting heart of mine;—
For joy at the thought of thy coming again
　　The clouds would break and shine.

Dear love, an' thou wert here,
  The driving rain and the misty air,
And the dark day drear
  Come no more anear ;
New joy, new earth, new heaven be fair,
  Dear love, an thou wert here.

An Old Town.

On The Riviera.

Up and down, up and down,
Through the winding streets of the quaint old town,
Now a glimpse through this sunlit archway—look !
Here, the stony path of a mountain brook,
There, palm and olive and orange tree,
Far down below, the glittering sea,
And sunny headlands keen and clear,
In the luminious, sparkling atmosphere.

  Up and down, up and down,
Through the narrow streets of the old, old town,
Up the rugged, well-worn, steep stone stairs
To the church where the peasants say their prayers ;
And the dark-eyed women, one by one,
Step from the shadow into the sun,
With linen down to the mountain's stream,
While the old crones chatter and nod and dream.
The jutting houses, sombre and high,
Almost shut out the warm blue sky,
The "earthquake arches" slant across,—
Here is a tuft of golden moss,—
A waving palm branch over there,
Bits of bright colour everywhere,
Lemons and oranges on the ground ;
From doorways dim the garrulous sound

Of the old crones' voices, the patois shrill
Of the children straggling down the hill.
The men are at work with olive and vine,
And the old ones bask in the warm sunshine.
Have they basked in the sun a hundred years?
Has anguish touched them, nor time, nor tears?
So long as the sun floods their southern sky,
They—they are happy—so am I.

DOROTHY CROWLEY.

DOROTHY, sister of E. M. Crowley, and youngest daughter of Alfred and Mary Catherine Crowley, was born at Bramley Oaks, Croydon, in September, 1874. She was educated at the High School, Croydon, and the Mount, York, and continued her studies during a six months residence in Switzerland. She has written poems since her ninth year, but has been very chary of publishing them. I hope soon, however, we shall have a collection of her verses in volume form. She married, in 1895, Dr. E. Vipont Brown, of Manchester.

LOVE.

O LOVE divine and perfect, deep and sure,
O mystic power, ne'er-ending, infinite,—
Shine ever onward, as this earth-life wanes,
Shine ever forward to the perfect light.—
O heaven-born power, divided not by time,—
The link between those oceans wide and free
Which roll around us, and about our way,
—The one that is, and that which is to be—
Bridge o'er the space between them made by Death,
That finite here and infinite above,—
For thou are constant, no division thine,
Since Life and Death are covered o'er with Love.

And guiding o'er the bridge between the two,
And growing fuller as we perfect grow,—
In fullest beauty in the dawning Life,
Shall be the Love we understood below.

PERFECTION.

What does it mean?—This beauty of Nature,—
Sky of soft blue with the glow in the west ;—
Last sunbeams slanting across the dim beeches,
South breezes lulling the tree-tops to rest.—
Sweet quiet stealing adown the fair meadows,
Peace all round, and deep peace in the sky,—
Fadeth the sun—but the afterglow brightens,
Where is the room for regret or a sigh?
Why does it all seem more sweet than before,
Sunset more lovely, and blueness more blue,
All that was wanting now perfect, completed?—
—Dear, 'tis that Love is there shining all through.
And Nature, now perfect in Beauty to me,
Whispers of Love, and—belovéd—of thee.

THOMAS ELLWOOD.

THOMAS ELLWOOD was born at Crowell, in Oxford-
shire, in October, 1639, and was the younger son of
Walter and Elizabeth Ellwood, both of whom belonged to
good, but decayed old families. At the age of seven, Thomas
Ellwood went to the Free School at Thame, from whence,
however, he was soon removed. He became expert in all
kinds of field sports, and was very waggish, and full of life and
spirit ; he afterwards reproached himself for much thoughtless
dissipation, but his worst crime seems to have been his trying
to run a ruffian, who had grossly insulted his father, through
the body with his sword. His mother and brother both died
in his youth, and in 1659 a great change came over the lively
high-spirited lad. He went with his father to pay a visit at
the Grange, Chalfont St. Peter's, Bucks, the home of Isaac
Pennington, son of Alderman J. Pennington, the regicide.
Pennington's wife, Mary, who had been the widow of Sir
William Springett, had been intimate with the Ellwoods in
London, and her daughter, Gulielma, had been Thomas's
especial playmate. The Pennington's had lately become
Quakers, and Thomas Ellwood and his father were much
interested, and paid them another visit in the same year to
learn more of these new doctrines. Thomas attended a
Friends' Meeting, and met there, it is said, Edward Burrough
and James Naylor; the former's preaching much impressed
him, and after attending another meeting at High Wycombe,
he formally joined the new sect, adopting their dress and
mode of speech. His father very strongly resented this,
thrashed him for wearing a hat in his presence, and kept him

a prisoner in his house during the winter of 1660. At Easter, however, the Pennington's managed to get him to Chalfont St. Peters, where he stayed until Whitsuntide, diligently attending meetings, and being, he declared, divinely inspired to write and print an attack on the established clergy, called "An Alarm to the Priests." He afterwards went to London, and met George Fox the younger. About this time Ellwood wrote to ask Thomas Loe, an Oxford Quaker, to attend meeting at Crowell. Unfortunately Loe was in prison, and the letter fell into Lord Falkland's hands; he was Lord Lieutenant of the County, and immediately sent a party of horse to arrest Ellwood, by way of answer to his epistle. They took him before two Justices, and he, having refused the oaths, was imprisoned in the house of the City Marshal at Oxford. His father managed to get him released, but vainly tried to persuade him to give up his Quakerism.

In 1661, the elder Ellwood, with his two daughters, went to live in London, and Thomas, by his father's orders, sold off all the cattle, etc., dismissed the servants, and lived in complete seclusion; often, however, visiting Aylesbury Jail, where many of his Quaker friends were imprisoned.

At a Friends' Meeting at the Pennington's house, he was again arrested, and though soon released, for no apparent reason he was again taken up, as a rogue and vagabond, while quietly walking home from Chalfont St. Peter's, through Beaconsfield; but after one night's detention was discharged once more. In 1662, Elwood caught the smallpox, and on his recovery went to London to study. Pennington had consulted Dr. Paget about his young friend, and Dr. Paget had arranged that he should read with Milton, who was then blind, and living a very retired life. Ellwood therefore took lodgings in Aldersgate, near Milton's house, and went there every afternoon, excepting Sunday, to read Latin with the poet, who taught him the foreign pronunciation. In October this same year he was arrested at a meeting at the " Bull and Mouth," and confined until December in the Old Bridewell, in Fleet Street.   At first he was nearly starved, but his father and the Penningtons sent him a few pounds, and he made night waistcoats of red and yellow flannel for a Cheapside hosier. On the 19th December he was taken before the Recorder of the Old Bailey, declined the oaths, and was sent to Newgate amongst the lowest felons and pickpockets.   The prison at that time was in a most unsanitary condition, and one of the Quakers having died, the Foreman of the Jury expressed great disgust at the Inquest at the treatment the prisoners received there.   After this Ellwood was removed to the Old Bridewell again, where he stayed some little time longer, and then became Latin tutor in the Pennington's family, and managed their estates in Kent and Sussex.   To obtain some ready money he consented to the sale of Crowell by his father. During the Plague he hired a cottage for Milton to retire to at Chalfont St. Peter's, and after his return from a month's imprisonment in Aylesbury Jail for attending a Friend's funeral at Amersham, the poet lent him " Paradise Lost " to read in manuscript.   Ellwood, when returning it, said :—" Thou hast said much of Paradise Lost, but what hast thou to say of *Paradise Found ?*"   When the questioner called on Milton afterwards, in London, he was shown " Paradise Regained," and the poet added :—" This is owing to you, for you put it into my head by the question you put to me at Chalfont, which before I had not thought of."

Isaac Pennington was himself in prison at Aylesbury for nine months during 1665 and 1666, his household was broken up, and Ellwood stayed with his pupils at Aylesbury, Bristol, and Amersham, but was again imprisoned for attending meeting, from March 13th to June 25th.

In October, 1669, he married a Friend called Mary Ellis, who was sixteen years older than himself; she died in 1708.

His father objected strongly to this marriage, and, contrary to a former promise, declined to help his son in any way.

Meanwhile Thomas carried on vigorous controversies, grew intimate with Fox and Penn, the latter of whom married his old friend, Gulielma, in 1668, and the former of whom he helped in his attempt to crush John Perrot in his controversy about wearing hats during meetings for worship. He travelled with Fox in his organising expedition through the West of England, and when the Conventicle Act became law in 1670, and the Quakers were at the mercy of corrupt Informers, he proceeded against two of them for perjury, and exerted all the ingenuity of his acute intellect to procure their downfall.

In 1674 he was engaged in controversy with Hicks, a Baptist who had written against Quakerism; he wrote also against tithes. His father died about 1684, and Thomas Ellwood was charged with not attending his funeral, and incurred much undeserved censure on this account. After this event he lived in great retirement, for the most part at Amersham, writing constantly against internal divisions in the Quaker ranks, and vigorously denouncing the heresy of George Keith.

In 1690 he edited George Fox's Journal, and was engaged for a considerable time on a History of the Old Testament. In 1707 and 1708 distraints were levied upon him for the non-payment of tithes. In 1708 his wife died; she was, according to his biographer, "a solid weighty woman," and he himself passed away in 1713, at his house at Amersham, and was buried at New Jordan, the Chalfont St. Giles Friends' Burial Ground.

He wrote "Davidei's," a sacred poem in five books, which has gone through several editions, the first being published in 1712. This poem was begun before 1688, and also before he had seen Cowley's "Davidei's." He published also "A Collection of Poems on Various Subjects."

FROM "DAVIDEI'S."

BOOK IV.

UNSTEADY Nature, varying like the Wind,
Hurries to each *Extreme*, th' *unstable* Mind.
At Sea *becalmed*, we wish some *brisker* Gales
Would on us rise, and fill our *limber* Sails.
We have our Wish; and strait our *Skiff* is toss't
So high, we are in danger to be lost.
At Land, we would be *foremost;* make a stir,
And Ride at *Neck-and-all*, with *Whip* and *Spur.*
We would *be*, would *have* all: are loath to stay
For what's our Right, till have't of right we may.
This is the Nature of *ambitious* Man,
Soaring as *fast*, as *high* too, as he can.
Whereas, would we but Bridle our Desire,
Till in due time we might rise safely higher.

DAVIDEI'S.

BOOK V.

How needful 'tis hot *Anger* to suppress!
Nor suffer *Wrath* to rise into *Excess!*
Not to give way to *Passion!*   Nor too high
Resent an apprehended *Injury!*
Much less to let the *Tongue*, upon Debate,
Break loose, in Words which may exasperate.
For Words oft times, like *Flint* on *Steel*, strike Fire,
And thereby the *Contention* raise the higher.
So have I seen what from a *Sparkle* came,
Blown, by hot Breath, into a furious *Flame.*

FRAGMENT.

"O that mine eye might closèd be,
 To what becomes me not to see!

That deafness might possess mine ear,
To what concerns me not to hear!
That Grace my tongue might always tie,
From ever speaking foolishly!
That no vain thought might ever rest,
Or be conceivèd in my breast!
That, by each word, each deed, each thought,
Glory may to my God be brought!
But what are wishes! Lord, mine eye
On Thee is fixed; to Thee I cry;
O purge out all my dross, my sin;
Make me more white than snow within!
Wash, Lord, and purify my heart,
And make it clean in every part;
And when 'tis clean, Lord keep it too,
For this is more than I can do."

SARAH HUSTLER FOX.

SARAH HUSTLER FOX was born on August 8th, 1800, at Undercliffe, near Bradford, Yorkshire. She was the only daughter of John and Jane Hustler, and married in 1825, Charles Fox of Falmouth. For many years they lived at Perranarworthal, where they exerted themselves to promote the welfare of their poorer neighbours in every possible way. Charles Fox offered prizes for improvements in the machinery for working mines, established a school at Perran, and followed this up by lectures, classes, and reading rooms, by which he endeavoured to supplement the instruction given in the school.

After their daughter's marriage, the Foxes removed to Trebah, Falmouth, which, originally a seaside cottage, was transformed by them into a complete and beautiful home. S. H. Fox published, in 1854, "A Metrical Version of the Book of Job." For this work she consulted the various translations and principal commentaries, carefully comparing disputed texts, and balancing probable interpretations. In 1863, she published "Poems, original and translated" by S. H. F. (Longman, Green & Co.), illustrated very beautifully by her niece, Elizabeth Tuckett, afterwards Mrs. William Fowler ; these illustrations add much to the value of the book, and won the approval of Ruskin. Sarah Hustler Fox was a true poet, her verse is instinct with that inspiration which comes from constant communion with those spiritual powers and influences, which are so much more real and authoritative to the poet and dreamer, than the material so-called realities by which they are surrounded in everyday life. Always thoughtful and musical, the poems reach in such pieces as

"The Brown Nuts," and "Scene in an Asylum," a depth of weird and tragic pathos, while "One more unfortunate," and "To have and to hold for better for worse," are suffused with that quenchless tenderness which a deeper wisdom than the merely human one embodied in the Statute Book draws from the pitiful sins and sorrows of life. The translations contained in this little volume are wonderfully faithful to the spirit of the originals, especially those from the German poets.

S. H. Fox was confined to her room with severe rheumatic gout for the last twelve years of her life, but her marvellous patience and brightness, through all those weary years of suffering, and her constant and deep sympathy with others, were most beautiful and striking. She died at Trebah in February, 1882.

SUNSET ON THE MOUNTAINS.

BENEATH the azure sky
They wait so solemnly,
Our human hearts are in their presence still'd ;
As if the ages old
Their secrets there did fold,
Until, Creation's purposes fulfilled,
Again shall sound the word,
Not as when Chaos heard
"Let there be light "—and darkness back did roll ;
But, over land and sea,
"Let time no longer be,"—
And earth shall crumble like a burning scroll.

And yet there is a time,
Before the vesper chime
From nestling birds, and odorous leaves ascending,
When, in the west, the sun,
His day's work almost done,
O'er purple clouds is for his farewell bending ;

Then every icy crest
And every marble breast
With sudden life doth seem to heave and glow ;
Touch'd by those ardent beams,
A golden glory streams
O'er adamantine heights and caves of snow,
And, blushing rosy red,
With joy, each radiant head,
In ether springs to meet the parting kiss—
Then every snow-white brow
Doth humbly seem to bow,
And sink to rest in quiet thankfulness.

EUTHANASIA.

I.

WITH meekly bended head, nor word, nor moan,
She turn'd her to the path none may retread,
Down the deep, solemn valley, dark and dread—
No hand to grasp in hers—alone—alone !
The watchers heard not as she hastened on,
So soft her footsteps fell ; when past them fled
A tremulous, low breath ;—and through the shade
They lifted up their eyes, and she was gone ;
But o'er the stream they saw one golden ray,
Beneath whose radiance the hush'd waves grew bright
And on her earth-worn garments by the shore,
Trac'd they the words that summon'd her away—
" Haste thee, and cast aside thy robes of night,
For thee the sun hath risen, to set no more."

EUTHANASIA.

II.

OH ! not alone ; for, ever as she went,
No lamps beneath, no stars above to guide,

He who, unseen, she lov'd was at her side ;
His was the pilgrim-staff whereon she leant ;
He, to restore her soul, His comfort sent,
Her Shepherd still, though to her sight denied,
She knew His footsteps, and was satisfied ;
A low sweet song breath'd from her soul's content,
For all but angel ears two lowly sweet—
"I fear no evil, for I trust in thee ;
I shall behold thee on that sun-bright shore ;
By the still waters thou wilt lead my feet ;
In thine own pastures green my rest shall be,
And I shall dwell with thee, and fall no more."

ROBERT BARCLAY FOX.

ROBERT BARCLAY FOX was born on September 6th, 1817. He married Jane Gurney Backhouse in 1844, and died March 10th, 1855. His life was outwardly uneventful, but was full of work for others, and has left a most fragrant memory behind for all those who knew him. He wrote some tender and touching verse, but most of it is unpublished, and is either in MS., or lost in the pages of old papers and magazines. His "War Song for the Times" shows how deeply and earnestly he felt on the subject of peace.

ON THE DEATH OF A. C.

SHE hath awaken'd from the dream of life,
And issued from her darkened chamber forth
Into the cloudless day.   O wherefore weep?
In throbbing expectation and delight,
Which leaves no place for hope, she goes to meet
Him whom, unseen, she loved—for He had been
The Life-spring of her soul—her Light, her Joy,
Her Consolation—all 'twixt God and her.

He came and called her in a vision sweet;
And she, with blissful haste, the call obeyed.
Bright forms, upon the sunny eastern hill,
Beckon'd her onwards, and she heard the tones
Of far-off music—how could she delay?
One kiss—one parting tear—and then she sped
To her appointed place.   O weep no more!

To the Moon.

Lonely pilgrim of the night,
Spherèd watcher, mildly bright,
    Whither art thou journeying?

Ever since Creation's morn,
Saw thee glide forth, Chaos-born,
Ladie of the mystic horn,
    Is it true that thou hast been
Treading that unvarying path,
    Round and round this globe of ours;
Heightening every charm it hath,
    With looks of light and silver showers?

Path to us unseen—unknown;
Trodden by thyself alone—
    Printless on the liquid ether;
Leaving far, to left and right,
Wandering worlds and spheres of light,
    Lov'd of one, but stay'd by neither.

Sleepless moon! athwart the sky,
Do thy mission—onward hie!
    Onward to the end of time.
Thou art more than something fair,
Voyaging aimless through the air,
Thou hast meaning high and rare,
    Writ in characters sublime!

Onward! for thy work's divine;
God who made thee sail and shine
    Twice three thousand years ago,
Sees thee work His will to-day;
Naught but He can bid thee stay;
O, if man could thus obey,
    Heaven again should dwell below.

Freely to the earth thou givest
Of the light which thou receivest,
    Unrequited, shining still ;
Like a kind and equal mother,
Blessing none above another,
    Blessing all, both good and ill.

Even though her shade enfold thee,
So that we can not behold thee,
    Yet we know that thou art there ;
Type of that mysterious grace,
Sin can hide, but not efface,
To the heart, its dwelling-place !
    Seen or unseen, ever near.

Holy—God, thy servants name thee,
Holy—all thy works proclaim thee,
    And in speechless *act* adore :
Man, whom thou hast lov'd and blest,
Far, how far beyond the rest—
Made him earth's most honor'd guest—
    Teach him, Lord, to love thee more !

MADNESS.

" A sunbeam gone astray "——
    A cloud-eclipsed star,
A fair child that hath lost its way
    In the wild woods afar.

A spirit disenthroned—-
    Yet a bright spirit still,
Fallen, alas ! —but not disowned,
    Such was the Maker's will.

One shade amid the shadows
    That sunbeam throws *aslant ;*

Dim lie the golden meadows—
    That accustomed haunt.

And the spirit's world is rife
    With strange and shadowy things;
Self-wrought, and lit to seeming life
    By the flashing of its wings.

And there its devious way
    It wandereth—unforgot;
For nought of God's so far can stray,
    As the place where he is not.

BENJAMIN GOOUCH.

BENJAMIN GOOUCH is descended from a family which settled in Ireland during the reign of William III., and which has for many generations belonged to the Society of Friends. He was born at Waterford, and his father being engaged in commercial pursuits, he was intended for a business life, but finding this very uncongenial, he determined to adopt the profession of teaching. He studied at the Flounders Institute and University College, London, where he took his degree, afterwards teaching in Friends' Schools until 1876, when he established a private school at Southport. In 1878 he published a volume of verse entitled "Life Thoughts and Lays from History." Many of these poems had previously appeared in magazines and papers, and their reception was so encouraging that the author commenced to prepare a second volume for the press, but owing to the stress of other work this volume has not yet been given to the public, although a few of the poems have appeared in various periodicals. Benjamin Goouch married, in 1876, Rebecca, daughter of the late John Sharp, Headmaster of Croydon School.

His verse has much power and beauty, and the piece entitled "The Leaf Fall," which I give, is full of a peculiar and delicate music, as though the poet had indeed stood in the autumn woods, and caught the very voice of the fragile whirling leaves as they fluttered by, borne on the wings of the relentless wind. The historical poems are very fine, both in diction and thought, and it is to be hoped that the half-prepared second volume will get itself finished with no longer delay, as I understand Benjamin Goouch has now more leisure than formerly.

ONCE MET.

THEY met, in summer's opening bloom,
    Beneath the linden trees,—
The soft air laden with perfume,
    And sound of humming bees:
Ne'er spoke they; 'twas a moment's glance,
    The gleam of kindling eyes,
A flush, as 'twere the rosy trance
    That falls from Alpine skies;
A sudden secret joy; a strife,
    With impulse in them stirred:
They lived into each other's life,
    Then passed without a word.

They met no more—but then they knew—
    Though still they know not how—
A secret bond between them grew;
    Their souls are kindred now:
The melody of that sweet hour
    Attunes their being yet,
And oft they ponder o'er its power,
    And wonder why they met.
They lead apart, in hope, alone,
    A life of long farewell;
But till they know as they are known,
    The *why* they cannot tell!

THE LEAF-FALL.

THE wind is now
That brings the dreary winter of the year,
Rending the blasted leaves, all red and sere,
    From the torn bough;
Wailing amidst the woodlands wild and lone
For the sweet summer day and the hours of sunshine gone.

Calling, calling,
Calling the spirits of the leaves to rest
'Neath the lone aisles with fading garlands drest :
And falling, falling,
Through the dim twilight of the short'ning day ;
Falling, falling, falling, they hear it and obey.

In the blear light,
Like spectres hovering on the verge of doom,
They float and whirl down through the airy gloom
From the lost height ;
And o'er the grave where silent they must lie,
Circling in airy ring, they whisper and they sigh.

Whisp'ring—yes, low
Their rustling voices mingle, as in fear—
" Break not our rest, O thou who drawest near :
Go ! scorner, go !
Thou too on earth from life's dishevelled bough,
A scorned and blasted thing shall fall, as we do now.

Leave us alone :
We that erewhile have with the zephyr played,
And, in our joyaunce, stirred the shadowy glade
With rustling tone,
We once again would commune with the wind,
Ere to the noisome clay in mouldering rest consigned.

But once we fall—
Once in the year, when sunshine is gone by,
And storms have darkened o'er the summer sky,
We hasten all
To our low rest ; but thou and thy proud race,
Oh ! who can tell your fall, its season, or its place ?"

And it is so!
O falling leaves! we wither day by day;
From our stripped homes the loved ones drop away;
    Fading they go
Through the sad autumn and the vernal bloom,
Through summer's golden light, through winter's stormy gloom.

    The passed away—
The loved of our young life, whose smiles have made
A summer sunshine in the wintry shade—
    Oh! where are they?
Where the warm love, whose mild and soothing power
Was to our opening hearts as dew on the young flower?

    Is it not so?
Where are the faces that were wont to meet us,
Where are the voices that were wont to greet us,
    Long, long ago?
Have we not mourned our dearest and our best,
Have we not seen them fade and laid them to their rest?

    And yet, ye leaves!
Though we may shed this frail mortality,
Though we may fade, we are not such as ye
    Whom the wind reaves;
And there is something in this dust enshrined—
Something that dwells not in your perishable rind.

    This is not vain:
When sleep has bound us with a death-like zone,
An unseen presence holds its darkened throne
    With mystic chain,
While thought and sense are locked in rayless night,
Linking the breathing frame still to the world of light;

But if that gem
From hence is parted, in the self-same hour
The empty casket shrivels, as a flower
On severed stem ;
Then is the endless sleep, and ne'er again
The mouldering flesh returns unto its place with men.

We know, we know
That all things earthly turn to dust and air ;
But what art *thou ? thy* fading is not there
With flesh laid low ;
Thy being is not as the things of earth—
Whence art thou, vital spring ? where is thy second birth ?

We know that when
Its chain is broken, shattered is the spell
That binds this breathing clay ; a leaf, a shell,
It falleth then.
True that we fade, as fade the herb and tree,
Yet, O ye falling leaves, we are not such as ye.

FANNY HARRIS.

FANNY HARRIS was born at Wimborne, Dorsetshire in 1846. Her family belonged to the Congregation-alists, but she became a member of the Society of Friends in 1878, and was recorded a minister in 1881. In 1882, she married Henry Vigius Harris, of Plymouth. Many of her pieces have appeared in "the Friend's Quarterly Examiner," and other magazines.

THE PRESENCE OF CHRIST.

My door is left ajar,
Earth's sights and sounds are free to come and go ;
What room is there for these within my heart,
When hope is burning low ?

No sun of joy hath set,
No radiant star been quenched in deepest night ;
And yet all glory from the face of Heaven,
Hath vanished from my sight.

For I have seen His face !
Just for one mingled hour of joy and pain,—
And souls that once have looked upon their Lord
Must die or look again !

O poor wayfaring man,
Turning aside amid the shades of night,
To rest beneath my humble roof,—and then
To vanish from my sight !

No robe of priestly white,
    No kingly grace I saw or worshipped then :
    Only a pilgrim garb, a " visage marred,"
        " More than the sons of men."

And yet my heart was glad,
    To see him pass across my humble floor,
    For 'mid the darkness, e'en a stranger's step
        Is welcome at our door !

But when the morning broke,
    And all the hills were bathed in golden glow,
    With speechless sorrow resting on His brow,
        I saw Him rise to go.

And once he seemed to pause,—
    " O weary heart, no more a passing guest,
    But as within thy home the Best-Beloved,
        How gladly would I rest ! "

And I ! the heavens were blue,
    And all the earth was gay with birds and flowers,
    And household tasks were waiting for my hand
        Through the swift noontide hours !

And so—I let Him go !—
    The lonely stranger with the veiléd brow—
    And orphaned, desolate, before *thy* door,
        O God, thou seest me now !

I cannot bid thee come,
    Only I cry with tears of bitter pain ;
    For souls that once have looked upon their Lord
        Must die or look again !

   .   .   .   .   .   .

Jesus, my Saviour-King !
    My soul hath rest beneath thy royal sway,

Each vacant chamber of my heart is filled,
  Thou art with me alway !

No more a stranger-guest,
  Turning aside to tarry for a night,
  In thine abiding presence there is peace,
    And infinite delight !

My Life of Life art thou !
  O, let thy perfect beauty in me shine,
  Till in the home of thy Redeemed I stand
    In loveliness divine.

JOHN HARRIS.

THE Cornish miner poet was born in October, 1820, to quote his own words in his auto-biography, "the place of my birth was a boulder-built cottage, with reedy roof, bare rafters, and clay floor, locally known as 'Six Chimnies,' on the top of Bolennowe Hill, Cambourne, Cornwall. The rough house had no back door, nor any windows looking northward, except one about a foot square in the little pantry, but on the south side it had four windows, and a porch of primitive granite, literally small unpolished boulders. The woodwork of the roof was all visible, and sometimes the stars through the thatch." His father was a copper miner, and also rented a small farm, on which he laboured mornings, evenings, and holidays, pursuing his work underground during the day. When he was ten years old, John Harris began helping the men who worked at the entrance of the mine, and had to walk three miles to the scene of his labours. He wrote poems afterwards in the evening hours, and when paper was scarce, pencilled them on the white-washed walls of his bedroom, or when ink failed, wrote them in blackberry juice! The miners used to place the boy poet on a hand-barrow, or heap of mineral, and gather round him while he recited his verses, marvelling at "the wonderful boy who could read a book like a parson!" When he was twenty-five he married, and took up his residence with his wife, in a two-roomed cottage in the village of Troon. For ten months after his marriage his earnings were only tenpence a day, yet the young couple contrived to live and keep out of debt; then luck changed, and John Harris soon found himself the happy possessor of two hundred pounds. With a portion of this money he built himself a house at Troon-Moor, by the river, continuing his work in the mine, and labouring at his home in the mornings and evenings, composing his poems as he worked, and soothing his hard and tiring labours with the poet's blissful visions.

In 1853 he published his first volume, "Lays from the Mine, the Moor, and the Mountain." This little book was well received, and was followed by a second and enlarged edition eighteen months afterwards. In 1858, soon after John Harris had removed to Falmouth, appeared his "Land's End, Kynance Cove, and other Poems." In 1860 his "Mountain Prophet, the Mine, and other Poems." In 1863, "A story of Carn Brea, Essays and Poems." In 1866, "Shakespeare's Shrine, an Indian Story. Essays and Poems." In 1868, "Luda, a Lay of the Druids, Hymns, Tales, Essays, and Legends." In 1870, "Bulo, Reuben Ross, a tale of the Manacles, Hymn, Song, and Story." In 1872, "The Cruise of the Cutter, and other Peace Poems." In 1873, John Harris began to issue a series of illustrated tracts, under the heading, "Peace Pages for the People", advocating arbitration instead of war, these were largely distributed. In 1874, he collected some of his best pieces, and published them under the title of "Wayside Pictures, Hymns, and Poems."

He also wrote for many magazines and papers, especially a series of articles on the land question. In 1875, he published "Walks with the Wild Flowers," and in 1877, "Tales and Poems." In 1878 he was suddenly seized with paralysis, but recovered sufficiently to bring out at the end of the year, his "Two Giants," which also contains his auto-biography, from which these particulars of his life have been chiefly drawn.

In 1879 he published "Monro," which was highly praised by Longfellow. In 1881 appeared "Linto and Laneer." Mr. S. C. Hall wrote to him very appreciatively about this book. But although he won much praise, his industry and poetic merit brought him small profit, and if it had not been for several grants from the Royal Literary Fund and Royal Bounty Fund, he would have been an actual loser by the publication of his works.   In the year 1879 he was received into membership with the Society of Friends, and in 1884 he died, having never completely recovered from the effects of the paralytic seizure.   His poems are wonderful productions, considering his lack of education and hard life; they are full of intense appreciation for natural beauty, and his landscapes and pictured scenes have been realised with the poet's intense vision, which sees *through* a thing, and in the beauty of form and colouring, recognises a deeper spiritual beauty.   His auto-biography is one of the most fascinating books ever written, and gives a terribly graphic picture of a miner's life, sweetened and glorified in the writer's case by the "angel of poetry," as he beautifully calls the spirit which soothed and comforted his darkest hours, whispering beautiful thoughts in musical rhymes, in the darkness of the mine, and amid the weariness of hard and protracted labour.

An Ode.

On the Anniversary of the birthday of William Shakespeare, April 23rd, 1864.*

*This poem won the first prize at the Tercentenary of Shakespeare, April, 1864.   Persons from all parts of the United Kingdom and America competed for it.

Over the earth aglow,
Peak-point and plain below,
The red, round sun sinks in the purple west;
Lambs press their daisy bed,
The lark drops overhead,
And sings the labourer, hastening home to rest.

Bathed in the ruddy light,
Flooding his native height,

A youthful bard is stretched upon the moss;
    He heedeth not the eve
    Whose locks the elfins weave,
Entranced with Shakespeare near a Cornish Cross.

    Men pass him and re-pass;
    The hare is in the grass;
The full moon stealeth o'er the hill of pines;
    Twilight is lingering dim;
    The village vesper-hymn
Murmurs its music through the trembling vines.

    Starts up the musing boy,
    His soul is hot with joy,
He revels in a region of delight;
    The winds are rich with song,
    As slow they sweep along,
And earth and sky are full of holy light.

    Tongues trill on every rock,
    Notes flow from every block;
The hawthorn shines with fairies; the clear rill
    With pointed rushes hid
    The pleasant banks amid,
Trickles its treasures tuning down the hill.

    A spell is on his soul:
    He scans the mystic scroll
Of human passions wakened by the wand
    Of England's noblest seer,
    Whom England holds so dear,—
Great, glorious Shakespeare, loved in every land!

    He hears the tramp of steeds,
    Sees war in gory weeds,

Roams through the forest with delighted eyes;
Bends to the tempest's roar,
Weeps for the monarch poor,
And sobs with sorrow when dear Juliet dies.

Thus lay that musing boy,
Whose soul was hot with joy,
Environed in a hemisphere of rays;
And in the mystic light
The genius of the height
Brought him a lyre, which he, enraptured, plays.

He sang of him, the great,
Shakespeare, of kingly state,
Who in his boyhood by clear Avon strayed,
Learning the lore of song,
From feeble thing and strong,—
The great tree towering and the tiny blade.

The welkin's solemn height,
The lightning's vivid light,
The thunder's mutter, the black whirlwind's roar;
The little child at play,
The red-breast on the spray,
The daisy nodding by the ploughman's door.

The hedges, hung in flowers,
The falling, pattering showers,
The dew-drops, glittering in the morning's shine;
The smallest film that be,
Which none but poets see,
All taught him lessons with a voice divine.

Dame nature ope'd her store,
Her secret inner door,

Boldly he revelled through her wondrous cell :
    And none the song-lines read
    Around and overhead,
Or knew the mystic chronicles so well.

    He solved the human heart
    Like mariner his chart,
And passion's every phase was known to him ;
    And when the full time came,
    Forth burst the mighty flame,
To blaze and brighten till the stars are dim !

    This greatly-gifted one
    Was labour's noblest son,—
The people's honour, leader, champion strong ;
    The glory of the soil,
    The towering prince of toil,
The matchless monarch in the realm of song.

    Loved now the wide world round,
    Where human hives are found ;
By prince, and peasant following the plough,
    The sailor out at sea,
    The yeoman on the lea,
The miner digging in the earth below.

    The shepherd in his plaid,
    The rosy village maid,
The warrior watching by the red camp fire,
    The mother with her child,
    The satchelled schoolboy mild,
The college student, daily pressing higher.

    The dweller of the street,
    In the great city's heat,

The mountaineer, within his lodge of reeds ;
 The silent solitaire
 On the wild desert bare :—
All own his witchery where the daylight speeds.

 Three centuries solemn span
 Since his great life began,
Have borne their burdens to the hidden sphere ;
 Each epoch ever found
 Him with new glories crowned,
Like the red sun when the wide west is clear.

 And so, great bard, to-day
 We weave thy natal lay,
And cluster gratefully around thy name ;
 England will ever be,
 Dear Shakespeare, proud of thee,
And coming ages but augment thy fame.

LUCRETIA'S GRAVE.

 'Tis where the tree-tops wave,
And gleam with glory 'neath the summer's sun,
And gentle breathings steal among the boughs,
 When busy day is done.

 'Tis where a tiny rill
Glides through the silence with a trickling fall,
And ivy-leaves, like holy epitaphs,
 Are clinging to the wall.

 'Tis where the grass is green,
And daisy flowers in snowy beauty lie,
And songs from fragrant field and forest screen
 Are sweetly gushing by.

'Tis where the village church
Among the dews its solemn shadow throws,
When silvery lyrics o'er the dingles float,
    At evening's gentle close.

    'Tis where the weary rest,
And age and beauty moulder in decay ;
And hope upon the silent green sward sits,
    Watching the slumbering clay.

    Above it shine the stars,
Around it woods and rocky mountains rise :
O, let it be my silent sepulchre,
    When death has sealed mine eyes !

HANNAH L. HARVEY.

THIS gifted lady was born near Waterford, in 1854, and still resides there. She is an ardent Nationalist, and resigned her membership in the Society of Friends many years ago.

THE JUNGFRAU.

ABOUT thy feet, O fair and awful maiden,
    The thunders roll,
And sombre clouds, with shooting death-fires laden,
    Appal the soul.

Giants with giants round thee are contending,
    With mighty throes,
As though the tumult of their wrath, ascending,
    Could shake thy snows.

Veiled in a robe of misty vapours streaming,
    A stately queen,
Beyond the clouds thy snowy peaks are gleaming,
    Unmoved, serene.

Awful as death, and glorious as a vision,
    Once more they rise,
And smiling forth celestial derision,
    Salute the skies.

O'er thee the lightnings flash in harmless anger,
    The thunders roll,
Thou bearest, high above the tempest's clangour,
    A stainless soul !

T. NEWENHAM HARVEY

W AS born near Waterford in 1837, and has, with intervals of travel, etc., resided there ever since. He married in 1870, Miss Huldah Bewley Jacob of Ballytore, who died in 1893. He has written a great number of fugitive pieces, which, although they have been much admired, have not yet been published in a volume.

A LAMENTATION.

Mourn for the great and brave !
For Jove, departed from the Olympian shore,
For his high court and retinue of yore,
　　All sunk into the grave.

　　No more the sea
Bears Neptune's car upon its sparkling foam,
No more fair Thetis plunges to her home
　　When winds are free.

　　No more the swain
To Ceres offers early fruits and flowers,
No more bright Phœbus drives the laughing hours
　　Along the plain.

　　No more the shield
And lightning sword of Mars are seen on high,
No more Bellona thunders through the sky,
　　Or shakes the field.

No more the maid
With footstep shy, fair Venus' shrine adorns,
No more Diana shows her crescent horns,
    Amid the glade.

No more we hear
The clang of Vulcan on his anvil sound,
No more his mighty hammer shakes the ground
    Or fills with fear.

No more the hills
Quake at the dreadful nod of sceptered Jove,
No more his eagle hovers high above
    Fair Ida's rills.

All, all are gone
All, all the well known forms have passed away,
And empty temples in the light of day,
    Appear alone.

O pleasant age
Of love and hope, and joy come back once more,
Teach us to live as on the Grecian shore,
    Lived child and sage.

Vain were such call
The present time in harsher mould is cast,
And every day but imitates the last,
    And love and romance fall.

Mourn for the lost,
For Jove departed from the Olympian shore,
For the loved faces that appear no more,
    On Helle's coast.

THOMAS HODGKIN, D.C.L., LITT. D.

DR. THOS. HODGKIN was born at Tottenham on the 29th July, 1831, and is the son of John Hodgkin and Elizabeth, his wife, who was the daughter of Luke Howard, the celebrated meteorologist and correspondent of Göthe. Thos. Hodgkin was educated partly in private, Thomas Hunton, the poet, being one of his teachers, and partly at Grove House School, Tottenham, and finally at University College, London, graduating there in 1851, with honours in classics. He married in August, 1861, Lucy Anna Fox, a cousin of Caroline Fox, the author of "Memories of Old Friends." L. A. Fox is the daughter of Alfred Fox of Falmouth, and his wife Sarah, née Lloyd.

Thos. Hodgkin's father was a barrister, and he himself studied for the Law, but delicate health forced him to relinquish that arduous profession, and he became a banker at Newcastle-on-Tyne, and devoted his leisure to literature.

He has already published six valuable volumes on "Italy and her Invaders," and is preparing the seventh and concluding volume.

His "Theodoric" appeared in the "Heroes of the Nations" series. Besides these works he has published the "Dynasty of Theodosius," and "Letters of Cassiodorus," and has written a number of valuable articles, critical and otherwise, in various magazines and papers, besides some fine poetry. Friends will remember his striking papers on Old Testament Criticism which appeared in recent numbers of "the Friend's Quarterly Examiner."

The Universities of Oxford and Durham bestowed on him

the hononary degree of D.C.L., and the University of Dublin that of LITT. D.

His poems are full of the scholarly spirit and cultured taste which distinguish his prose work, and are very beautiful in their union of lofty thought and musical diction. He has the true poet's gift, that which most markedly distinguishes the seer from the versifier, viz., the faculty to "look thro' the sign to the thing signified," to see beyond the outside symbol, the hidden verity; and so his poetry is representative of what I believe to be the highest and truest meaning of Quakerism, the spiritual sense which is enclosed but not hidden in all visible things in the flower, as in the gospel; in everyday man, as in the Christ.

ODE.

Sung at the Opening Ceremony of the Royal Mining, Engineering, and Industrial Exhibition, Newcastle-on-Tyne, 11th of May, 1887 (Queen Victoria's Jubilee).

UPON a bleak Northumbrian moor,
    Behold a palace raised.   Behold it filled
    With all that fingers fashion, deftly skilled.
    With all that strongest fibred brains have willed,
    When they, like natures self, have vowed to build
Structures that shall for centuries endure.

    How came these marvels hither?   By what power
    Have all been gathered in the self-same hour,
Upon a bleak Northumbrian moor?
    Why should both East and West for ever pour,
    The willing tribute of their golden store
    In ceaseless tide upon thy storm-swept shore?
Oh little island in the northern main!
    Oh little isle between two oceans' spray!
Deep lies the answer.   Endless is the chain
That binds the far-off ages with to-day.

Here, when the north wind raved,
The giant tree-ferns waved,
We see them o'er the unimagined tracts of time.
Yet never eye beheld
Those woodlands fair of Eld;
No hand those tree-trunks felled,
Scarred by the summer's flash, silvery with winter's rime.
For countless years the sun
Through steaming vapours dun,
Beheld their growth renewed
In sylvan solitude.
While the green-mantled earth slept in her innocent prime.
Wave! fronded forests! wave!
Sink gradual to your grave
Beneath some nameless river's oozy bed,
Roll! myriad ages! roll!
So shall the treasure, coal,
Be stored for some new race, creation's crown and head.

But vain is nature's store,
Vain as the golden ore
Upon some barren isle for famine-wearied men,
Unless her sons be true,
Mighty to dare and do,
And prompt to bind at need the social bond again.
Patience and mutual trust,
And courage to be just,
And the frank, fearless gaze that seeks a brother's eyes,
And loving loyalty.
Law-bound yet ever free—
Upon these deep-set stones enduring empires rise.

Thus hath our England grown,
E'er since, long years agone,

She first did turn her face towards freedom's holy light,
When Alfred, best of kings,
Beat back the raven's wings,
And gave her law for war, sweet day for barbarous night.
Till now, when Alfred's child
Sees 'neath her sceptre mild,
Wide ocean-sundered realms in loyal love unite.

Lady! who through thy tears,
Surveyest the traversed years,
The bright, the sad, the strange half-century,
The people's shouts acclaim
Thy loved, victorious name.
Oh, be that name the pledge of conquests yet to be,
O'er want and grinding care,
Faction and fierce despair,
Dark ignorance in her lair,
And all that mars, this day, our joyous jubilee.

Lord of the ages!   Thine
Is the far-traced design,
That blends earth's mighty past with her to-be.
Slowly the web unrolls,
And only wisest souls
Some curves of thine enwoven cypher see.

Power fades and glory wanes,
But the Unseen remains,
Thither draw our hearts, and let them rest in thee.

EMORI NOLO:

MORTUUM ME ESSE NIHIL ÆSTUMO.*

* " Dying I abhor : I care nothing about being dead." Translated and
adopted by Cicero, in his Tusculan Disputations, I. 8, from Epicharmus,
the Sicilian comic poet. The circumstances of Cicero's death are well
known. Epicharmus died at the age of 95. Sir T. Browne (Religio
Medici) erroneously attributes the sentiment to Cæsar.

ONE wrote of old, " The struggle of this dying
          Is all I dread :
I shall not heed when men above me, sighing,
          Say, ' He is dead.' "

Not in such words, oh Father of our Spirits,
          Speak we again :
A fear, a hope each child of us inherits,
          Making them vain.

Awful the hour, and shall be through the ages,
          That closeth Life ;
With the worn soul the weary body wages
          Self-torturing strife.

Till far, so far from loving eyes around them,
          One journeyeth lone,
And that close wedlock that for years hath bound them
          Ends with a groan.

The pale still form, so late so dear a treasure,
          Its fate we know ;
The dust, the worm, its depth of ruin measure
          Where it lies low.

But the vast doubt wherewith our souls are shaken
          Outlasts the tomb !
" Where, in what regions shall the wanderer waken,
          Gazing on whom ? "

Father ! I live or die, in this confiding,
          That Thou art King ;
That each still star above me owns Thy guiding,
          Each wild bird's wing.

That Nature feels Thee, great unseen Accorder
          Of all her wheels,
That tokens manifest of Thy mightier order
          Her strife reveals.

8

And that without Thee, not a wave is heaving
     Nor flake descends,
That all the giant Powers of her conceiving
     Are thy Son's friends.

Yet, I beseech Thee, send not these to light me
     Through the dark vale ;
They are so strong, so passionlessly mighty,
     And I so frail.

No ! let me gaze, not on some sea far reaching
     Nor star-sprent sky,
But on a *Face* in which mine own, beseeching,
     May read reply.

For more than Poet's song or Painter's seeing
     Of fiery Hell,
Thrills me this dread of waking into Being
     Where no souls dwell.

Such was my cry : hath not the mighty Maker
     Who gave me Christ,
Hath he not granted me a sweet Awaker
     For the last tryst ?

Given a Son who left the peace unbroken
     That reigns above,
That he might whisper God's great name unspoken,
     The name of Love !

Have I not known him ?   Yes, and still am knowing,
     And more shall know ;
Have not his sweet eyes guided all my going,
     Wept with my woe ;

Gleamed a bright dawn-hope when the clouds of sadness
     Made my soul dim,
And looked their warning when an alien gladness
     Lured me from Him ?

Lord, when I tread this valley of our dying,
  Sharp cliffs between,
Where over all, *one* ghastly Shadow lying
  Fills the ravine,

E'en then, thy kingly sceptre being o'er me,
  I will not fear,
Thy crook, my Shepherd, dimly seen before me,
  My way shall clear.

And when the grave must yield her prey down-stricken,
  When sleep is o'er,
When the strange stirs of life begin to quicken
  This form once more.

Oh Son of Man, if Thee and not another
  I here have known,
If I may see Thee then, our first-born Brother,
  Upon Thy throne.

How stern soe'er, how terrible in brightness
  That dawn shall break,
I shall be satisfied with thy dear likeness
  When I awake.

DAVID HOLT.

DAVID HOLT'S father was a successful cotton spinner at Holt-town, Manchester, where the poet was born in 1828. The family having suffered reverses, David Holt began a commercial life, but retained the passionate love of poetry which had distinguished him as a child. At the age of seventeen he published a volume entitled "Poems Rural and Miscellaneous." This book appears to have contained nothing remarkable, but five years later, by the appearance of his "Lay of Hero Worship and other Poems," he was recognised as a poet of promise, and his third volume, "Janus, Lake Sonnets, etc," confirmed the critics in their verdict. In 1868 he was induced to issue a small volume of selected pieces, entitled "Poems by David Holt," in which several new poems of great beauty were included. His outer life was entirely uneventful ; he was engaged in a railway office for thirty-four years, and was seldom absent from Manchester. He married in 1853, and his marriage was a perfectly happy one. His family of three sons survived him. He died in 1880, and was buried in the beautiful churchyard of Bowden. He had resigned his membership in the Society of Friends on his marriage, and had joined the Church of England. He seems to have been a man of great learning and much humour, his heart turning ever to the fields and rivers, though his feet were set to tread the streets of a great city. His poetry is not particularly strong or imaginative, but it is full of melody and sweetness ; full, too, of the ordered charm of happy love and placid faith.

THE WOODLANDS.

O 'tis sweet, 'tis sweet to wander in the greensward-paven
    alleys,
With the laden boughs above us, and the moss-clad trunks
    around,
Or to lie and dream with Nature mid the fern-clad hills and
    valleys,
In a harmony of silence far surpassing sweetest sound.

O the woodlands, O the woodlands, O the sweet and shady
    places,
Lone romantic hollows haunted by the wild bird and the bee ;
Ye may gaze for hours together on the sweet upturnéd faces
Of the flowers, whose gentle smiling it is almost heaven to see.

And they smile upon you ever with the pure and holy smiling
Of their lovély human sisterhood, and ever as you pass
Look up to you beseechingly, as though they were beguiling
You to take your seat beside them on the warm and sunny
    grass.

And think you they will answer if with gentle words ye woo
    them ?
O trust me they have voices sweet as any singing bird,
But they speak to those who love them, and who lean their
    souls unto them ;
And by such, and by such only, are their gentle voices heard.

They will tell you tales of fairy-bands that come and dance
    around them,
And sing them songs of joyance through the livelong summer
    night,
Tracing circles in the greensward when the quiet moon hath
    bound them
In the mystery of beauty with a veil of silver light.

And the merry, merry streamlet, as it plays amid the pebbles,
Chiming in with happy chorus to the wild birds' sunny song,
With its softly murmur'd tenor, and its liquid-trilling trebles,
Makes the woodland ring with music as its light waves dance
    along.

Ye may almost dare to fancy that ye will behold the issue
Of some naiad from the waters with her eyes of liquid blue,
With rounded form of beauty, and with lips of vermeil tissue,
Sent expressly by the Muses to hold converse sweet with you.

Or, if graver mood be on you, from the antique trunks all
    hoary,
Ye may list for dryad-voices with their sad and solemn strain,
Bewailing to the passing winds their far and faded glory,
And lamenting days departed which may never come again.

O, to couch on beds of violets, in a foliage-curtained pleas-
    aunce,
There to feast upon their beauty, and to breathe their sweet
    perfume,
Meet to be inhal'd by angels so etherial is its essence,
Whilst they are meet for angel's gaze, so holy is their bloom ;

'Twere a joy almost too blissful for mere mortal to inherit ;
Yet a simple joy, and Nature hath a thousand such in store
For all those who woo her beauties with a pure and constant
    spirit,
And for every fresh revealing, love those gentle beauties more.

Yes, to live mid leafy shadows, and to note the hours flit by us
By the sunbeams on the foliage, were a happy life to lead,
And a life according sweetly with the pure and natural bias
Of some hearts devote to Nature, and well-skilled her lore to
    read.

But the world hath claims upon us, and our social duties ever
Call us forth to crowded cities there to jostle with the throng ;
Yet methinks it were much happier to depart from Nature
    never,
But to dwell amid the wild woods, and to pass our life in song.

MARY HOWITT.

MARY BOTHAM, afterwards Howitt, was born on the 12th March, 1799, at Coleford in the Forest of Dean, whither her parents had gone to look after some ironworks. Her father was Samuel Botham of Uttoxeter, and her mother was Anne Wood, a convinced Friend, and a grand-daughter of that Wood the patentee, so bitterly attacked by Swift in " The Drapier Letters."

Soon after Mary's birth the family went back to Uttoxeter, and she gives a very graphic picture of her childhood in her autobiogrophy. Scarcely any teaching, excepting to read and write, seems to have been given to the children, and very few books save those of a mystical character allowed. Their dress was a source of trouble to Mary and her sister, who loved beauty, and by their long wanderings in Needwood Chase had grown accustomed to lovely form and colouring. When Mary was nine, and her sister Anna a year and a half older, they went to a school which a Mrs. Parker kept next door to their parent's house ; but after less than a year Mrs. Parker left Uttoxeter, and the young Bothams were sent to a Friend's school at Croydon, from whence they were recalled by their mother's serious illness. After some time at home, Mary was taken to a school at Sheffield, conducted by Hannah Kilham, the widow of Alexander Kilham, founder of the New Methodist Connection, who, with her stepdaughter and a niece were convinced Friends. In 1812, she left Sheffield, and the master of the only boy's school in Uttoxeter, Thomas Goodall, was engaged to teach her and Anna "spelling, Latin, the globes, and, indeed, whatever else he could impart." When he died, the girls seem to have pursued their studies pretty much as they liked, and were allowed twice a week to teach some poor children of the place in a stable-loft, which their father had fitted up for them ; they also taught their younger sister and brother, and were very busy with household matters. They were omnivorous readers, and Mary soon began to write verses herself.

In the autumn of 1818, she first met her future husband, William Howitt, and became engaged to him before the close of the year. "On the 16th of Fourth Month, 1821," she says in her autobiography, "we were married, I wearing my first silk gown—a very pretty dove-colour—with bonnet of the same material, and a soft, white silk shawl. For a wedding-tour my husband took me to every spot of beauty or old tradition in his native county—romantic, picturesque Derbyshire."

The newly-married pair went to live at Hanley for nearly a year, and after some visits, and a tour in Scotland and the north of England, they settled in Nottingham, and produced many of their books there. They pursued a course of joint authorship, at first chiefly in periodicals and annuals, but they published "The Forest Minstrel and Other Poems," in 1823, and "The Desolation of Eyam and Other Poems," in 1827 ; both these volumes were very successful. Mary Howitt was entirely wrapt up in her husband ; all their pursuits and studies were conducted together, and with the exception of a few days now and again, she was only separated from him during his Australian journeys. Their life seems to have been an ideally happy one, and the glimpses we get of these two poets in their various homes are very bright and delightful. Their friends and correspondents embraced almost every eminent man and woman of the day, and they were themselves so sweet-natured and highly-cultured, and carried with them, wherever they went, that indefinable serene charm and quiet beauty, which the spirit of true Quakerism gives, both to life and manner, quite apart from any conformity to the outward peculiarities of the

Society of Friends, that they seem to have won the admiring affection of all those who came into contact with them.

She published in 1833, "Sketches of Natural History" in verse, and in 1834 "The Seven Temptations." In 1837, a volume of verse entitled "Birds and Flowers" appeared. In 1840, the Howitts went to Heidelburg, not returning to England until 1843, when they settled at Clapton. During their stay in Germany, they studied the German, Swedish, and Danish languages, and began the translations of books in those tongues, which they continued with great success after their return to England. In 1847, Mary collected her ballads, miscellaneous poems, and some poetical translations, which were published in one volume. In August of this year she writes to her sister, "Thou wilt be glad to hear that we have drawn up our resignation of membership, signed it, and when thou readest this, it will be noised abroad that we are no longer Friends." She wrote at this time "The Heir of West Waylan."

In 1848, the Howitts left Clapton, and went to live at Upper Avenue Road, Regents Park. They became contributors to "Household Words" from its commencement; Mary writing many ballads, and both she and her husband many stories for it; she also wrote at this time for the "Illustrated News," "Ladies Companion," and other papers and magazines. Throughout the year 1851, the Howitts were working hard at "The Literature and Romance of Northern Europe." In June, 1852, William, with his two sons, set sail for Australia, to visit his brother, Dr. Godfrey Howitt, who was settled at Melbourne, and Mary, with her daughters, removed to the Hermitage, Highgate. She took at this time a very active part in the protest of English women against slavery, which had been aroused by Mrs. Stowe's "Uncle Tom's Cabin." The signatures of the "Ladies' Address to their American Sisters on Slavery," reached the number of 576,000, and Mary Howitt was on the Committee with Lady Shaftesbury and

others to get up this address.   In 1856, she interested herself
with other eminent women, in the attempt to amend the law
relating to the property of married women ; this petition was
only successful, however, in modifying the law of marriage and
divorce.   In 1857, the Howitts left the Hermitage, and took
another house at Highgate ; they had become much interested
in spiritualistic phenomena, and devoted a good deal of their
time here to investigations into the truth of Spiritualism ; they
appear to have accepted its pretensions, although still holding
the Christian Faith as before, indeed, regarding the
spiritualistic manifestations as strongly corroborative of
Christianity.

In 1866, the Howitts settled at the Orchard, near Esher,
where they remained until 1870, when they left England for
Switzerland and Italy, and never returned.   They passed their
remaining summers in the Tyrol, and their winters in Rome.
In 1879, a pension from the Civil List, of £100 a year, was
conferred on Mary.   The Stockholm Literary Academy
awarded her a silver medal, and she received innumerable
marks of consideration and admiration from eminent people
wherever she went.   In 1882, she was baptised into the
Catholic Church, and was one of the English pilgrims received
by the Pope in January, 1888.   A few days after this ceremony,
which she describes as filling her with spiritual joy and peace,
she expired, and was buried by the side of her husband in the
Protestant cemetery, by permission of the Cardinal Vicar of
Rome.

The Howitts had been all their lives great wanderers ; they
would journey for weeks or months at a time, chiefly on foot,
through England, Wales, or Scotland, and the Continent, and
knew intimately and minutely every place they wrote about.
Their literary industry was marvellous, as is shown by appended
list of books.   Mary Howitt's name was attached, either as
author, editor, or translator, to 110 works !   She was sole

author of the following, besides those she wrote with her husband.

Sketches of Natural History	1834
Wood Leighton, or a Year in the Country	1836
Birds and Flowers	1838
Hymns and Fireside Verses	1839
Hope On, Hope Ever, a Tale	1840
Strive and Thrive	1840
Sowing and Reaping	1841
Work and Wages	1842
Which is the Wiser	1842
Little Coin, Much Care	1842
No Sense like Commonsense	1843
Love and Money	1843
My Uncle, the Clockmaker	1844
The Two Apprentices	1844
My Own Story	1845
Fireside Verses	1845
Ballads and Other Poems	1847
The Children's Year	1847
The Childhood of Mary Leeson	1848
Our Cousins in Ohio	1849
The Heir of West Waylan	1851
The Dial of Love	1853
Birds and Flowers	1855
The Picture Book for the Young	1855
M. Howitt's Illustrated Library for the young, a series	1856
Liliesleaf, or Lost and Found	1861
Little Arthur's Letters to his Sister Mary	1861
The Poet's Children	1863
The Story of Little Cristal	1863
Mr. Rudd's Grandchildren	1864
Tales in Prose for Young People	1864
M. Howitt's Sketches of Natural History	1864

LITTLE STREAMS.

LITTLE streams are light and shadow,
Flowing through the pasture meadow,
Flowing by the green way-side,
Through the forest dim and wide,
Through the hamlet still and small—
By the cottage, by the hall,
By the ruined abbey still;
Turning here and there a mill,
Bearing tribute to the river—
Little streams, I love you ever.

Summer music is there flowing—·
Flowering plants in them are growing;
Happy life is in them all,
Creatures, innocent and small;
Little birds come down to drink,
Fearless of their leafy brink;
Noble trees beside them grow,
Glooming them with branches low;
And between, the sunshine, glancing
In their little waves, is dancing.

Little streams have flowers a many,
Beautiful and fair as any;
Typha strong, and green bur-reed;
Willow-herb, with cotton-seed;
Arrow-head, with eye of jet;
And the water-violet.
There the flowering rush you meet,
And the plumy meadow-sweet;
And, in places deep and stilly,
Marble-like, the water-lily.

Little streams, their voices cheery,
Sound forth welcomes to the weary,
Flowing on from day to day,
Without stint and without stay;
Here, upon their flowery bank,
In the old time, pilgrims drank—
Here have seen, as now, pass by,
Kingfisher and dragonfly;
Those bright things that have their dwelling,
Where the little streams are welling.

Down in valleys green and lowly,
Murmuring not, and gliding slowly:
Up in mountain-hollows wild,
Fretting like a peevish child;
Through the hamlet, where all day,
In their waves, the children play;
Running west, or running east,
Doing good to man and beast—
Always giving, weary never,
Little streams, I love you ever.

PHILIP OF MAINE.

FROM "THE SEVEN TEMPTATIONS."

ACT 5. SCENE 2.

Evening—The gallery of the castle—Philip pacing about in deep thought.

ON, on unto the topmost verge of power;
And, as I yet ascend, still more doth grow
The grasping wish for more;—the aspiring wish
Higher and higher to rise.   This petty lordship,
Why not a sovereign dukedom?   Wherefore not
The Duke of Maine as good as Duke of Suabia?
And Kronberg dead; the path is right before me.
Ambition and revenge shall have their way!—
But where is Gaston? he, the ready tool
Who does not start and cry "alack, my lord!"
Ha! here he comes!

GASTON.

No moment may be lost—
Fabian and Segbert, and Count Nicholas
Are hence.   As firebrands in the standing corn
Are they among the people; and a rumour
Has reached the town, that Suabia draweth near
With a strong army for the aid of Kronberg.
Do quickly what thou dost, and rid thyself
Of one foe ere another takes the field!

PHILIP.

Thou hast access unto the tower.   Go thou,
Poison or steel, use thou the surer means!

GASTON.

Nay, 'twill be tenfold vengeance from thy hand.

PHILIP *(feeling at his dagger)*.

'Tis sharp and true, but do thou mix a cup

Of subtle poison.   I would liefer that—
And if he will not pledge me, why, there's this!

GASTON.

I'll mix a cunning potion that will do.

Enter the LORD OF MAINE.

My son! my son! hast thou decreed his death?

PHILIP.

I have.

LORD OF MAINE.

Nay, do not tell me so.

PHILIP.

I have.

LORD OF MAINE.

Didst thou not love his gentle angel daughter?
Remember her, and do not harm his life.

GASTON.

And be himself the victim!

LORD OF MAINE.

It is thou
That counsellest my son to these bad deeds!
Philip, she gave me life and liberty,
And but for her, thy father had been dead!

PHILIP.

Whose hate was't doomed thee to the gallows-tree?
Hence! hence! thou dost not know, for urgently
The hour calls for his blood!

LORD OF MAINE.

I leave thee not,
Till thou hast given his life unto my prayer.

GASTON, to PHILIP.

Fortune is slipping through your hand, my lord,
While you stand dallying thus.   Away, old man!

PHILIP.

I'm ready.   Let's begone.

(*They go out together*).

LORD OF MAINE.

                        Then, may the Avenger
Take from thee thy ill-gotten power and station!
This is a place of blood and horrible outrage:
I will away; men's hearts are turned to stone.
Better it were to hide with desert-beasts,
Where 'tis a natural instinct to be cruel!

(*He goes out*).
(*After a short time re-enter Philip*).

PHILIP.

I did not quail, nor did my heart upbraid me,
When thousands lay beneath my conquering step,
And from the helmet-crown unto the heel
I was dyed crimson; why then faints my soul,
Trembling and drooping 'neath a mountain's weight
Of miserable remorse for one man's blood?—
Ne'er till this moment, when my debt is paid,
When I have conquered my great enemy,
Quailed I, or wished undone aught that was done!
But hark! what sounds are these—quick, coming steps
And hurried voices?   Am I grown a coward?

Enter GASTON.

Philip! Philip! now is a time for action:
Why dost thou stare as one who walks in dreams?

PHILIP.

Whence come those hurried sounds?   Whose are those
        steps?

GASTON.

The disaffected thousands from the fields
Are on the walls—within the very castle!

9

PHILIP.

How got they access?

GASTON.

             Even as thou didst;
By the old rock-path.   Hundreds more have entered—
Thy portals have they fired; and hark their cries—
Vengeance and blood!

PHILIP.

         Hence; draw the soldiers out,
And man the walls. Strike every villain down
That sets his foot within the castle gate.

GASTON.

They fight with us for every inch of ground;
They are within the walls—the place is fired;
Accursed knaves, born for the gibbet-tree!

PHILIP, drawing his sword.

I'll teach them what the cry of vengeance meaneth!

        (*He rushes out—Gaston follows him*).

        (*A confused noise, and yelling cries are heard
        approaching, and a rabble force their way in,
        with torches in their hands*).

WILLIAM HOWITT.

WILLIAM HOWITT was born on the 18th December, 1792, at Heanor, in Derbyshire; his father, Thomas Howitt, had become a member of the Society of Friends three years before his marriage with Phœbe Tantum, a young Quakeress possessing a considerable fortune. Mary Howitt, speaking of her husband after his death, says:—" His birth-place, Heanor, was an obscure and rural nook linked to the outer world by the carrier's cart, retaining many traces of feudal rudeness, and filled with a motley assemblage of eccentric, undisciplined, but often very humorous, individuals, whose odd sayings and doings amused my husband throughout his life. Indeed, the scenes and characters of his secluded youth produced upon him the same permanent fascination as those of mine had done in my case, and which imparts a biographical rather than inventive quality to our works of fiction. The bold happy lad, to whom Nature had been nurse, guide, and guardian, never had his brain dwarfed by excessive study, and gradually amassed a vast stock of learning. As a young man, when the use of tobacco was not carried to the present excess, he for a short time accepted that indulgence, but perceiving the power it might gain over him, and resolving never to become the slave of any enjoyment, he speedily and entirely relinquished it. He never accustomed himself to the use of wine or spirits, or the habit, either for pleasure or labour, of turning night into day. He was through the whole of his literary career a steady, industrious worker. He faith-fully fulfilled every engagement in the accomplishment of task-work; and maintained with equal exactitude his regular relaxation and refreshment, and that simply of fresh air and exercise. Thus preserving a sound mind in a sound body, he reached his eighty-seventh year without the failure of any mental or physical faculty. He traversed much of Great Britain on foot, principally to gather up personal knowledge for his "Rural Life in England," his "Visits to Remarkable Places," and his "Homes and Haunts of the Poets." He was very conscientious in never describing as known to him what he himself had never visited. Hence he became familiar with the character of England, its scenery and its people as existing half-a-century ago. He had immense sympathy and an infinite fund of humour : wherever, therefore, he paused for a night, or sat to rest by the wayside with peasant people, he left behind him a memory that long survived."

Until the age of ten, William Howitt seems to have been allowed to run wild in the country surrounding his home, and, excepting for a short attendance at a village school, kept by an oddity, who joined the trades of schoolmaster and baker, was practically his own master, roaming about for long distances with his grey pony Peter Scroggins and his white terrier Pry. He was afterwards sent to Ackworth, where he remained between three and four years, and began writing verses. Some stanzas on Spring were sent to the "Monthly Magazine," the journal in which Lord Byron's first effort appeared.

After a short time at home, where he continued a wide course of reading, he was dispatched to a Friends' seminary at Tamworth for a year; but at the end of that time his eyes became much injured from the effects of over-study, and so for about two years he remained at home engaged in his old rural pursuits. At seventeen he was apprenticed to Richard Hallam, a Mansfield Friend, who carried on a mixed business of builder, carpenter, and cabinet-maker. Here he remained until he was twenty-one, when, tearing up his indentures, he returned to his father's farm, and besides his work there, diligently continued his reading, acquiring also French, Latin, and Italian, and pursuing his experiments in chemistry, botany, and medecine. "In the autumn of 1818," he says, "I paid a visit to a relative, Susanna Frith, at Uttoxeter, and thus first saw Mary Botham, destined to become my best friend, truest companion, and wife. . . . Early in 1821 a chemist of Derby, who had opened a concern at Hanley, in the Staffordshire Potteries, wished to dispose of this business. As a commencement, though with no view of permanent settlement there, I purchased it; and on April 16th, 1821, I married Mary Botham in the little meeting-house at Uttoxeter, and we went to reside at Hanley."

They stayed at Hanley less than a year, when William Howitt sold the business very advantageously, and after short visits to Uttoxeter and Heanor, he and his wife made a long tour, chiefly on foot, through the North of England and Scotland. On their return they went to live in Nottingham, and, in 1823, published "The Forest Minstrel and other Poems." This was followed, in 1827, by "The Desolation of Eyam and other Poems." These volumes were very favourably received, and Wordsworth, David M. Moir, Mrs. Hemans, and others, wrote saying how much pleasure they had derived from them.

In December, 1829, the Howitts paid a short visit to London, staying at the house of Alaric Watts, who had married Jeremiah Wiffen's sister Zillah. Here they met L. E. L., Mrs. Hofland, Thomas Pringle, T. K. Hervey, the S. C. Halls, and many other celebrities, including Allan Cunningham and Miss Jewsbury. In 1831, William Howitt published "The Book of the Seasons." In January, 1834, he was deputed, together with the Rev. Joseph Gilbert and Mr. Hugh Hunter, to present a petition to Government, from Nottingham, for the Disestablishment of the Church; his "History of Priestcraft" had led to this appointment. The deputies had an interview with Earl Grey, who, after hearing them, declined to consider their proposition, declaring that he considered it the duty of every Government to maintain an established religion.

In 1835, William Howitt published "Pantika," and, in 1836, the Howitts had another delightful tour in the North of England and Scotland, meeting at Edinburgh, at a dinner given to Campbell, "Christopher North," Professor Ferrier, and other remarkable people. In Edinburgh, too, they were introduced to the "Blackwood," "Tait," and "Chambers' Journal" sets, and the little group gathered round the Quaker artist William Miller.

At Michaelmas, 1836, the Howitts removed to West End Cottage, Esher, where they rejoiced in a garden, orchard, and meadow of their own. Their letters at this time are full of the enjoyment they felt in their country life. In 1837, William published his "Rural Life in England;" in 1838, "Colonisation and Christianity;" in 1839, "The Boy's Country Book;" in 1840, "Visits to Remarkable Places" (first series). In this year also the Howitts left Esher, and went to live at Heidelberg, principally for the sake of their childrens' education. G. P. R. James and his wife, and Captain Medwin, were then living there, but the Howitts, on account of their children, chiefly sought German friends, they read German and followed German customs. In 1842, William published "Visits to Remarkable Places" (second series), and "Rural and Domestic Life in Germany." While at Heidelberg, he made a complete study of the Swedish and Danish, as well as the German, languages.

In 1843, the Howitts returned to England, and settled for a time at The Elms, Lower Clapton, where they continued their translations of Swedish, German, and Danish books begun at Heidelberg. William published, in 1847, "Homes and Haunts of the Poets;" in 1850, "The Year Book of the Country;" in 1851, "Madame Dorrington of the Dene" (a novel). In 1846, he had become editor of "The

People's Journal," but at the end of the year he grew dissatisfied with it, and in January, 1847, be began "Howitt's Journal;" this, however, like its predecessor, proved a pecuniary failure, and was discontinued.   In 1847, the Howitts drew up and signed their resignation of membership in the Society of Friends.   At Michaelmas, 1848, they left Clapton, and took a house near Regent's Park, and when Charles Dickens commenced the publication of "Household Words," they were among the earliest contributors to the new venture.   In June, 1852, William Howitt, with his two sons, sailed for Australia, and Mary Howitt left the house in Avenue Road, and took up her abode at The Hermitage, Highgate.   In December, 1854, William and his son returned, and soon afterwards the Howitts became·interested in the investigation of so-called spiritualistic phenomena.

In 1857, they quitted The Hermitage, and took West Hill Lodge, Highgate.   In 1866, they made another move, renting The Orchard, at Claygate, near Esher, where they luxuriated in a large garden and country life again.   While at West Hill Lodge, William had, besides continuing his literary labours, spent much time in arranging *séances* with Home, the spiritualist; he also contributed to the "Spiritual Magazine" more than one hundred articles describing his experiences, but their new belief did not interfere with the Howitt's faith in Christianity, indeed they looked on the strange phenomena of spiritualism as a strong confirmation of the Christian truths.

In 1865, William received a pension, £140 a year, from the Civil List, and, in 1870, the Howitts settled themselves in Rome, where, the next year, they celebrated their golden wedding.   In this year, too, 1871, he published "The Mad War-Planet and other Poems."   While at Rome he interested himself greatly in forming a Society for the Protection of Animals, and also formed a project for planting the Campagna with eucalyptus globulus.

For the remaining years of William's life the Howitts spent their summers at Dietenheim, in the Tyrol, and their winters in Rome, where, on March 3rd, 1879, William died from heart disease and bronchitis, and was buried in the Protestant Cemetery.

His life had been one of unfailing industry, and the works written by William and Mary together, or alone, would form a small library themselves, as may be seen from the following list :—

Book of the Seasons	1831
History of Priestcraft	1833
Pantika (2 vols.)	1835
Rural Life in England (2 vols.)	1838
Colonisation and Christianity	1838
The Boy's Country Book	1839
Visits to Remarkable Places (1st series)	1840
The Student Life of Germany	1841
Visits to Remarkable Places (2nd series)	1842
Rural and Domestic Life in Germany	1842
Peter Schlemihl, a translation	1843
Wanderings of a Journeyman Tailor	1844
German Experiences	1844
The Life and Adventures of Jack of the Mill	1844
Life in Dalecarlia, a translation	1845
Homes and Haunts of the Poets	1847
The Hall and the Hamlet	1848
The Year Book of the Country	1850
Madame Dorrington of the Dene	1851
A Boy's Adventures in the Wilds of Australia	1854
The History of Magic, a translation (2 vols.)	1854
Land Labour and Gold (2 vols.)	1855
Tallangetta the Squatter's Home (3 vols.)	1857
The Man of the People	1860
The History of the Supernatural	1863

The History of Discovery in Australia, etc. (2 vols.) 1865
Woodburn Grange   1867
The Northern Heights of London   1869
The Mad War-Planet   1871
The Religion of Rome   1873

William Howitt also wrote a popular history of England, and, in conjunction with his wife, many other volumes.

SPRING-FLOWERS.

(FROM "THE COUNTRY YEAR BOOK.")

BUT, oh, ye spring-flowers! oh, ye early friends!
    Where are ye, one and all?
The sun still shines, and summer rain descends,
    They call forth flowers, but 'tis not ye they call.
        On the mountains,
        By the fountains,
In the woodland, dim and grey,
Flowers are springing, ever springing,
But the spring-flowers, where are they?

Then, oh, ye spring-flowers! oh, ye early friends!
    Where are ye?   I would know
When the sun shines, when summer rain descends,
    Why still blow flowers, but 'tis not ye that blow.
        On the mountains,
        By the fountains,
In the woodlands, dim and grey,
Flowers are springing, ever springing,
But the spring-flowers, where are they?

Oh then, ye spring-flowers! oh, ye early friends!
    Are ye together gone
Up with the soul of nature that ascends,
    Up with the clouds and odours, one by one?
        O'er the mountains,
        O'er the fountains,

O'er the woodlands, dim and grey,
Flowers are springing, ever springing,
On heaven's highlands far away!

Hotter and hotter glows the summer sun,
    But you it cannot wake,
Myriads of flowers, like armies marching on,
    Blaze on the hills, and glitter in the brake.
        On the mountains,
        Round the fountains,
In the woodlands, dim and grey,
Flowers are springing, ever springing,
But the spring-flowers, where are they?

Oh! no more! oh, never, never more!
    Shall friend, or flower, return,
Till deadly Winter, old, and cold, and frore,
    Has laid all nature lifeless in his urn.
        O'er the mountains,
        And the fountains,
Through the woodland, dim and grey,
Death and winter, dread companions,
Have pursued their destined way.

Then oh, ye spring-flowers! oh, ye early friends!
    Dead, buried, one and all;
When the sun shines, and summer rain descends,
    And call forth flowers, 'tis ye that they shall call
        On the mountains,
        By the fountains,
In the woodlands, dim and grey,
Flowers are springing, souls are singing,
On heaven's hills, and ye are they!

    FROM "THE COUNTRY YEAR BOOK.

    ROSE! Rose! open thy leaves!
        Spring is whispering love to thee;

Rose ! Rose ! open thy leaves !
  Near is the nightingale on the tree.
      Open thy leaves,
      Open thy leaves,
And fill with balm-breath the sunlit eaves.

Lily ! Lily ! awake, awake !
  The fairy watcheth her flowery boat ;
Lily ! Lily ! awake, awake !
  Oh ! set thy scent-laden bark afloat.
      Lily, awake !
      Lily, awake !
And cover with leaves the sleeping lake.

Flowers ! Flowers ! come forth, 'tis spring !
  Stars of the woods, the hills, and the dells !
Fair valley lilies, come forth and ring,
  In your green turrets, your silvery bells
      Flowers, come forth,
      'Tis spring ! 'tis spring !
And beauty in field and woodland dwells.

THE DEPARTURE OF THE SWALLOW.

    AND is the swallow gone ?
        Who beheld it ?
        Which way sailed it ?
    Farewell bade it none ?

    No mortal saw it go :—
        But who doth hear
        Its summer cheer
    As it flitteth to and fro ?

    So the freed spirit flies !
        From its surrounding clay
        It steals away
    Like the swallow from the skies.

Whither?   Wherefore doth it go?
'Tis all unknown ;
We feel alone
That a void is left below.

FROM "THE FOREST MINSTREL."
BY WILLIAM AND MARY HOWITT.

AWAY with the pleasure that is not partaken !
  There is no enjoyment by one only ta'en :
I love in my mirth to see gladness awaken
  On lips, and in eyes, that reflect it again.
When we sit by the fire that so cheerily blazes
  On our cozy hearthstone, with its innocent glee,
Oh ! my soul warms, while my eye fondly gazes,
  To see my delight is partaken by thee !

And when, as how often, I eagerly listen
  To stories thou read'st of the dear olden day,
How delightful to see our eyes mutually glisten,
  And feel that affection has sweetened the lay.
Yes, love,—and when wandering at even or morning,
  Through forest or wild, or by waves foaming white
I have fancied new beauties the landscape adorning
  Because I have seen thou wast glad in the sight.

And how often in crowds, where a whisper offendeth ;
  And we fain would express what there might not be said,
How dear is the glance that none else comprehendeth ;
  And how sweet is the thought that is secretly read.
Then away with the pleasure that is not partaken !
  There is no enjoyment by one only ta'en :
I love in my mirth to see gladness awaken
  On lips, and in eyes, that reflect it again.

RICHARD HOWITT.

RICHARD HOWITT was born at Heanor in Derbyshire, in 1799. His sister-in-law, Mary Howitt, says of him in her autobiography :—" This younger brother of my husband was my contemporary, and at the time of which I am writing (1823), our fellow-inmate. He possessed a most poetical, sensitive mind ; was caustic, humorous, a quiet punster, deeply versed in nature, and sympathising in all noble movements and vital human interests. Although thoroughly awake in congenial society, he would lose himself in some poetical dream when uninterested in his companions. This reminds me that once a very ordinary individual walked with Richard from Nottingham to Heanor, and asked him suddenly, 'What bird that was ?' No reply was vouchsafed for the distance of several miles, then without uttering another word, the wished-for information was given. He was well versed in literature, and was fond of old-fashioned poetry, but it must be choicely good."

Richard Howitt, at first in partnership with his brother William, and afterwards alone, conducted a chemist's and druggist's business in Parliament Street. Here Wordsworth once visited him, here also came James Montgomery and John Edwards, here Thomas Bailey showed him his son's MS. of " Festus," and here constantly came Millhouse, Henry Wild, Thos. Miller and Sidney Giles, Danby and Samuel Plumb, and all the celebrated characters and oddities the neighbourhood possessed. Richard Howitt never married, having, Spencer T. Hall says, been twice disappointed in love. After a time he retired to Edingley, where he had a small farm, and lived in great seclusion. Mary Howitt says, "The young clodhoppers helping him at his work thought him a strange man, and one of them observed to the housekeeper, ' He fancied Mester completely *lost*, for when plucking the orchard fruit he would give no reply, and often pause as if going asleep.' If silent and meditative, he was active and eloquent in the service of the careworn and oppressed. When elected guardian of the poor by a large majority, blue and white flags fluttered gaily from the cottage windows, and for more than an hour the church bells of his village were merrily rung."

He published in 1830, a volume of poems called "Antediluvian Sketches," which won high praise, and in 1840 were followed by "The Gipsey King." Many of his poems appeared first in "Tait's Magazine," and "Dearden's Miscellany." In 1839, Richard Howitt, with his brother, Dr. Godfrey Howitt, emigrated to Australia, where the latter remained and settled at Melbourne; Richard, however, returned in 1844, and published his "Impressions of Australia Felix, Notes of a Voyage round the World, Australian Poems," etc, a miscellany of prose and verse.

In 1868, he published "Wasp's Honey," and in 1869, he died at Edingley. Mary Howitt thus speaks of his funeral :— "On February 5th, 1869, Richard Howitt breathed his last. His tenants and his poorer neighbours, according to country custom, one by one visited their old friend and champion, as he lay robed for the tomb ; and as they stood beside the coffin, each one laid his or her hand in blessing upon the cold brow, in the belief that this 'laying on of hands' gives rest to the dead. His relatives accompanied his revered remains, in a mist of soft rain, across the district of old Sherwood Forest to his grave in the burial-ground of the Society of Friends at Mansfield."

Richard Howitt was a fine poet. With a decided lyrical faculty, he united deep thought and noble idealism ; and many of his poems, impressive by their transparent simplicity, will be remembered when the more ambitious work of his brother and sister, William and Mary, are forgotten. In reading his poems, we are frequently met by snatches of delicious music, breaths of pure poetry, beautiful thought embalmed in amber-clear language, such as the following, quoted almost at random :—

No matter where his labours close :
 No matter where his ashes lie :
A breath, the odour of the rose—
 Will breathe about him from the sky.

. . . . .

A gladsome sight it is to see,
In blossom thy mimosa tree.
Like golden moonlight doth it seem,
The moonlight of a heavenly dream ;
A sunset lustre, chased and cold,
A pearly splendour, blent with gold ;
That in its loveliness profound,
The waters have a mellower sound.

. . . . .

A lovely sisterhood of nuns ye seem,
 White-hooded, in your cloister of the snow ;

. . . . . .

Some of his sonnets, as the one just quoted from, "Snow-drops," are very beautiful, and many of the lines cling to the memory almost with the persistent force and haunting melody of Wordsworth's.

STAND OUT OF THE WAY, OLD TIME.

Written on seeing the dial in ruins in the *pleasure*-grounds of Southwell Union Workhouse.

STAND out of the way, Old Time !
 With your scythe and weary wing ;
You, in this poverty-palace
 No longer may reign as king,

Your symbol is shattered and rent;
  Its pillar crumbled and strown;
So pitch elsewhere your tent,
  And find you another throne.

They who have lost life's trial,
  By fortune beggared and shorn,
Care not for clock or dial,
  Nor whether 'tis even or morn.

O, were there good in the future—
  They here by the hour might watch;
Would hope come to the doorstep—
  Or love lift up the latch.

They have had a visit from grief—
  Have strayed in error's den;
And find the cross and crown of thorns
  The bitter portion of men.

They care not for the morrow—
  They weary of to-day;
So break the dial that the hours
  May blindly ebb away.

Death is a visiting justice,
  Who will not his hour neglect;
Of all inspectors, the welcomest
  That comes here to inspect.

Poor things! from life's dread battle,
  Persued by wind and wave—
They run unto death for safety,
  And anchor fast by the grave.

EVENING AND NIGHT.

A Soliloquy of Abel.

THE flowers are closing, and the few first stars
Are dimly twinkling in the deepening blue ;
The dewy mist, that riseth from the river,
In crystal drops is beaded on the stems,
On the fresh leaves, and on the tinted flowers.
Few of the songs which cheered the open day,
Few, yet more loud, the evening cheer and charm.
No more the elephant beneath the shade
Reposeth, where the shadowy palm was cool ;
No more the lion in the thicket lies,
Retired from noontide heat ; the pard no more
Is, where the fountain gushed beside him couched ;
The eagle, too, hath left his mountain home,
And with the lion will he share the prey.
Surely the eventide hath power to wake,
With its calm might in all things energy ;
That thus all powerful natures are abroad,
Deserted thus, the eyrie and the lair.

The light that is a wanderer now departs,
Following its giver through the glorious west ;
Following the faded crimson of the clouds.
Awake, O nightingale ! voice of the night !
The melody of darkness body forth
The songs of loneliness.   Now, mighty things
Of solemn mood are present ; now, the earth
Is hushed to hear thy music ; wake ! awake !
Silence is sad until thy strain be heard.
Sing, that the river's song be lost in thine,
And sigh of leaves, wind-stirred.   Awake, that we
No more may deem we hear our beating hearts
Listening intense amid the nightfall's hush.

10

The night in now thine auditor,—the stars
Lamps in thy temple of immortal song.
Sing ! 'till thou only seemest in the world,
Stilling all life—all life by thee entranced—
Binding all souls in bands of ecstacy !
Fair is the dome of heaven ; the stars intense
Burn in the blue, the blue without a cloud :
Dark is the earth, the heavens are clearly dark,
And leaves and flowers seem darkling of one hue,
Yet, beautiful is night ! and silence here
In the awed soul stirs music ; whilst the stars
Lead the free thoughts to follow in their track,
Paths to the throne of God ; till the full heart
Pours forth its wealth in worship unconfined !

RAILWAY SONNETS.

RUDE railway-trains, with all your noise and smoke,
I love to see you wheresoe'er ye move ;
Though nature seems such trespass to reprove,
Though ye the soul of old romance provoke,
I thank you that from misery ye unyoke
Thousands of panting horses.   Science pleased,
Sees by machinery lungs and sinews eased,
And mercy smiles as suffering ye revoke.
Calm sanctities, deem not such march profane :
Sweet meads give up your flowers and emerald sod :
Small fields resign your being without pain :
For, thinking on old roads in anguish trod,
Not to the heart of nature can be vain-
Humanity, which serves both man and God.

Lawns, shaven smooth ; parterres all summer fair,
With rarest flowers from farthest regions brought :
Groves dedicate to friendship and sweet thought :

These, touched by railways, wither in despair,
Die in strong light, and the obtrusive air.
For gardens, crofts, old owners are distraught,
For cottages, home-hallowed, scorned as nought ;
Leisure made public, and retirement bare.
Thank God it is so.   Hence, in order due,
To countless blessings these distractions tend :
Good to the million, social gifts ensue :
The anxious lover, and the heart-warm friend,
Parents and children long-lost sweets renew,—
All quickly met, as 'twere from the world's end !

THOMAS HUNTON.

THOMAS HUNTON was born at Yarmouth on the 27th April, 1818, and was educated at Rochester and Ackworth Schools. He took his B.A. at London University in 1841, being the first Friend to do so. After being for some years a private tutor, he became superintendent of Grove House School, Tottenham, which position he occupied from 1849 to 1860; since that date he has resided at Torquay.

His first verses appeared in "The Friend"; he has also contributed poems to the "Friends' Quarterly Examiner." In 1890 he published a volume of verse entitled "Scenes from the Past," and in 1894 "Scenes from the Past," Part Second, from which the following poems are taken.

TORQUAY IN MARCH 1891.

THE snow and the north-east wind came down
In a fierce descent upon Torquay town;
"Repel the invaders," exclaimed the Mayor,
Or more correctly the Town Surveyor;
"Seize such weapons as seize ye can,
Think of your country, and play the man."
Then from their houses they hastened quick,
With spade and shovel, with broom and pick;
From the dark recess came the McIntosh,
Boots and leggings, and stout golosh.
Blenheim and *Waterloo* heard again
The roll of carts and the tramp of men;
By "*Linden* lay the untrodden snow,"
But another sight it was soon to show,

For out of *the Nest*, and down from the *Towers*,
From *Kilmaurie*, and from proud *Kilmauers*,
From *Glenholme* and *Glenrock*, and twenty *glens*,
From *Holmes* by dozens, and *Leighs* by tens,
From *Lebanon*, *Hermon*, and *Stuart Mount*,
From *hills* as many as fingers count,
From *Sunnymead* and from *Sunnyside*,
From *Edenhurst* and from *Eventide*,
From *Limefield*, *Crossfields*, and bright *Boveen*,
From steep *Gonvena* and sweet *Clareen*,
From *Smyrna*, *Florence*, and *Fontainebleau*,
Rushed muffler'd heroes to fight the foe.
Wellesley and *Raglan*, and stout *Glendower*,
Brave, as of old, faced the pelting shower ;
Saints in their snow-white garb were there,
Cecilia, *Mary*, and lovely *Clare ;*
From the *Pines* and *Firs* were white volleys thrown,
And the ground with many a limb was strewn ;
From the *Elms* a crashing sound was heard,
By the war-like blast were the *Cedars* stirred ;
Many and swift were the balls they sent
From *Cambria's* "snow-white battlement,"
And from roof to pavement the foe they threw,
From *Wanganui* and from Wooloomooloo.

A JOURNEY WITH THE SUN.

'TWAS in the month of November
    When the bright sun said to me,
"I am going my daily journey,
    Will you my companion be?
Pleasant I think you'll find it,
    For there's much both to hear and to see."

"Thank you, good Sun," was my answer,
    "But the burning heat I fear,

And so high is your path in the heaven,
    That Earth's sounds one would fail to hear,
And now, with old age pressing on me,
    I can only see things that are near."

   .   .   .   .   .

And bright as the brightest silver,
    The Ocean rolled around,
And the waves as they chased each other
    Gave forth melodious sound,
And the tops of the snow-clad mountains
    With purple light were crowned.

And from verdant plains emerging,
    Wide forests rose on high,
And winding as winds a serpent,
    The rivers glided by;
And over all was stretching
    The arch of the azure sky.

"Sure 'tis a blessed lot," said I,
    "Thus o'er the world to range,
And, free from fear, to gaze on scenes
    So wondrous fair and strange;
But is the prospect always thus?
    Does Time produce no change?"

"For countless years," replied the Sun,
    "I've journeyed on this track;
And Time and Space such difference make,
    That nought of change I lack;
Aye, sometimes on the changes seen,
    I look, bewildered, back.

   .   .   .   .   .

And last, I saw man's race arise,
    Excelling all in might;
With all who would not own his sway
    Joining in deadly fight,

And in the varied acts of power
 Finding his chief delight.

Works he has raised, you see them there,
 Defying envious Time,
And now he tries my speed to reach,
 Passing from clime to clime,
And Nature's barriers to subdue
 He deems a task sublime."

"But if," said I, "he holds the power
 The Earth to make more fair,
Adding fresh charms to land and sea,
 Trying to soar through air ;
Can't he his home unchanged retain,
 And dwell for ever there?"

"Nay," said the Sun, "to laws of change
 Men yield like all before ;
Ten times ten thousand every day
 Will see my face no more,
And learn that gifts I take away
 Earth never can restore.

But yet more numerous still are they,
 Who with each rising morn,
For the first time behold my light
 In their life's early morn,
Nor dream for what high destiny
 Perchance they have been born."

And is it then their destiny
 To live, then pass away,
Yielding their place to some new race
 More powerful than they,
Fitted more exploits to achieve,
 And nobler aims display?"

'Twas thus I asked, and then the Sun
    In thoughtful mood replied :—
"No light of mine can pierce the clouds
    Which future changes hide ;
But tho' some changes sorrow bring,
    Yet others joy provide.

Of change of race I see no trace,
    But many a change must be,
Ere Want and Wrong, and War and Woe,
    From yonder Earth shall flee,
And homes inured to Sorrow's wail
    Resound with notes of glee.

I know not if my light will last
    Such progress to behold,
For not through me returns to Earth
    The fabled age of gold,
But earnest men their aid must lend
    Its glories to unfold.

All hail to those whose daily life
    Illumes and cheers like mine,
Whose love, like heat that warms the Earth,
    Tells of a source divine,
And on the gloomiest human heart
    With cheering light can shine."

"Well said," I cried, "but now 'tis time
    Homeward my course to bend ;"
"Then," said the Sun, "you'll find it best
    Yon rainbow to ascend ;"
And so I did, and gliding down,
    My dream was at an end.

JAMES HURNARD.

JAMES HURNARD was born at Boreham, a village near Chelmsford, in Essex, on the 3rd March, 1808. In 1815, the family removed to Kelvedon, where his father had taken a mill. This was the year of the battle of Waterloo, and James Hurnard speaks in his autobiography of the constant state of excitement in which the village was kept by soldiers continually passing through it on their way to embark for the Continent. In 1818, he was sent to a boarding school at Earl's Colne, about eight miles from Kelvedon, kept by William Impey, a minister in the Society of Friends; he did not stay here long, however, as his father, being in business difficulties, resolved to emigrate to America, and they left England in April, 1819.

After a short tarriance at New York and Philadelphia, they went to Wilmington, and set up a school, beginning with four or five boys, which number increased to thirty in the course of a few months. James Hurnard traces his first love of poetry from this period, when, by his mother's advice, he read Falconer's "Shipwreck." In 1824, having had a legacy left to them, the Hurnards returned to England, and again settled at Kelvedon, where James devoted himself to writing poetry, many of his youthful productions are to be found in the memoir of him edited by his widow. He had an epic about half finished at this time on the wickedness of war; but incited by the preaching of William Impey, his old schoolmaster, who had laid great stress on the sacrifice of "delectable things," he burned this, although with much pain and regret.

In 1828, the Hurnards removed to Colchester, and James

seems to have devoted himself to composition in earnest, although with scant success; he says in the memoir before alluded to :—"Third month, 3rd, 1835. My birthday. The fourth and fifth cantos of my poem, 'The Phantom Land,' having been rejected in the last two numbers of the 'Monthly Magazine,' my hopes of bringing myself into notice as a poet seem now to be extinguished. Every avenue of literary distinction seems to be closed against me, and with a heavy heart I submitted to my lot. . . . But I did not for one moment relinquish my attachment to poetry, and I determined still to write, though I might never be read."

He took a very active part in the agitation for the repeal of the Corn Laws, and a sonnet he wrote was printed with passages from Byron, Cowper, Elliott, and others in the pamphlets distributed by the Anti-Corn Law League. In 1845, he wrote a poem on Biard's picture of the "Slave Mart," which gained a prize, and also introduced him to the notice of Benjamin B. Wiffen, who wrote to him highly extolling his poem, and this proved the beginning of a friendship which lasted until the close of Wiffen's life.

In 1849, James Hurnard attended the Peace Congress in Paris, Victor Hugo being called to the chair; he was much interested in French oratory, and in visiting the various public buildings, museums, etc., in the French capital. The death of his father in 1866 left him entirely at liberty, and he gave up the house and business at Colchester, and, after various short stays with different friends and relatives, he became engaged to Louisa Bowman Smith, whom he had known from her childhood. They were married in 1867, and, after passing their honeymoon in the Isle of Wight, they settled at Colchester, Here he finished the long poem by which he is chiefly known. "The Setting Sun," which was published in 1870. In the same year his only son, Samuel Fennell, was born. And, in 1873, having inherited a considerable fortune, he bought a lovely country home for himself at Lexden, near Colchester. Here, with his wife and child, many friends, and a large and varied literary correspondence, his life seemed at last perfectly stable and peaceful, but he fell into delicate health, and passed away, after only about an hour's illness, on the 26th February, 1881, in the seventy-third year of his age. He was buried in the Friends' Cemetery, Roman Road, and his funeral was very largely attended.   He had been made an alderman as a mark of respect, and by his kindness and generosity, not only to causes in which he believed, but to individuals, had made himself much beloved.

"The Setting Sun" is a very remarkable poem, full in places of deep thought and true poetry, and brimful of originality, but, as a whole, lacking in that unity of motive which would make it a grand work of art, and it gives one more the idea of a series of extremely clever and interesting sketches than a perfect poem.   Mrs. Hurnard has also written some graceful verses, besides editing her husband's memoir.

SONNET.

OH! for a mind congenial with my own!
Loving whatever is divine in thought,
And beautiful in vision.   Life is short,
My youth is past, and I am still alone.
Oh! for a friend with kindred feelings fraught
To love me, cheer me, and, with skill untaught,
Forth from my heart-strings call each slumbering tone;
One of the true imaginative sort
To whom I might, confidingly, make known
What glorious pageants sometimes sweep athwart
My visual range, and vanish into nought,
Whither the poet's bubble worlds are blown.
Is there a voice that can respond to mine?
Or must my life in loneliness decline?

FROM "THE SETTING SUN."

I AM a member of the Sect of Friends,
A sect reviled and ridiculed and flouted
With quirks and quibbles of the penny-a-liners,
And even learned men who should know better,
Men who know little of the things they talk of.
Sects dimly read each other's inner life,
And so through ignorance misjudge each other ;
The best things in the world are most abused ;
So has it happened with the Sect of Friends ;
And yet its members individually
Are mostly treated with respect and praise.
A sect in numbers inconsiderable,
Diminished to a very few in England
By rigid rules and unwise regulations,
And over-prudence in contracting marriage ;
But growing rapidly across the Atlantic.
A sect whose doctrines being little known,
And nothing popular, are therefore freely
Misrepresented by the outside world ;
And yet a noble sect, who boldly stood
For liberty of conscience and for truth
In the dark days of bigot persecution ;
Who, when more numerous sects shrunk cowardly
Into safe garrets, or down into dark cellars,
To worship God by stealth, in fear and trembling,
Assembled boldly in their meeting-houses,
And, when expelled by brutal soldiery,
Stood in the open streets to worship God ;
Yes, even in the streets of Colchester !
Till hurried off with blows and violence,
Inflicted equally on men and women,
To dungeons dismal as the times were dark !
Thousands were thus imprisoned wrongfully,

And hundreds perished in most loathsome cells
By cruel usage and by prison fevers.

.   .   .   .

Friends were the real and valiant Protestants;
They took their stand for liberty of conscience,
And perfect freedom in the forms of worship;
Protested against hireling ministry;
Protested against human interference
Between the soul of man and his Creator;
Protested against empty forms and ceremonies,   .
And outward ordinances employed in worship,
As superseded by the coming of Christ,
And non-essential to the soul's salvation;
Believing that the saving grace of God
Is freely offered to the human family;
Protested against war in all its forms;
Protested against oaths and imprecations;
Protested against human slavery,
And capital punishment for any crimes;
Protested, on the other hand, in favour
Of peace, and progress, and humanity;
Of justice, godliness, and temperance;
Of woman's mission to proclaim the Gospel,
And relative equality with man;
The free diffusion of the Holy Scriptures;
And of the education of the people.

FROM "THE SETTING SUN."

.   .   .   How many men mistake their mission!
How many a cobbler thinks himself a Solon!
Mistaking the ambition for the power,
And, listening to the flattery of the heart,
Grows noteless to the warnings of the brain.
I have beheld a borough magistrate

Sitting in glory on the Bench of Justice,
Who had been better picking plums at home.
I have beheld a preacher, bold and noisy,
With brow perspiring, hammering on a text,
Who had been better hammering on a lapstone.
I have beheld a member of Parliament,
One of the actual makers of our laws,
Who had been better sitting on a board
With thread and needle and a brother goose,
Making the breeches of the British people.

.   .   .   .

True greatness calmly smiles at insolence,
'Tis littleness that promptly takes offence—

.   .   .   .

There never was a doctrine so absurd
As not to find disciples to adopt it ;
There never was a theory so Utopian,
So shallow, crass, jejune, and contradictory,
As not to find shrewd men to swallow it,
Write for it, fight for it, and at last go mad for it.
One fool draws other fools into his net ;
This is the law of Natural Selection.

.   .   .   .

Slaves all ! slaves all ! slaves all ! we all are slaves !
Some to a foolish crotchet of the brain,
Some to an idle habit formed in youth,
Some to a treacherous glass of sparkling liquor,
Some to a pipe of villainous tobacco,
But most of us to other people's eyes.
    Unnumbered are the forms that slavery takes :
We choose our master when we form a habit.

.   .   .   .

But all the world is one great auction room,
In which men struggle for the various lots.

It is for them to choose which lots to strive for,
And what they are content to pay for them.
Some buy bad bargains when they hope for good,
And others good beyond their expectations.
Experience is the most expensive thing,
When you are forced to buy it as you want it,
'Tis wiser far to borrow other people's.
Some trust to mother-wit to help them on,
And some to luck, and some to providence,
But Heaven helps those the best who help themselves.

WILLIAM KITCHING.

WILLIAM KITCHING was born in 1837 at Gainsboro,' and is the youngest son of William and Sarah Hopkins Kitching. He was educated at Ackworth and Bootham Schools, became a junior teacher at York, and afterwards continued his studies at the Flounders Institute under Isaac Brown and Dr. Willis. In 1860 he went as a teacher to Sidcot, and after two years there, settled down for eighteen at Ackworth as a senior master. He married Louisa Wilmot, of Bristol, who had been a teacher on the girls' side at Sidcot.

In 1880 William Kitching removed with his family to Southport, where he established a very successful private school known as Ackworth Lodge. This was disposed of in 1894, and he removed to Clevedon where he still resides.

The greater portion of his poetry was written during his residence at Southport, and much of it has appeared in different magazines and papers, amongst others in " The Friend," " British Friend," " Friends' Review," " Christian," " Herald of Peace," " All the world," etc., etc., In 1893 he published " Verses for my Friends " (Edward Hicks, Jun., London), and has, I understand, nearly sufficient pieces for another volume already written. William Kitching was recorded a minister in 1872, and has earnestly advocated the Temperance, Peace, and Anti-opium movements, both with voice and pen. He is an ardent lover of nature, and many of his most musical verses were written, he says, amid the heather and gorse on the Yorkshire moors, or under the influence of the grand sea and mountains.

To the Reader.

(Prefixed to Verses for my Friends).

DEAR READER, may these verses prove
A welcome messenger of love !
Tho' slight their depth and small their power,
They may beguile a passing hour
With thoughts of what is surely good,
And helpful to our brotherhood.
Thus sends the writer forth to-day,
His " maiden speech " his first essay ;
Pray criticise with kindly ear
The many faults that must appear,
Nor let thy strokes be too severe.
May peace within thy bosom dwell
Throughout life's journey.   Friend, farewell !

From Nature's Music.

THE sages of the ancient world
  Perceived, with awe-struck ears,
Mid silence of the universe,
  The music of the spheres.

The midnight star-bespangled sky
  Their fertile fancy woke,
Until they deemed that soothing sounds
  The awful silence broke.

  .   .   .   .   .   .

And yet what music meets the ear
  Where nature's voice is heard ;
We hear it in some fountain's fall,
  Or trill of tiny bird.

The roll of thunder through the sky,
  Its echo from the hills,
The patter of the falling rain
  The air with music fills.

11

When musing on the lonely shore,
　Beside the surging sea,
The rolling of the ocean waves
　Is music, too, to me !

The breeze that stirs the forest boughs
　I fondly love to hear,
And loudly though the storm may howl
　'Tis music in mine ear.

　.　　.　　.　　.　　.　　.　　.

O cuckoo ! thy enchanting voice,
　My heart yet thrills with joy ;
How oft, enraptured, to thy strains
　I listened when a boy.

The sea-mew screaming o'er the wave,
　The swift upon the wing,
Remind me of those bygone years,
　The joyous days of spring.

Ah ! then full oft a still small voice,
　Like music soft and low,
Played o'er my spirit's tender strings,
　And caused the tears to flow.

MARY LEADBEATER.

MARY LEADBEATER was the daughter of Richard Shackleton (by his second wife, Elizabeth Carleton), and grand-daughter of Abraham Shackleton, Edmund Burke's schoolmaster; and was born at Ballitore, in 1758. She was highly educated, her literary studies being aided by Aldborough Wrightson, a man of great ability. In 1784, she went to London with her father, and paid several visits to Burke's town house, where she met Sir Joshua Reynolds, George Crabbe, and many other celebrated people; she also went to Beaconsfield, and wrote a poem in praise of the place and its owner, which was acknowledged by Burke in a long eulogistic letter.

In 1791, she married William Leadbeater, a former pupil of her father's, and they settled down at Ballitore. William Leadbeater, who traced his descent from the Huguenot family of Le Batre, was a small farmer and landowner, and Mary kept the Post Office. She had from time to time written poems, and in 1794 published anonymously in Dublin, "Extracts and original anecdotes for the Improvement of Youth," which begins with an account of the society of the people called Quakers, contains several poems on secular subjects, and concludes with "divine odes."

She was in Carlow on Christmas Day, 1796, when news arrived that the French fleet had been seen off Bantry; and she gives a graphic description of the march out of the troops. In 1798, Ballitore was occupied, first by yeomen and soldiers, then by insurgents; it was sacked, and the Leadbeaters narrowly escaped death. She thought her food tasted of blood, and had horrible dreams of massacres. In 1808, she published

"Poems," with a metrical version of her husband's prose translation of Maffœus Vegio's 13th Book of the Œneid. In 1811, she published "Cottage dialogues among the Irish Peasantry," of which four editions had appeared by 1813, with additions and alterations. In 1813, she published "the Landlord's Friend," which was intended as a sequel to "Cottage Dialogues." In 1814, "Tales for Cottagers" appeared which she had written in conjunction with Elizabeth Shackleton; this book concludes with a curious moral play, "Honesty is the best Policy." In 1822, she published "Cottage Biography," and "Memories and Letters of Richard and Elizabeth Shackleton," compiled by their daughter.

Her biographical notices of members of the Society of Friends resident in Ireland, came out in 1823: this book is a very curious one, being a summary of their spiritual lives, with a scanty record of events. Her last work, "The Pedlar's Tale," was published in 1824. She also wrote a large number of poems, essays, characters, and tales, many of which appeared in various periodicals. Beside Edmund Burke, she corresponded with Maria Edgeworth, George Crabbe, Mrs. Melusina Trench, Thomas Wilkinson, and other interesting or famous people; and from her ninth year kept a journal. She died at Ballitore, in June. 1826, and was interred in the Quaker burial-ground there. Her best work is, perhaps, "the Annals of Ballitore" (2 vols.), which was not printed until 1862; the 2nd volume contains unpublished letters from Burke, and her correspondence with Crabbe and Mrs. Trench.

ON THE DEATH OF EDMUND BURKE.

'Tis o'er—that lamp is quench'd in endless night,
Which Nature kindled at her purest flame,
By Science fann'd,—if Science could enhance
A genius from which Science caught new rays—
No, 'tis not quench'd; the spark ethereal lives,

And it shall blaze along the track of time,
While we, who 'joy'd beneath the radiant beam,
Shall mix unheeded with our kindred clay.

That star is set, on earth to shine no more,
On which admiring nations wond'ring gaz'd :
That pow'rful stream of eloquence is dry,
Which with commanding force o'erwhelm'd the mind.
O mourn for this, that from a barren world
Such excellence is fled !—But public care
Apart, in pensive solitude retir'd,
Lamenting friendship drops the silent tear.
There tender recollection calls to mind
The sweet benevolence which marked that mien ;

That mien which unadmiring who could view ?
'Tis her's, with soft regret and pleasing pain,
To trace the social and domestic scene,
Where, ever shining, most of all he shone.
She saw the liberal hand the healing balms
Dispense unboasting ; and to haggard eyes,
Bedimm'd with poverty, and pain, and care,
The vivid rays of health and hope restore.
Th' unvarying friendship, and the candid mind,
Prompt to forgive and ready to atone,
Were his.—And O, how close the tender ties
Of father, husband, brother, bound his heart !
Why droops that noble soul ?   Alas ! he mourns
A brother's fate, companion of his youth,
By death relentless sever'd from his side.

Yet still remain'd that son, the only pledge
Of a long happy union ; and on whom
Paternal love had fix'd the ardent gaze
Of fond presaging hope, from infant years
To manhood's ripen'd bloom, and now retir'd

Th' illustrious father from the public scene,
And onward mov'd the son to fill *his* sphere
On life's conspicuous stage.—Ah, what avail,
Fame, youth, and health! for Febris' fiery dart
The throbbing temple smote, and soon dislodg'd
From the frail tenement the spark divine.
O blasted hope! O bitter streaming tears!
O childless parents! mourning o'er the tomb
Where duteous love, cold and unconscious lies
Of pangs that filial heart had bled to heal!—
The blow was struck, and life's delights were o'er.

Three suns roll'd joyless o'er that honour'd head:
Yet trembling hope, with lowly fear, survey'd
The op'ning scenes of hope and rest secure,
Where sorrows cease, and tears are wip'd away:
For well that meek, that noble spirit knew
This meed, which fame nor genius dare demand:
Though great his claim on both, a higher claim,
DIVINE PHILANTHROPY, he held on thee.

Farewell, O ever honour'd, ever dear,
And long lamented: may thy matchless voice,
Which never more shall charm terrestrial ears,
Th' immortal choirs of Hallelujah join!

WILLIAM HENRY LEATHAM, M.P.

WILLIAM HENRY LEATHAM was born on July 6th, 1815, at Wakefield. He was the second among the nine children of William Leatham, the banker, and author of "Letters on the Currency," which had attracted a good deal of favourable notice. One of his sisters became the wife of John Bright, and another married Joseph Gurney Barclay, the banker. W. H. Leatham was educated at Bruce Grove, Tottenham, and at Darlington, and afterwards continued his studies with a private tutor. At the age of nineteen he entered his father's bank, and was made a partner in 1836. In 1851 he left the bank in favour of a younger brother, and two of his sons were admitted at the same time.

In 1835 he made a tour on the Continent, and shortly after his return he began the publication of his poems at brief intervals. He married in 1839 Priscilla, fourth daughter of Mr. Samuel Gurney of Upton, Essex, and they settled at Woodthorpe, Sandal, and a few years after their marriage left the Society of Friends, and joined the Church.

In 1832 W. H. Leatham had greatly assisted in the return of the first member for Wakefield, a Liberal, and in 1852 he contested the town in the Liberal interest himself, but was defeated: at the General Election in 1859, however, he was returned by a small majority, but was unseated on petition. Both Leatham and his opponent were prosecuted for bribery, but a *nolle prosequi* was ultimately entered by the government.

In 1865 Leatham was again returned, and his native town, to show its appreciation of his character, and indignation at the unjust prosecution to which he had been subjected, returned him free of expense, and presented him with a testimonial signed by 8,700 non-electors.

He did not offer himself for re-election in 1868, but in 1880 he was returned for the S. W. Riding of Yorkshire.

In 1851 he purchased Hemsworth Hall, now in possession of his eldest son, and devoted much time to its improvement, and to his magisterial duties; he was considered one of the best magistrates in the West Riding, and was placed on the Commission of Peace in 1850, made Deputy-Lieutenant soon afterwards, and Deputy-Chairman of Quarter Sessions in 1870. After his partner, Mr. Tew, died, he became Chairman of Wakefield Petty Sessions, and altogether took a most active part in municipal and national affairs; he also delivered many lectures at different mechanics' institutes, and the list of his principal publications shows the unremitting industry, and unabated vigour of his literary occupations and faculties. His poetry has hardly been appreciated at its real worth; it is marked by great strength of diction, and tenderness of thought, but its author was so prominent in other walks of life, and so well known and revered for his political and social labours, that people often forgot how true a poet he was. He died rather suddenly at the White House, Carleton, near Pontefract, in November, 1889. His chief works are :—

A Traveller's Thoughts	1837
The Victim, a Swiss Tale	1838
Sandal in the Olden Time	1839
Henrie Clifforde and Margaret Percy	1841
The Siege of Granada	1841
Emilia Monteiro	1841
Strafford, a Tragedy	1842
Cromwell, a Drama	1843
The Widow and the Earl	1843
The Batucaes and other Poems	1844

Montezuma	1845
The Red Hand and other Poems	1845
Life hath many Mysteries	1847
Selections from Lesser Poems	1855
Later volume of Selections	1879
Tales of English Life and Miscellanies, (2 vols.)	1858
Two volumes of Lectures	

Life's Enigma.

Life hath many mysteries!
Ceaseless when we close our eyes,
Whilst our frame in slumber lies. —

Then the soul breaks forth in gleams—
Bodiless her passage seems
Through fantastic, airy dreams.

Then we meet the dead again,
Hear them speak, and see them plain—
Morning snaps the magic chain!

Time and place are one in sleep,
Thoughts unbidden o'er us creep—
Then we smile, and then we weep.

Life's stream owns a double flow,
One is real—one but show;
Which the real—who can know?

Body, so alive all o'er,
Feeling breathes from every pore,
What can sentient life do more?

Conscious of a mind within,
Great in thought, though soiled by sin,
Still our upward course we win!

Soul has pledge of endless life—
Doubt with her can have no strife—
Immortality is rife!

But the body—when it lies
Dead before our weeping eyes—
Where's the hope that it may rise?

Look at yonder giant tree,
Think how dead its germ must be,
Is it not a type of thee?

What is matter? all we see,
Touch, or taste's a mystery—
How such things from nought could be!

Mind or matter—what are they?
Tenants both of unknown clay,
Past our knowledge, some may say.

Mind, ethereal, cannot be
Else than spirit's property—
Tho' from matter not yet free.

My Sister.

Sweet, my sister! sweet to me
Is the thought that dwells with thee!
Dimly through this vale of tears
Thy angelic form appears ;
I can see thy radiant brow
'Mid the white-robed seraphs now!
I can see thy heaven-born smile
Turned in love to earth awhile.

How it speaks of perils past,
Weepings o'er, and joy at last!
How it beckons us away,
From the trifles of to-day!

Sweet, my sister ! sweet to me
Is the thought that dwells with thee !

Thou hast left a track behind
All who follow thee must find ;
Simple faith and truthful love
Plumed thy wings to realms above,
And the savour of thy life
Is with roseate perfume rife.

Beautiful that life appears
· As it glimmers through my tears,
Memory blends thy days in one ;
They are here, but thou art gone !
Sweet, my sister ! sweet to me,
Is the thought that dwells with thee !

LONDON LODGINGS.

MEM'RY ! what of London ?—what of London ?   Canst thou
    tell ?
Of palaces and courts, where rank and fashion dwell—
Of music rich and rare ; of beauty dressed for show—
Of eloquence in senates, fired with patriot's glow—
Of military pomp—of parks, alive with flowers—
Of carriages and horses—of light, convivial hours—
Of worship, in dim aisles—of throng'd and lighted streets—
Of chill, November fogs—of sultry summer heats—
Of these can mem'ry tell—but they form but part of life,
'Tis of the daily spot we dwell in that memory is rife.

Out from the bustling street—a stone-throw, but not more,
Where the eye may view the thronging—the ear may catch the
        roar—
But it passes harmless by you—is a home I know full well,
Of that little spot in London, my memory can tell.

I mount the airy story—my pictures look so neat—
My hearth is trimly swept—I look across the street.
There sits the little Milliner, who never ceases work ;
There swings the parrot in his cage, as gaudy as a Turk.
My letters lie unopen'd—my papers by their side—
The easy chair is set for me—its arms are open'd wide.
Then soon the cocoa-pot comes in—the curtains snugly
        drawn—
Who says a London Lodging is cheerless and forlorn?

THOMAS LISTER.

THOMAS LISTER, the poet-naturalist, was born at Old Mill Wharf, Barnsley, February 11th, 1810. He was the youngest of fourteen children, and his father, Joseph Lister, was a small farmer and gardener, who had formerly been employed in the linen industry carried on at Barnsley. Thomas was a very delicate child, and but for the kind care of an old Friend, Margaret Parrington, would probably not have lived to reach manhood. He went to Ackworth in 1821, where he became acquainted with John Bright, and made himself notorious for astonishing athletic feats and great physical courage. He was a remarkable "new boy" in every way, on the first evening of his arrival, he mounted a wall, from the top of which he recited long passages from Pope's *Iliad*, to an astonished and appreciative audience.

He obtained a good English education at Ackworth, as well as that great love for natural objects and outdoor life, which ever afterwards pervaded his work and writings. After leaving school, he worked with his father for some years, driving a horse and cart, and wearing a long smock and strangely-shaped hat, and being usually intent on Homer as he drove along.

In 1832, he was introduced to Lord Morpeth at the Parliamentary Election, when the latter contested the West Riding. Lister wrote effective political squibs in his favour, and was afterwards offered the Postmastership of Barnsley. But the young quaker declined to take the necessary oaths, so the post was given to another. In 1839, however, affirmation being then allowed, he was made Postmaster, which office he retained until 1870. In 1834, he published "The Rustic Wreath," of which 3,000 copies were quickly sold, and after visiting Spencer T. Hall, and becoming acquainted with Ebenezer Elliott, he made a tour, chiefly on foot, through the Lake District and into Scotland, where he met John Wilson, the Chambers, and Miller the artist. In 1838, he travelled through France, Italy, Switzerland, and the Netherlands, and wrote many of his poems for Tait's Magazine. In 1837, he published "Temperance Rhymes," and in 1862, "Rhymes of Progress." He also contributed many papers on natural history and meteorology to various publications. He had always been an enthusiastic naturalist, and became President of the Barnsley Naturalists' Society. He was also a member of the British Association, and regularly attended its meetings, reading in 1882 a valuable paper on the distribution of Yorkshire spring migrants. In 1884, he accompanied the British Association to Montreal, and took the opportunity to visit the chief towns and points of interest in Canada and the United States. He was one of the founders of the Barnsley Mechanics' Institute and Literary Society in 1837, and frequently lectured there in after years, being also an active temperance worker.

He married in 1841, Miss Hannah Schofield, who proved a perfect helpmate and companion in every sense; they had no family. He died at Barnsley, March 25th, 1888.

Thomas Lister is said to have been of a very inquiring nature, and made a point of being introduced to every celebrated person who came to Barnsley; this was very agreeable to most visitors, as the poet-naturalist was the most interesting companion possible, and although sometimes asking odd and searching questions, full of all kinds of knowledge and imformation, which he was always willing to pass on to his companions.

GENERAL MEETING AT ACKWORTH SCHOOL.

THIS day, the sweetest of the year,
Hope-lov'd—in memory treasur'd dear—
 Glad-utter'd by each tongue—
When friends, long parted, warmly greet,
And bonds of love, more kindly meet,
 And age once more seems young,—

Tells of a fond-remember'd time,
When life exulted in its prime,
 Here bless'd with golden dreams.
Hail! walls, where peace and joy abide,
Bowers, gardens, cloth'd with summer's pride
 And ye mead-loving streams.

Those cupolas,—where morning's smile
Plays bright,—that noble central pile—
 Gigantic in embrace;
Whose wings on either side extend,
To guard, to cherish, and befriend
 The tender rising race:—

The green—that sport-inviting ground,
The shed—where skippers lightly bound,
 While whizz their cords in air,—
To me, like well-known friends, are dear,
Who once was blithe as any here,
 And knew not more of care.

Thought rushes from its secret springs,
While memory swift before me brings
 The scenes of former years;—
When here the first firm stone was laid,
The virtues lent their holiest aid,
 Mov'd by the foundling's tears.

Benevolence, with offer'd dower,
And Pity,—gentle soothing power,
  Smil'd kindly on the place :
And Charity,—of higher birth,
Descending gracious, came on earth,
  To feed the helpless race.

Time saw a change—for here, the mind
As yet in chains of sloth confin'd,
  Assum'd its noble throne :—
A people came—who once withstood
Reproach and hate, while humbly good,
  They bow'd to One alone.

Here, choosing learning's pleasant seat
Within this order-ruled retreat,
  They placed their offspring dear,—
Who, train'd with care by guardians kind,
Are taught to store with Truth the mind,—
  And her pure laws revere.

The fair, the serious, the gay,
Plain, neat their garb—-are seen to-day—
  Beauty unplum'd is here ;
Yet, simpler were their sires of old,
Who, strong in toil, unflinching, bold,
  Walk'd firm, with Truth severe.

Not the bare word, nor barer form,
Sustain'd them in their morn of storm,
  Heaven was their light—their guide ;
So long as men on Heaven rely,
They will the worst of foes defy—-
  Strife—fraud—ensnaring pride.

Thus warm my feelings as I gaze
On these dear scenes of early days,

Where my young mind acquir'd
The seeds of that augmenting store,
Which daily culture ripen'd more,
   While glowing hope inspir'd.

Yet, here, what hours I mourn as lost :
Since then, by cheerful breezes toss'd,
   All lore was laid at rest ;
Till late, once more the flame aspir'd,
By some strange secret impulse fir'd,
   Too strong to be repress'd.

Where'er around I cast my eyes,
What long forgotten thoughts arise,—
   A rapid, fleeting train :
The well-known grounds I traverse o'er,
Each room—each favourite haunt explore,
   I feel a boy again.

The youngsters, eyeing my advance,
With their peculiar schoolboy's glance,
   Their varied sports pursue ;
Unknown to me each prying face,
Save that in some a kindred trace
   Of former friends I view.

.   .   .   .   .   .

THE FIRST FOUND FLOWER.

To thee, though not the first of spring's young race,
   The earliest wild flower, greeting yet mine eye ;
Ev'n ere the crocus bursts in golden dye,
   Or primrose pale unveils its modest face—
To thee small celandine I yield first place.
   For thou dost greet me, earliest of the band,
That comes as sweeteners, after storms and cares.
   Remembrance of past pleasures ! moments bland,

12

Pledge of rich joys the coming season bears!
   Well might thy starry cup of golden bloom—
Thy lowly virtues—one pure mind awake,
   Who sought, before the art-emblazon'd dome,
The flower-crowned mountain, and the reedy lake—
   Thee! hallow'd Wordsworth sang—I love thee for his sake.

CHARLES LLOYD.

CHARLES LLOYD was born in Birmingham, on the 12th February, 1775, and was the eldest son of Charles Lloyd, the well-known banker and philanthropist, and the translator of portions of the Iliad and Odyssey, and the epistles of Horace. He was educated by a private tutor, and was intended to enter his father's bank; but having literary tastes, he strongly objected to this, and in 1795 he published a first volume of poems at Carlisle.

In 1796, he became acquainted with Coleridge, and when the latter visited Birmingham, to obtain subscribers to his " Watchman," Charles Lloyd was so fascinated by his conversation, that he offered him £80 a year in return for three hours' daily instruction. For some little time the two lived together at Kingsdown, Bristol, and at the close of 1796 Lloyd went with the Coleridges to Nether Stowey. It is believed that Coleridge's sonnet "To a Friend," on the birth of Hartley, and his lines "To a Young Man of Fortune," were addressed to Charles Lloyd. The latter had already printed, ready for publication in London, a volume of elegiac verse to the memory of his grandmother, Priscilla Farmer; this volume was introduced by a sonnet from Coleridge, and ended by Charles Lamb's " The Grandam." Soon after they settled at Nether Stowey, Lloyd was attacked by fits, and Coleridge described his condition as very alarming; but he shortly afterwards went to London, and devoted himself to cultivating Charles Lamb's friendship. He appears, however, to have practically lived with the Coleridges until the summer of 1797. In the autumn of that year, Cottle appended to a second edition of Coleridge's

poems, all Lloyd's pieces which were considered worth preserving, together with various poems by Charles Lamb. This
volume was headed by an elegant Latin motto composed by
Coleridge, on the friendship existing between the authors. He
afterwards, however, ridiculed both Lamb's and Lloyd's con-
tributions; declaring it was only at their earnest solicitation
that he had allowed them to be published with his own.

Lloyd published in 1797 "Edmund Oliver," a novel in letters,
which was a polemic against Godwin's views of marriage. In
the same year appeared "Blank Verse by Charles Lloyd and
Charles Lamb." In 1799, Lloyd married Sophia, daughter of
Samuel Pemberton of Birmingham, with whom he eloped by
proxy; employing, according to De Quincey, no less a person
than Southey to carry her off for him!

The young couple lived first at Barnwell, near Cambridge,
and the prosaic and quiet landscape around them, provided
subjects for some of his best poetry. About August, 1800,
however, he took Low Brathay, a small place near Ambleside,
where he received the Southeys, on their return from Portugal,
and where De Quincey made his acquaintance in 1807.

He seems to have been at this time perfectly happy; his
father made him a good allowance; he was surrounded by a
charming family, while Mrs. Lloyd, according to De Quincey,
was "unsurpassed as mother and wife." He carried on a lively
correspondence in French with Miss Watson, the daughter of
the Bishop of Llandaff, and in 1805 began the translation of
Ovid's Metamorphoses, which he did not finish until 1811, and
of which only portions were published. In this year, Lloyd
began to suffer from distressing auditory illusions, which
increased into serious illness. His translation of Alfieri, however, appeared in 1815, dedicated to Southey, who reviewed it
in the *Quarterly*. In 1820, he published "Isabel, a Novel."

Meantime he had been obliged to be confined in an asylum
at York, from whence he escaped sometime in 1818, found his

way to Westmoreland, and suddenly appeared at De Quincey's cottage.

De Quincey afterwards told Woodhouse that Lloyd tried hard to convince him that he (Lloyd) was the devil! He said to another friend, that he was lost, and that his wife and children were only shadows. He seems to have been afflicted in much the same way as Cowper, as soon after his interview with De Quincey, he temporarily recovered his reason, and went with his wife to London. Here he seems to have been very beneficially affected by seeing Macready perform in Rob Roy, and this he expressed in a copy of verses, printed in the actor's " Reminiscences."

For a time he displayed great literary activity, publishing in 1819 "Nugæ Canoræ," in 1821 "Desultory Thoughts in London," "Titus and Gisippus, and other Poems," and " Poetical Essays on the Character of Pope," in 1822 "The Duke d'Ormond," a tragedy written in 1798, and "Beritola," a metrical tale in the Italian manner, and in 1823 another small volume of poems.

His latter days seem to have been clouded by insanity ; but although in such a depressed condition, with regard to himself, he could still discuss speculative questions with interest and acumen. Eventually he went to France, and died in a maison de Santé, near Versailles, on the 16th January, 1839; his wife died at Versailles also, about the same time. De Quincey compares Charles Lloyd with Rousseau, in his love of nature, and sentimental pensiveness, and also his fine descriptive powers. He had besides a marvellous gift of analysis, and great discriminative faculties. His poetry is very powerful in parts, but gloomy and sad, rarely rising into joy or lightness.

STANZAS.

OH, that a being in this latter time
  Lived such as poets in their witching lays,

Feigned were their demi-gods in nature's prime!
  The Dryad sheltered from noon's scorching rays
By leafy canopy ;—the Naiad's days
  Stealing by gently wedded to some spring,
In pure connatural essence ; while the haze
  Of twilight in the vale is lingering,
The Oread from the mountain-tops the sunrise welcoming.

Oh, that a man might hope to pass his life,
  Where through lime, beech, and alder, the proud sun
His leafy grot scarce visited ;—where strife
  Is known not ;—to absolve—to impeach him none ;—
His moral life, and that of nature, one :—
  Where fragrant thyme, and crisped heath-bells prank
The ground, all memory of the world to shun,
  And piercing, while his ears heaven's music drank,
Nature's profoundest depths, the God of Nature thank.

   .   .   .   .

My God! this world's a prison-house to some ;
  And yet to those who cannot prize its treasure,
It will not suffer them in peace to roam
  Far from its perturbation and its pleasure.
No! though ye make a compact with its measure—
  Except to one or two by fortune blest !—
'Twill only mock your efforts ; thus your leisure,
  Yielded to her, becomes a sad unrest ;—
It pays the fool the least that worships her the best.

Yet, on the other hand, if ye forego
  Her haunts, and all her trammels set aside,
Though 'tis her joy ungratefully to throw
  Scorn on her slaves, her vassals to deride—
" Hewers of wood, drawers of water," plied
  With daily drudgery know this truth full well—
She will from pole to pole, through time and tide

Still follow you with persecuting spell,
And by her whispers foul, make solitude a hell

Therefore breathed I this prayer, that as in years
 Long parted, beings were supposed to live
Exempt from human ties ;—from human tears,
 And human joys ;—endowed with a reprieve
From friends to flatter, or foes to forgive ;
 So it might fare with me !—Oh, Liberty,
I ask for thee alone ;—with thee to weave
 Quaint rhymes, to breathe the air, were heaven to me ;
To dream myself the only living thing, save thee !

When Heaven has granted thought and energy,
 Passion, Imagination, Fancy, Love,
Pleasures and pains, hopes, fears, that will not die,
 'Tis surely hard to be condemned to rove
In a perpetual wilderness ; to move
 Unblest by freedom and humanity ;—
I blame not those for whom the world has wove
 Spells that to them are best reality—
Some are there 'twill not serve, nor yet will let them fly.

Oh ! for an island in the boundless deep !
 Where rumour of the world might never come ;
Oh ! for a cave where weltering waves might keep
 Eternal music ! round which, nightwinds roam
Incessantly, mixed with the surging foam ;
 And from their union bring strange sounds to birth ;—
Oh, could I rest in such an uncouth home,
 No foes except the elements ;—the earth,
The air ;—though sad, I'd learn to make with them strange
  mirth.

I'd learn the voices of all winds that are,
   The music of all waters ; and the rude
Flowers of this isle, although both " wild and rare,"
   Should be by me with sympathy endued.
I would have *lovers* in my solitude ;
   Could animal being be sustained, the mind,
Such is *her* energy, would find all good ;
   And to her destiny eftsoons resigned,
In solitude would learn the infinite to find.

Oh ! thou first cause, thou giver of each blessing,
   E'en were *I* cursed, so vain a thing I'm not
As to suppose *nothing* is worth possessing ;
   That misery's the universal lot.
A cold hand lies on me ;—a weight ;—from what,
   Whence, where, or how—boots it not here to tell :
I only wish that I could be forgot,
   And that I might inherit some small cell,
With blessings short of heaven, and curses short of hell.

ELIZABETH S. LUCAS.

ELIZABETH S. LUCAS was born in January, 1816, at Broxbourne, near Hoddesden, Herts; she belongs to an old Quaker family, and married, in 1862, the late Samuel Lucas, of Hitchin (well-known as a good amateur artist), of whom a notice may be seen in the "Dictionary of National Biography" (Smith, Elder, & Co.).

Elizabeth S. Lucas has been for many years a contributor of verse to "The Friend," "Friends' Quarterly Examiner," and other papers and magazines. She obtained a prize in 1846 for a poem on Biard's picture of the "Slave Mart," then in the possession of the late Samuel Gurney.

THE LORD'S SUPPER.

VAIN is the consecrated shrine
    If Jesus be not there;
Nor, need we outward bread and wine,
    His sacred feast to share.

Oh! who amid the Gospel Light,
    Pour'd round us from above
Shall dare to make a shadowy rite,
    Our passport to His Love?

To all believing on His word,
    He gives the living bread;
These at the table of their Lord
    From His own hand are fed.

Christ is himself that Bread Divine,
　　The manna sent from Heaven ;
His precious blood the strengthening wine,
　　To fainting thousands given.

Spirit and life the words He spake,
　　Enjoining us to feed
On Him, that so we may partake
　　Of meat and drink indeed.

Lord ! daily grant this rich repast,
　　Our sustenance to be ;
Till sanctified we find at last,
　　Eternal life with Thee.

A LULLABY ON THE SEA.

FROM THE GERMAN.

SLEEP, my boy ! while round us wide,
Madly heaves the troubled tide ;
Dream not of these dangers dark,
Ready to o'erwhelm our bark.

Hush ! oh, hush ! ye angry deeps !
See how soft my baby sleeps.
Ha, how waves contending dash !
Slumber on, nor heed the crash.

Sleep, my boy, till ocean's breast,
Like thine own is rocked to rest ;
Till the glorious beams of day
Laugh once more around our way.

Sleep, good night, thou know'st not why,
Weeps thy mother's wakeful eye ;
Oh, how sweet his peace must be,
Who in storms can rest like thee.

MARY E. MANNERS.

THIS promising young poet is the daughter of George and Louisa Wallis Manners. Her father, who died in March, 1894, was for twenty years the representative of the Ward of Farringdon Without, in the Corporation of the City of London. Mary E. Manners was born at Penge, in Surrey, and has lived for the greater part of her life at Croydon ; she was educated at Dunedin, Redhill, by E. and C. Sharp, those excellent and enlightened ladies, who have since removed to Reading, and who have done so much for the education of our younger Friends. Many of her humorous pieces made their first appearance at a social gathering of Croydon Friends, called "Our Circle," but her first published poem appeared in "Sylvia's Home Journal," and was entitled "Wonderland."

The poem by which she is almost universally known, "The Bishop and the Caterpillar," was published in the Summer number of "The Boy's Own Paper," 1888. It immediately attracted mirthful attention, and was afterwards recited by Brandram, and has proved a perennial resource to reciters and readers since. It was published in book form, "The Bishop and the Caterpillar and other Pieces," by Messrs. James Clarke & Co., in 1892.

Mary E. Manners has written many pieces for "The Christian World," "The Literary World," "The Family Circle," "The Woman's Penny Paper," etc., and other magazines and papers. She contemplates publishing another collection of her poems in book form by-and-bye, but can fix no date for its appearance. I have quoted "The Bishop and the Caterpillar" and "Pickled Cockles" from "The Boy's Own Paper," *by special permission of the editor.*

The whole of her little book is so brimful of healthy fun and innocent laughter, so full, too, of clever rhyming and acute perception, with all its drollery, that is it a veritable feast of fun and laughter, unmingled with any shade of bitterness or scorn.

It is not often we are allowed in literature to peep behind the scenes, and see the fun and humour which season at favourable moments the gravity of Quakerism, but this young Friend has enabled us to do so, and as she pokes her innocent fun at the peculiarities of her sect we feel that she is none the less a staunch Friend in its essentials; like the "excellent young Quaker" Joseph of her poems, she has evidently seen a fairy, and been awakened to the mystic meaning of life and Nature, until

> ".   .   .   the sound of human laughter,
> And the songs of human gladness,
> Seemed no longer sad and sinful."

PICKLED COCKLES:

A QUAKER STORY.

In the old-fashioned "Friendly" days,
    When Quaker garb and Quaker ways
Had not died out—when Quaker phrase
Was heard in every Friendly greeting,
And not merely reserved for "Preparative Meeting."
        When old and young
        Used the Quaker tongue,
        Said "thee" and "thou,"
        Declined to bow,
        And thought a song
        Most improper and wrong ;
In the days which we love to hear about
(They were less amusing to live in, no doubt,)
There dwelt just outside a suburban town
A dear old Friend named Tabitha Brown.

Now Tabitha Brown was clad always
In the softest of drabs and most dove-like greys ;
With the whitest of caps on her silver hair,
And apron and mittens and "all to compare ;"
While out of doors she was just the same,—
Most spotless, quiet, and free from blame ;
Her shawl was neatly folded in,
And kept in its place by a white-headed pin ;
The sweet placid face, 'neath the silver hair
(Showing lines of sorrow, but none of care),
Looked out from a bonnet quaint and shady,—
She was what one might call a real "Quaker Lady,"
Thy excuse, gentle spirit,—I apprehend
Thou wert what's better still, a true "Woman Friend.'

Tabitha Brown was well skilled in the arts
Of making pies, and puddings, and tarts ;
Of pickling, preserving, and baking, and brewing ;
Of boiling and roasting, and frying and stewing,
            Cheese-pressing and churning—
            In all sorts of learning
Connected with thrifty household ways,
Tabitha Brown was above all praise.
In fact, there was nothing she couldn't make,
From a whole-meal loaf to a wedding-cake !

            While for dusting and rubbing,
            And scouring and scrubbing,
And subjecting all things to the process called "tubbing,"
For swilling and mopping, for sweeping with brooms,
For turning the furniture out of the rooms,
For shaking of beds and for beating of chairs,
For taking up carpets and cleaning the stairs ;
For polishing pots, pans, dishes, and kettles,
And everything else that is made of bright metals ;

For leaving blackbeetles and spiders no peace,
For using that article termed "elbow-grease."
Together with soap, sand, bath-brick, and black-lead,
Emery paper (or what was then used instead),
For keeping the house without spot, speck, or stain,
There never was servant like Phœbe Jane!
In short, and most boys will, I think, grasp my meaning,
She kept up *all the year* one perpetual "spring-cleaning."

Phœbe Jane was tidy and trim,
But no Quaker dress could make her look prim ;
And, notwithstanding her "Friendly" gown,
She failed to resemble Tabitha Brown.
Her bonnet and shawl were just as plain,
Yet they looked somehow different on Phœbe Jane ;
While rebellious curls would sometimes stray
From her cap in a most unorthodox way,
And, though she persistently brushed them o'er,
They only curled tighter than before.
Her temper, too, was none of the best ;
And if anyone, either mistress or guest,
Her peculiar notions chanced to offend, she
   Her feelings expressed
   (It must be confessed)
In Quakerly speech which was not always "Friendly ;"
And Tabitha Brown wrote these words in her diary :
"P. J.'s heart—it is good, but her temper—is fiery."

This quiet household contained a third,—
A jackdaw, a really remarkable bird !
From the day he left his parental nest
In Quaker language he'd been addressed ;
And he talked in quite as "Friendly" a strain
As Tabitha Brown or Phœbe Jane.

No schoolboy's freak
Had e'er taught him to speak
Of "awfully jolly," or "stunning," or "fine,"
Or to whistle sad airs
About "oysters" and "stairs,"
And "Ehren," or "Bingen," or "Bonn" "on the Rhine."
Sedate and grave,
He knew how to behave;
On points of decorum his feelings were sensitive;
Friends scarce had erred
Had they sent this bird
To the "Quarterly Meeting" as "Representative."
Tho' no doubt he would not have failed to declare
That he certainly "did not expect to be there."

But not even beneficent Quaker law
Can eradicate mischief from a jackdaw,
And a failing bad
He once had had,
Which is common to all his species and genus
(Pray let it be kept a secret between us)—
He had not a conscience sufficiently fine
To discriminate clearly 'twixt "mine" and "thine."
On thimbles and keys
Button-hooks and green peas,
Spoons ("tables" or "teas")
He would suddenly seize
Without saying "please,"
And convey them to places not reached with great ease—
To the top of tall trees,
Rocked by Spring's "gentle breeze,"
Or to crannies through which your hand could not squeeze.
Once, when many degrees
Of cold made it freeze,

And Tabitha Brown 'gan to cough and to sneeze,
She sent for her doctor, the best of M.D.'s,
And this model jackdaw ran away with the fees.
      But 'twas long ago
      Since he'd acted so ;
And Tabitha gently said, "Thee know,
We ought to have charity, Phœbe Jane ;
I do not think 'twill occur again."

Now of all the receipts which Friend Brown possessed,
She prized one more highly than the rest,
Which, from mother to daughter handed down,
Had for years belonged to the race of Brown ;
'Twas for pickled cockles, and Friends would declare,
When they tasted the "Monthly Meeting" fare,
That this dish indeed was beyond compare.
So, though Tabitha looked with benignant eyes
On the rapid consumption of puddings and pies,
And showed, indeed, very small reserve
In the matter of marmalade and preserve,
She was somewhat "exercised in her mind,"
On entering the store-room one morning to find
That the jar she had thought was filled to the brim
With dainty molluscs in orderly trim,
Was in truth half empty ; and in some pain
She mentioned the fact to Phœbe Jane :
"They'll not last until cockles come round again."
But Phœbe Jane was very cross,
And, as she gave her head a toss,
Replied, "I thought thee couldn't know
That the stock was getting low
      Of pickled cockles."

Tabitha quietly withdrew,
Yet still alas ! 'tis very true

That neither mistress nor maid could guess
How day by day the store grew less
    Of pickled cockles.

And Phœbe Jane took it into her head
That her mistress didn't believe what she said,
And remarked, as she took the breakfast up,
"I know thee think that I dine and sup
    On pickled cockles."

And, though Tabitha calmly assured her that she
Had not the least doubt of her honesty,
Phœbe still declared that she couldn't remain
If her character wasn't freed from the stain
    Of those pickled cockles.

One afternoon it chanced that she
Was filling the little brass kettle for tea ;
When, turning round, with surprise she saw,
On the ground beside her, the grave jackdaw
    Eating pickled cockles.

The kettle falls, the waters pour
Over jackdaw, grate, and kitchen floor ;
And Phœbe cries, with excited feeling,
"Oh ! Friend, I see that thee've been stealing
    The pickled cockles !"

The poor jackdaw became very bald
From the dire effects of that terrible scald ;
He looked a most deplorable fright,
And he never after could bear the sight
    Of pickled cockles.

For a year and a day this poor little bird
Never opened his mouth to speak a word ;
At the end of that time an event occurred
Which caused his voice once more to be heard.

13

Tabitha Brown had a brother-in-law,
As strict a Quaker as ever you saw ;
His coat was long, and his collar was straight ;
You knew him at once as a " Friend of weight."
He wore a broad-brimmed beaver hat,
And rejoiced in the name of " Nathaniel Pratt."

Now this " weighty Friend "
Came up to attend
The famed " Yearly Meeting," of which you have heard,
Which begins, so Friends say,
" On the first Fourth day
Which follows the First day, in order the third,
Of the Fifth month."   Pray
Might I venture to say
That this is rather a roundabout way
Of describing the third or fourth Wednesday in May ?

'Twas First-day morning, and eight or nine
Most " well-concerned Friends " had met to dine
At Tabitha Brown's.   Nathaniel Pratt,
Who on the right hand of the hostess sat,
Still wore, sedately, his broad-brimmed hat ;
But having thus borne his testimony
In a manner in which he stood quite alone, he
Began to think that he now was free
To consider himself at liberty
To consult his comfort in some degree ;
So he took off his hat, and exposed to view
A massive head, which, I assure you,
Might have served as a model for Giunta of Pisa,
Who loved to paint
A benevolent saint
As bald—as bald as Julius Cæsar,

With the halo instead of the laurel rare
Which the Senate permitted the latter to wear
To conceal the scarcity of his hair!
(For further particulars see Lemprière).
The jackdaw, whom nobody thought of heeding,
Took a lively interest in the proceeding;
And though he had never studied geology,
And had no acquaintance with natural laws,
It was plain to this cleverest of jackdaws.
That effect, as a rule, must proceed from cause.
Then, not stopping to make the slightest apology,
   With a knowing air
   He perched on the chair
Of the "weighty Friend" who had lost his hair,
   And exclaimed in his ear
   In tones loud and clear,
But yet with a touch of pity sincere
(Inspired no doubt by a fellow feeling),
"*Ah, Friend! I see that thee've been stealing*
  The pickled cockles."

    Moral.

Don't steal pickled cockles—fresh ones are not dear,
And if in your mind you are not quite clear
Concerning the pickling, look out the receipt on
Page three-ninety-one of the late Mrs. Beeton.
Thirdly, and lastly—I speak with due cause—
I should certainly strongly advise you to pause
Before you put faith in the best of jackdaws!

  THE BISHOP AND THE CATERPILLAR.

THE Bishop sat in the schoolmaster's chair:
The Rector, and Curates two, were there,
   The Doctor, the Squire,
   The heads of the Choir,

And the gentry around of high degree,
A highly distinguished company ;
For the Bishop was greatly beloved in his See !

And there below,
A goodly show,
Their faces with soap and with pleasure aglow,
Sat the dear little school-children, row upon row ;
For the Bishop had said ('twas the death-blow to Schism)
He would hear those dear children their Catechism.
And then to complete
The pleasure sweet
Of those nice little children so pretty and neat,
He'd invited them to a magnificent treat !
And filled were the minds of these dear little ones
With visions of cakes, and of " gay Sally Lunns,"
Of oceans of tea, and unlimited buns
(The large ones called " Bath," not the plain penny ones).

I think I have read,
Or at least it is said :
" Boys are always in mischief, unless they're in bed."
I put it to you,
I don't say it is true,
But if you should ask for my own private view,
I should answer at once, without further ado :
" I don't think a boy can be trusted to keep
From mischief in bed—unless he's asleep !"

But the Schoolmaster's eye hath a magic spell,
And the boys were behaving remarkably well—
For boys ; and the girls—but 'tis needless to say
Their conduct was perfect in every way ;
For I'm sure 'tis well known in all ranks of society
That girls always behave with the utmost propriety.

Now the Bishop arises, and waves his hand ;
And the children prepared for questions stand,
With admiring eyes his form they scan ;
He was a remarkably fine-looking man !
His apron was silk of the blackest dye,
His lawn the finest money could buy ;
His sleeves and his ruffles than snow were whiter,
He'd his best shovel-hat, and his second best mitre.
With benignant glance he gazed around—
You might have heard the slightest sound !—
With dignified mien and solemn look
He slowly opened his ponderous book,
And proceeded at once the knowledge to try
Of those nice little children standing by.

Each child knew its name,
And who gave it the same,
And all the rest of the questions profound
Which his Lordship was pleased to the school to propound.
Nor less did secular knowledge abound,
For the Bishop, to his great pleasure, found
That they knew the date when our Queen was crowned,
And the number of pence which make up a pound ;
And the oceans and seas which our island bound ;
That the earth is nearly, but not quite, round ;
Their orthography, also, was equally sound,
And the Bishop, at last completely astound-
Ed, cried,
In a tone of pride,
"You bright little dears, no question can trouble you,
You've spelled knife with a *k*, and wrong with a *w*.

"And now that my pleasing task's at an end,
I trust you will make of me a friend :

You've answered my questions, and 'tis but fair
That I in replying should take a share;
So if there is aught you would like to know,
Pray ask me about it before I go.
I'm sure it would give me the greatest pleasure
To add to your knowledge, for learning's a treasure
Which you never can lose, and which no one can steal;
It grows by imparting, so do not feel
      Afraid or shy,
      But boldly try,
    Which is the cleverer, you or I!"
Thus amusement with learning jealously blending,
His Lordship made of his speech an ending
And a murmur went round of " How condescending!"

But one bright little boy did not care a jot
If his Lordship were condescending or not;
      For with scarce a pause
      For the sounds of applause,
      He raised his head,
      And abruptly said:
" How many legs has a Caterpillar got?"

Now the Bishop was a learned man,
Bishops always were since the race began,
But his knowledge in that particular line
Was less than yours, and no greater than mine;
And, except that he knew the creature could crawl,
He knew nothing about its legs at all—
Whether the number were great or small,
One hundred, or five, or sixty, or six,—
So he felt in a "pretty consid'rable fix!"
But, resolving his ignorance to hide,
In measured tones he thus replied:

"The Caterpillar, my dear little boy,
Is the emblem of life and a vision of joy!
It bursts from its shell on a bright green leaf,
It knows no care and it feels no grief."
Then he turned to the Rector, and whispered low,
"Mr. Rector, how many? You surely must know."
But the Rector gravely shook his head,
He had not the faintest idea, he said.
So the Bishop turned to the class again,
And in tones paternal took up the strain:
"The Caterpillar, dear children, see,
On its bright green leaf from care lives free,
And it eats, and eats, and grows bigger and bigger,
(Perhaps the Curates can state the figure?)"
But the Curates couldn't; the Bishop went on,
Though he felt that another chance was gone.

"So it eats, and eats, and grows and grows,
(Just ask the Schoolmaster if he knows)."
But the Schoolmaster said that that kind of knowledge
Was not the sort he had learned at College.
"And when it has eaten enough, then soon
It spins for itself a soft cocoon,
And then it becomes a chrysalis—
I wonder which child can spell me this?
'Tis rather a difficult word to spell—
(Just ask the Schoolmistress if she can tell)."
But the Schoolmistress said, as she shook her grey curls,
"She considered such things were not proper for girls."

The word was spelled, and spelled quite right,
Those nice little boys were so awfully bright!
And the Bishop began to get into a fright,
His face grew red—it was formerly white—
And the hair on his head stood nearly upright;

He was almost inclined to take refuge in flight,
But he thought that would be too shocking a sight;
He was at his wit's end—nearly—not quite,
For the Pupil Teachers caught his eye,
He thought they might know—at least he would try—
Then he anxiously waited for their reply:
But the Pupil Teachers enjoyed the fun,
And they would not have told if they could have done.

So he said to the Beadle, "Go down in the street,
And stop all the people you chance to meet,
      I don't care who,
      Anyone will do;
The old woman selling lollipops,
The little boys playing with marbles and tops,
Or respectable people who deal at the shops;
The crossing sweeper, the organ grinder,
      Ask any or all,
      Short or tall,
    Great or small, it matters not—
How many legs has a Caterpillar got?"
The Beadle bowed, and was off like a shot
From a pop-gun fired, or that classical arrow
Which flew from the bow of the wicked cock-sparrow.
Now the Bishop again put on a smile,
And the children, who had been waiting meanwhile,
In their innocent hearts imagined that these
      Remarks applied
      (They were spoken aside)
To the weighty affairs of the Diocese.

"The Caterpillar is doomed to sleep
For months—a slumber long and deep.
      Brown and dead
      It looks, 'tis said

It never even requires to be fed ;
And except that sometimes it waggles its head,
Your utmost efforts would surely fail
To distinguish the creature's head from its tail.
But one morning in Spring,
   When the birds loudly sing,
And the earth is gay with blossoming ;
   When the violets blue
   Are wet with dew,
And the sky wears the sweetest cerulean hue !
   When all is seen
   The brightest sheen—
When the daisies are white, and the grass is green ;
   Then the chrysalis breaks,
   The insect awakes,—
To the realms of air its way it takes ;
   It did not die,
   It soars on high,
A bright and a beauteous butterfly !"

He paused, and wiped a tear from his eye ;
The Beadle was quietly standing by,
And perceiving the lecture had reached its close,
Whispered, softly and sadly, " Nobody knows !"

The Bishop saw his last hope was vain,
But to make the best of it he was fain ;
So he added, " Dear children, we ever should be
Prepared to learn from all we see,
And beautiful thoughts of hope and joy
Fill the heart, I know, of each girl and boy !
Oh, ponder on these, and you will not care,
To know the exact allotted share
Of *legs* the creature possessed at its birth,
When it crawled, a mere worm, on this lowly earth.

Yet if you know it, you may now tell,
Your answers so far have pleased me well."

Then he looked around with benignant eye,
Nor long did he wait for the reply,
For the bright little boy, with a countenance gay,
Said, "Six, for I counted 'em yesterday !"

Moral.

"To all who have children under their care,"
Of two things, nay, three things, I pray you beware—
Don't give them too many "unlimited buns,"
Six each (Bath) is sufficient, or twelve penny ones ;
Don't let them go in for examination,
Unless you have given them due preparation,
Or the questions, asked with the kindest intention,
May be rather a strain on their powers of invention.
Don't pretend you know everything under the sun,
Though your schooldays are ended, and theirs but begun,
But honestly say, when the case is so,
"This thing, my dear children, I do not know ;"
For they really must learn, either slower or speedier,
That you're not a walking Encyclopædia !

JOHN MARRIOTT.

JOHN MARRIOTT was born at Edgend, a small village near Colne, in Lancashire, in 1762. He received a very careful education, and made rapid progress in his studies, especially in his knowledge of Greek and Latin. He was of a gentle and amiable disposition, somewhat saddened by an early disappointment in love. He spent much of his time in his garden, building arbours, and writing inscriptions on trees, and otherwise amusing himself in beautifying and improving what his biographer terms "a little wilderness."

In 1795 he married Ann Wilson, who is described as a very worthy and amiable young woman, and they began their married life with every prospect of happiness; but about two years after his marriage he was attacked by a painful disorder, which terminated in his death the next year. He left a widow and one little son.

The poem quoted was addressed to a beloved cousin who nursed him in his last illness with great devotion.

FAREWELL TO THE MUSES.

ONE simple effort more, and then farewell
    The tuneful cadence and the measured strain;
Then sleep, for ever sleep, my vocal shell,
    For thou hast sounded; I have sung in vain!

A few sad numbers more to grief belong;
    Friendship's loved name should once more grace my lay,
And gratitude's, whose fondly-melting tongue
    Still loves to mention what she cannot pay.

When one fond hope has long the heart amused,
  And many a year supplied its darling theme,
O'er all its clouds the softest light diffused,
  In all its sunshine lent the brightest beam ;

Should such a hope, so tender and so dear,
  Though fond and foolish, from that heart be torn,
How the frame shudders at the wound severe,
  How sinks the soul in helpless anguish lorn !

How all its sunshine sickens into shade,
  While every cloud assumes a deeper dye !
Ah me, my feelings need not fancy's aid—
  That woe-struck frame, that sinking mind have I.

Say, will Amanda lend a patient ear
  (While thus her melancholy friend complains),
Whose wishes rise above this changeful sphere,
  Whose hopes are fixed where endless sunshine reigns?

Yes, though herself the noblest path has trod,
  And, heaven-directed, 'scaped each wildering maze,
The breast that bleeds beneath affliction's rod,
  She still will pity, though she cannot praise.

When on the couch of sickness pale I lay,
  Disease infectious threatening deaths around,
In vain, to fright my generous friend away,
  Discretion reasoned, and contagion frowned.

Full many a night she watched that couch beside,
  With eye as mournful, look as full of care,
As if my life to thousands health supplied,
  As if my death would damp the general cheer.

Yes, 'twas that voice, whose lenient accents mild,
  When yielding reason helpless dropt the rein,
Hushed my vain tremors, smoothed my questions wild,
  And calmed the tumults of my erring brain.

O should the tide of still increasing grief
    Quench the last quivering, intellectual ray;
Should e'er thy friend, disordered past relief,
    A poor lymphatick through thy woodland stray;

Say, wouldst thou fly me?—no; too feeling maid,
    Even then thy breast with sympathy would thrill;
Even then thou oft wouldst lend thy gentle aid,
    And, as a brother, sometimes love me still.

Ah, dear Amanda, mayst thou still eschew
    The paths of passion and affection blind!
For oft the unwary heart has cause to rue
    The entire dominion of the most refined.

Still to the world superior mayst thou live,
    Possessed of peace, and calm, supernal joy,
That genuine peace, which nor the world can give,
    Nor all its restless turbulence destroy!

Too feeble verse to speak a grateful mind:
    What but good wishes have I to repay?
May these, my friend, acceptance hope to find?
    Ample the wishes, though but poor the lay.

Silent, yet zealous, those shall ever glow;
    This the sharp tooth of time shall soon corode;
Those for Amanda ne'er shall cease to flow;
    Conclusive this, if right my heart forbade.

Grief, gratitude, and friendship's cordial swell
    Till life's last throb, this breast must sure retain,
Yet sleep, for ever sleep, my vocal shell,
    For thou hast sounded, I have sung in vain.

MARY MOLLINEUX.

MARY SOUTHWORTH was born in 1651, and married in February, 1685, Henry Mollineux, with whom she had become acquainted in Lancaster Castle, where they were both imprisoned for attending Friends' Meetings. She died in November, 1695. Frances Owen, her cousin and close friend, in her account of Mary Mollineaux prefixed to the first edition of her "Fruits of Retirement," tells us in the quaint fashion of the day, "she was one who, in her Childhood, was much afflicted with weak eyes, which made her unfit for the usual employment of girls; and being of a large Natural Capacity, quick, witty, and studiously inclined, her Father brought her up to more Learning, than is commonly bestowed on our sex; in which she became so good a Proficient, that she well understood the *Latin Tongue,* fluently discoursed in it; and made a considerable progress in Greek also; wrote several *Hands* well; was a good *Arithmetician,* yea, in the best Arithmetick; *for she so numbered her days as to apply her Heart unto Wisdom*; as also to the study of several useful Arts; had a good understanding of Physick and Chyrurgery, the Nature of Plants, Herbs, and Minerals; and made some inspection into divers profitable Sciences; delighting in the Study of Nature . . . and tho' Verse is not so commonly used in Divine Subjects, as Prose, and but too much abused by the extravagant Wits of the age; yet she, like a skilful Chymist, had learned to separate the Purer Spirits, and more Refined Parts of Poetry, from the Earthly, Worthless dross; and made use of her Gift, rather to Convince and Prevail upon the Mind, to affect and raise the Soul upon Wings of Divine Contemplation, than to please the airy Fancy with strains of Wit, and Unprofitable Invention; which she was ever careful to avoid."

From various other "Testimonies," as they were called, she seems to have been a wonderfully learned woman. On one occasion, having argued with Entwistle, Bishop Stratford's chaplain, and silenced him, Entwistle's brother, a lawyer, said to him, "I wonder you should trouble yourself to discourse with that woman. She hath so much learning, it makes her mad." She was very clever as a doctor, and wrought, her husband tells us, several cures freely, among those who were sick and poor. She seems to have been one of those beautiful spirits, who, dowered with every gift and grace, learned, gracious, fascinating—a poet, a healer, a good classical scholar, and a most loving and beloved wife and mother, are yet perfectly simple and lowly in their minds: "having," as her cousin says, "I believe, meaner thought of herself, than anyone else had of her, who knew her qualifications." She died when only forty-four, and in her last illness had no regret, save in leaving "My Love and my little Lads," as she tenderly called her husband and two children.

Her poetry is brimful of the quaint tenderness and mystical passion, which are so characteristic of the writings (whether prose or poetry) of the early Quakers, and apart from the interest it possesses on that account, is beautiful and musical in an uncommon degree, and permeated with a noble spirit of resignation and true religion. Her collected poems were published after her death, and the volume was entitled " Fruits of Retirement," the book bears date 1702.

CONTEMPLATION.

My Life, My Love, my Joy,
Who can enough admire
The sweetening Influence
Of *Shiloh's* stream, from whence

Virtue abounds unto thy Plants, whereby
The *Lily* sprouts, free from the Choaking Bryar;
Thy *Trees* do likewise bring forth Fruit, and flourish,
To th' Praise of Thee, who dost both Prune and Cherish.

    The time that is employ'd
    In holy Meditation
    Of Thy Prevailing Love,
    Engaging from above
The upright Heart, (wherein it is enjoy'd)
In humble Fear, and sacred Admiration,
Is best Improv'd; for this indeed doth tend
To true Content and Peace, World without end.

MEDITATION.

    ALAS, Alas! this Day
    Seems almost past away;
       What shall I say? My Love
    Doth hide his face from me,
    Who Sorrows in Perplexity:
Ah, shall not Sighs and Groans prevail to move

    Unto Compassion? Shall
    My drooping Spirit call
       And cry, but find no Ear,
    No Entrance, no Access,
    To ease my Heart in great Distress?
Ah, Lord! How long canst Thou forbear to hear?

    Great Dreadful Majesty,
    Whose Omnipotency
       Is Omnipresent? Doth not Love
    Always abound with Thee?
    Yea surely, though it be
Thine holy Pleasure thus sometimes to prove.

Especially when we
Have slighted Thee,
    Or to thine enemy inclined,
Or have not kept retired,
Nor fervently desired
Thy Presence with a right composed Mind.

    Worthy art thou to be
Sought to in Fervency,
    The Careless ones shall not prevail :
Thou, Gracious Prince indeed,
Favours the Wrestling Seed ;
This, in its Expectation cannot fail.

    Thy sweet Encouragement,
In season does prevent
    All Doubtings and Distrust that can
Arise, if faithfully
Our Hearts depend on thee ;
Thou waits to manifest Thy Love to Man.

    O teach my Soul to wait
At th' Posts of Wisdom's gate,
    In holy Fear ! So to be found
Prepar'd to meet with thee
In true Sincerity,
In whose sweet Presence Heav'nly Joys abound.

AMELIA OPIE.

AMELIA OPIE was born at Norwich, on November 12th, 1769. She was the only daughter of Dr. Alderson, a physician there, and as her mother died when she was only fifteen, she became at that early age the head of her father's house. Amelia was a clever, lively, and accomplished girl, and soon became much sought after in the brilliant literary society of Norwich at that time.

While her mother lived she seems to have been somewhat severely disciplined: she was a very timid child, afraid of black beetles, and skeletons, so her mother gave her a skeleton to play with, and made her hold black beetles in her hands until she lost her terror of them. "One of my earliest recollections," she says, "is of gazing on the bright blue sky as I lay in my little bed before my hour of rising came, listening with delighted attention to the ringing of a peal of bells. I had heard that heaven was beyond those blue skies, and I had been taught that *there* was the home of the good, and I fancied that those sweet bells were ringing in heaven."

In 1798 she married John Opie, the artist, and encouraged by him published in 1801 a tale, "Father and Daughter," and in 1802 "Poems." The Opies lived in London after their marriage, and Amelia knew most of the literary and artistic celebrities of the day. Godwin, Mrs. Siddons, Mrs. Inchbald, Erskine, Me. de Staël, Sydney Smith, Byron, Sheridan, Walter Scott, Wordsworth, and many others were amongst her friends and correspondents. She was herself extremely fond of society and amusement, and says in a letter to a friend: "If I would stay at home for ever, I believe my husband would be merry from morning till night—a lover more than a husband."

She was particularly fond of flowers, and had a perfect passion for prisms; in her old age she had several set in a frame, and mounted like a screen, so that the flashing colour flew about round her little room, as she sat there in a prim Quaker dress.

Amelia Opie had been baptised at the Norwich Unitarian Chapel, where her uncle was for ten years the minister, and where her father and many of the literary people of the place regularly attended. After the death of her husband she returned to live with her father, and went with him to this chapel until 1814, when she began regularly to attend the Friends' Meeting. In 1825 she became a member of the Society of Friends, adopted the plain speech, and wore the Quaker dress. "Great was the conflict" says Joseph John Gurney in his notice of his beloved friend, "when she found herself constrained to make an open profession of Quakerism. I remember her telling me of the agony of her mind in the view of changing her dress, and of addressing her numerous friends and acquaintances by their plain names, and with the humbling simplicity of 'thee' and 'thou.'"

A few months afterwards her father died, to her great grief; she still stayed on at Norwich however, "a lonely woman," as she called herself, despite her many friends, but always bright, gracious, and charming, as in her younger days. The vision of beauty which appeared to Opie the first time he saw her, when he sprang up exclaiming, "Who is that?" and never rested until she became his wife, seems always to have drawn and impressed those who saw Amelia Opie: the S. C. Halls describe her in her old age as equally charming, fresh, and youthful-looking; gracious and graceful alike in her worldly and "Friendly" days. She died on the 2nd December, 1853, and was interred in the Friend's burial ground, Gildencroft, Norwich.

Her tales were much admired when she published them, though little read now, and some of her poems are very beautiful. The Edinburgh Review said of the song, "Go Youth Beloved," "it is scarcely surpassed by any in our language," and it was highly praised both by Sydney Smith and Sir James Mackintosh.

SONG.

Go, youth beloved, in distant lands,
 New friends, new hopes, new joys to find !
Yet sometimes deign, midst fairer maids,
 To think on her thou leav'st behind,
Thy love, thy fate, dear youth to share,
 Must never be my happy lot ;
But thou may'st grant this humble prayer—
 Forget me not, forget me not !

Yet should the thought of my distress ;
 Too painful to thy feelings be,
Heed not the wish I now express,
 Nor ever deign to think on me ;
But oh ! if grief thy steps attend,
 If want, if sickness be thy lot,
And thou require a soothing friend,
 Forget me not, forget me not !

A LAMENT.

There was an eye whose partial glance
 Could ne'er my numerous failings see ;
There was an ear that still untired,
 Could listen to kind praise of me.

There was a heart time only made
 For me with fonder feelings burn ;
And which whene'er, alas ! I roamed,
 Still pined and longed for my return.

There was a lip which always breathed
    E'en short farewells with tones of sadness ;
There was a voice whose eager sound
    My welcome spoke with heartfelt gladness.

There was a mind, whose vigorous powers
    On mine its fostering influence threw ;
And called my humble talents forth,
    Till thence its dearest joys it drew.

There was a love that oft for me
    With anxious fears would overflow ;
And wept and prayed for me, and sought
    From future ills to guard—but now.

That eye is closed, and deaf that ear,
    That lip and voice are mute for ever !
And cold that heart of faithful love,
    Which death alone from mine could sever

And lost to me that ardent mind,
    Which loved my varied tasks to see ;
And, oh ! of all the praise I gained,
    This was the dearest far to me.

Now I, unloved, uncheered, alone,
    Life's dreary wilderness must tread,
Till He who loves the broken heart,
    In mercy bids me join the dead.

But, " Father of the fatherless,"
    O ! thou that hearest the orphan's cry,
And " dwellest with the contrite heart,"
    As well as in " Thy place on high."—

Elland Clare ... ... daughter of William
E ... ... and of Ellen,
daughter ... ... his wife, and was
born at ... ... married in 1873 Edward
Pearson ...

During ... ... accompanied Eli and Sybil
Jones ... ... Egypt, Syria, and Palestine,
and wrote ... ... entitled, "Eastern
Sketches ... ... published by W. Oliphant & Co.,
Edinburgh.

In ... ... Jane Lucy Fox of Falmouth, she
succeeded ... ... London and Dublin Yearly
Meetings ... ... Palestine and Syria, receiving a
fund ... ... what is now known as
the Friends ...

In ... ... Jane Miller accompanied
Robert and ... ... South and East of France,
where they ... ... sympathy for the suffering
people ... ... Yearly Meeting. They also
distributed ... ... Out of this journey
sprang the ... ... Justine Dalencourt in Paris,
and other ... ... different parts of France.
Many of her ... ... poems have appeared in
Quaker Magazines ... ... pamphlet form, and in 1894
John Heywood, ... and London) published a
volume of her collected poems entitled "A Dream of a
Garden and other Poems." Many of these are beautiful in
thought and ... ... of modern verse will, I
think, care to ... ... of this little book.

"Awake and Sing, Ye That Dwell in the Dust."
(Isa. xxvi., 19.)

UNDERNEATH the larch's shade,
     Where there fell
Flickering lights and shadows, made
     By the spell
Of the sun and breeze, I lay
On an early Summer day,
Heard the waters far away
     Down the dell.

Damp the moss grew in the nooks,
     Overhead :
Trailed the ivy from the rocks ;
     Softly spread
All around a dreamy glow ;
Waved the branches to and fro,
As the wind would come and go,
     Fancy-led.

And I heard a tiny peal,
     Low and clear,
Softest music seemed to steal
     To mine ear,
Not the sound of bird or bee,
Not of stream, or breeze, or tree,
But a gentler melody,
     Yet more near.

All among the grass there grew
     'Neath the trees,
Flowers of fairest form and hue,
     'Twas from these,
From the petals, lightly swung,
Of the hyacinth, that hung
Her blue bells, which softly rung
     On the breeze.

And this music seemed to swell,
          Faintly heard,
From each tiny swinging bell,
          Lightly stirred,
"Oh! a joyous life is ours
With its golden Summer hours,
Breeze and sunshine, dewy showers,
          Bee and bird!

When the sunny smile of Spring
          Warms the air,
Bids the woods awake and sing
          Music rare,
Then we burst our Winter tomb,
Cast aside our robes of gloom,
Clothe us in our Summer bloom,
          Fresh and fair.

To our blossoms sweet and free,
          Wild bees throng;
Oh! a gladsome life have we
          The woods among,
Till the Autumn winds blow cold,
Then our tender buds we fold,
Sink beneath the kindly mould,
          The Winter long.

And though loud the storm may beat,
          Wild and drear,
We, within our safe retreat,
          Feel no fear;
For we know that Winter's sway,
Yields to Spring's delicious May,
And to Summer's golden day,
          Year by year!"   .   .   .   .

Such their music—it enfolds
    Thoughts of faith ;
Thou, whose soul long Winter holds,
    Night and death,—
He who bringeth by His might
Life from death, from darkness light,
Holdeth precious in His sight
    Thy soul's breath.

He who keeps the Summer flowers
    'Neath the sod,
Sees thee in thy darkest hours,
    All down-trod,
He, whose hand, with tenderest might,
Bathes with dew and paints with light
These frail creatures, knows *Thy* night,
    Is *Thy* God.

Oh ! thou dweller in the dust,
    Lift thine eyes,
Look to him with holy trust,
    Thou shalt rise ;
Look to Him, so will He bring
For *Thy* Winter, joyous Spring ;
Thou too shalt awake and sing
    To His praise.

DAVID LIVINGSTONE.

Born at Blantyre, Scotland, March 19th, 1813. Died May 4th, 1873.
Buried in Westminster Abbey, April 18th, 1874.

FROM out the grass-roofed hut in far Illala,
 . Beneath the shadow of the tropic palm,
Where sudden on that life of heat and labour
    There settled evening's healing cool and calm ;

When he, who through long years of toil had wandered,
  Folded his hands for ever on his breast,
And they who watched him, drawing near with reverence,
  Whispered, "The mighty master is at rest";

Up from the tangled groves and reedy thickets,
  By lake and river's dank and marshy shore,
O'er mountain and o'er plain, 'mid foes and danger,
  With faithful hands the cherished form they bore.

Thus many moons had come and gone upon them,
  Until at last they reached the longed-for strand,
And then they brought their dead across the ocean,
  And laid him down within his father's land.

Yes, long and grand the funeral march they gave him,
  Those sons of Afric', bringing home their trust,
Like them of old, who through their desert journey
  Bore up from Egypt Joseph's treasured dust.

Oh! traveller from that unknown wild's recesses
  For thee may Britain well her hands outspread
Well may she seek to give thee noblest burial,
  And lay thee with the mighty of her dead.

No warrior thou, borne home from fields of slaughter,
  With earthly pride and blood-bought honour crowned
But greater far, for deeds of highest daring,
  Of mercy, and of Christian love, renowned.

Wails of the vanquished, groans of the despairing,
  Mar not the music of thy funeral hymn,
And with no smoke of burning kraal in ruins,
  Or lands deserted, is thy glory dim;

For thou went'st forth to loose the iron fetters,
  The spoiler's deeds of darkness to unveil,
And in the spirit of thy Heavenly Master,
  The broken-hearted and oppressed to hail.

So, ages hence, when from her shores enlightened,
　Glad voices peace and liberty proclaim,
Shall Africa thy blessèd memory cherish,
　And teach her sons this noble white man's name.

And worthy sepulture she too had found thee,
　Beside the long-sought fountains of her Nile,
Within the shadow of her ancient mountains,
　Or where Marava's silver waters smile.

But fitter that with us thy dust should slumber,
　And since two lands must mourn their fallen brave,
That Afric's hut should be thy funeral chamber
　While Briton gives her long-lost son a grave.

Yet wherefore reck where Livingstone is lying?—
　For long before our portals opened wide,
With pomp and state to give those ashes burial,
　And lay the dust its kindred dust beside,—

Straight from that lonely hut of pain ascending,
　A soul had touched the everlasting shore,
And joyful at the heavenly city's gateway
　A spirit entered to go out no more.

MRS. FREDERICK PRIDEAUX.

FANNY A. PRIDEAUX was born in April, 1826, and was the daughter of Richard and Mary Ball, of Taunton, and the niece of William Ball, the poet. In her poem, " Philip Molesworth," which is partly autobiographical, she gives a vivid description of the happy life of her childhood at her parents' charming home.

She married in April, 1853, her second cousin, Frederick Prideaux, so well-known in legal circles as the author of a standard work on Conveyancing, and also as having been for nine years Professor of the Law of Personal and Real Property to the Inns of Court.

Mrs. Prideaux resigned her membership in the Society of Friends, and has been for many years a member of the Church of England. Her poetical creed, she says, may be summed up in the words of one of her favourite Welsh Tryads, quoted at page 61 of " Claudia."

> " Eye that sees nature, heart that feels her power,
> And resolution that dares follow her : "

and this creed has been no empty formula for her, as every page of her books testify. Her poetry is instinct with the love for, and insight into, Nature, both animate and inanimate. Her descriptions of scenery are exquisite, truthful, and lifelike, yet with that wonderful gleam over them which transforms the guide-book into the poem ; the light and shadow which Turner painted, and which make his pictures stand apart in memory from all others, seem in a measure to have suffused Mrs. Prideaux's poems, and one feels in reading many of them that unique and delicious sense of etherialised reality which is experienced on a warm afternoon in spring, as one wanders beneath the crimson-budded larch boughs, and breathes the odour of lilac flowers borne from the distant gardens by the soft winds, while high up over all, a rain of melody translates the enveloping sweetness, as the larks sing on unseen in the delicate blue of the quiet sky. Mrs. Prideaux published "Claudia" in 1865; "The Nine Day's Queen" in 1869; "Philip Molesworth and other Poems" in 1886; and "Basil the "Iconoclast" in 1892.

These volumes have, as they deserved, been very well received by the leading reviews, and their author will, eventually, I believe, take very high rank among the poets of the day. Her dramas are very finely wrought, the characters well defined, and the interplay of thought and action worked out most naturally, and yet with great dramatic force. She is perhaps too real and great a poet to be very widely popular; the thin and shallow music of Lewis Morris attracts many, whose ears are deaf to the deeper melody, the richer harmony of poetry like Mrs. Prideaux's; but to all lovers of beautiful work her books will bring an ever-increasing joy and satisfaction. She died in September, 1894.

At Festiniog.

A little stretch of mountain road
  Silvered with moonlight, for on high
The harvest-moon's full glory showed
  The vastness of the vaulted sky :
  Nor knoll, nor tree, nor roof was nigh
To narrow up the spangled tent,
That on the distant ranges leant.

And all the sleeping land was still
  Save the far murmur of the fall
Deep in the gorge, and one near rill

That trickled by us, soft and small,
  Under the shadow of the wall.
To walk the earth and breathe the air
Seemed almost like a trespass there.

We could not speak : a solemn grace
  Poured through the senses of the soul :
We stood within the holy place,
   We saw the tide of life that stole
  From life itself and heard its roll,
Through deep and deeper channels drawn
For ever since creation's dawn.

Then something moved amidst the haze
  And dimness of the road below :
A woman, bending down to raise
  A burden dragged with motion slow :
  Then two child-shapes began to grow
Behind the first, and we could see
They bore a blasted sapling tree.

Close, close upon us ; gone too soon
  'Ere clearly seen : for as they passed
A little vapour hid the moon
  And all about in shade was cast.
  But in the silence deep and vast
One long-drawn, heavy sigh we heard :
Only a sigh, no sob, no word.

Only a sigh, a human sigh,
  Yet eloquent of many woes,
Of weariness and poverty,
  Of scanty fire in winter snows,
  Perchance of widowhood, who knows ?
And often since, subdued yet clear,
That deep-drawn sigh I seem to hear.

Should I have spoken ? laid a hand
　　Upon the burden that she bore—
The cross that through the careless land
　　She carried, weary and footsore ?—
　　Dear Lord ! had I but loved thee more
I might have caught thy tender touch
And learned the way to succour such.

Her face was hid from me : it seemed
　　A sort of disembodied sigh
That indistinct as if I dreamed,
　　Rose through the mist and passed us by.
　　Yet still that feeble step draws nigh,
And still in my remorseful ear
That deep pathetic sigh I hear.

ONE OF MANY.

　　Gone out of sight ! but where ?
　　　　Like all the rest,
　　　　Where it is best,
Where only it is fitting she should be.
We search and peer but cannot find or see
　　　　Where of God's grace
　　　　Is her right place :
　　Howbeit, she is there.

　　Dull, pining life of pain
　　　　In hovel dim,
　　　　Filled to the brim
With hungry, naked, clamourous infancy,
But all things else in barren scarcity,
　　　　From earliest days
　　　　Stinted all ways ;
　　In purse and pulse and brain.

Her last poor babe was weak,
   Languished and died ;
   At which she sighed,
Sadly content to let it gasp and go,
Saying its ceaseless wailings wore her so ;
   And as she spoke
   No warm tears broke
Over her pallid cheek.

Her eldest born but one
   Lost her good name,
   Yet showed no shame.
She fought her battle for her, scarcely seemed
To see disgrace or vice, or so we deemed ;
   But from that day
   She drooped away,
Spoke little, soon was gone,

Pathetically dark,
   No inward eye
   That could descry,
The vast encircling sphere of unseen things ;
Yet moving on her being's deepest springs,
   The spirit divine
   Made light to shine,
Though but a feeble spark.

Dumb, groping sense of need
   Of One above,
   Whose awful love
Can brook for love's own sake no smallest sin,
Yet draws the sinner in safe arms within
   His Fatherhood
   By Jesus' blood :—
Served as her simple creed.

15

Will our's at the last test
   Be better found?
   More form, more sound;
But pare it down to its essential core,
The creed of noblest saint is nothing more.
   Our clearest light
   Is as the night
Or glimmering dawn at best.

Ah! let us ponder more
   That strange, stern word
   That our dear Lord
Puts of His wisdom in the patriarch's mouth.
"Son, who alive nor hunger felt nor drouth,
   Thy good things thou
   Then hadst, but now
He has the richer store."

Gone out of sight! but where?
   Wherever rest
   In softest nest
The weary, humble, earth-defeated ones;
Wherever God's best stream of comfort runs,
   Where through fair meads
   The Shepherd leads,
She is most surely *there*.

ANTHONY PURVER.

ANTHONY PURVER was born at Uphurtsborn, near Whitchurch, in 1702. He lost his father when quite young, and was brought up by an uncle, who, at the age of ten, had him taught reading, writing, and arithmetic; the boy's memory seems to have very early developed, as, at this time, he is said to have learned twelve long chapters of the Bible in twelve hours. He was afterwards apprenticed to a shoemaker, who was also a farmer, but at the age of twenty he opened a school at Uphurtsborn. Soon after this he removed to London, and published "The Youth's Delight," and learned Hebrew. About this time also he became a member of the Society of Friends, and shortly afterwards returned to his native place and reopened his school. While visiting at Coggleshall he wrote "Counsel to Friend's Children," a tract in verse. In 1737 he fixed his residence at Bristol, and engaged in the study and translation of the Scriptures. In 1738, however, on his marriage with Rachel Cotterell of Fenchay, he opened a school there, and published his translation of *Genesis*. In 1758, he again removed his residence to Andover, and there completed his translation of the Bible, which was published in two volumes at the expense of Dr. Fothergill. Anthony Purver died at Andover in 1777, aged seventy-five. Besides the "Counsel to Friend's Children," he wrote a very quaint poem, "To the Praise of God," from which I quote portions.

FROM A POEM TO THE PRAISE OF GOD.

WHILE wanton Love to others is a theme,
And stains the paper with the writer's shame;

While some the page with bloody battles fill,
Praising them most, who most, alas! do kill;
And while *this* flatteries, *that* does Satyrs write,
And *one* for profit and the *one* for spite:
Be *mine* a nobler task, to lay in view
What *Homer* thought not, nor yet *Virgil* knew!
If God assist, why should I be afraid?
The lowest poet with the highest aid?
Do thou Great Being, then, whom I adore,
Whom fear and love, direct me how to soar:
Strengthen me, plume with eagle's wings, to fly;
And bear above *Parnassus*—to the sky.

.   .   .   .   .   .

To thee, my Dear, and of myself the part,
In marriage join'd and join'd in soul and heart,
I this address, that thou with me may'st bear
In praising God (the subject here) a share.
A fever, close confinement, mind intent,
Me long ago to proper lowness bent:
Fit school to learn, and fittest place to find
The frequent sallies of th' Eternal Mind.
How oft, awak'd, distress'd, I've went alone,
To seek my long'd for, my beloved one;
Witness thou moon, you glitt'ring stars of lights,
That led my steps amidst the glooms of nights!
Nor led in vain, as rose, and blest the way
The sacred sun, which turned my night to day.
And witness darkness, where I had, conceal'd
From mortal view, immortal things reveal'd!
Then to my bed with peace and joy return'd;
How alter'd now, from him who fear'd and mourn'd!
So well rewarded, home the lab'rer goes,
And toil and joy invite to sweet repose.

Now praise with me, who hast such footsteps trod,
And known such wonders as confess the God :
May I especially his thanks rehearse,
And may this stand a monument in verse ;
Which shall the humblest gratitude enshrine :
Yet living praises breathe along the line.

   .   .   .   .   .   .

But work more pleasant, not more void of care,
To feed the lambs, is also Peter's share,
Who loves his Lord, has been himself forgiv'n :
For such returns requires impartial Heav'n :
The nurse is pleas'd her lisping care to hear ;
Whose childish words the name of witty bear,
Of manly infant deeds, and blemishes of fair.
So plays the prudent with the young convert,
And wins the soul by winning of the heart.
With what delight he sees th' undaunted youth
Treading the steps himself has trod of truth,
Say who hast went this way, and him that eyes
The rising train, that shall for ever rise.
For truth remains unchang'd, divinely bright ;
Warms with its flame, discovers with its light.
See to its standard future crowds repair !
See them still coming, still abiding there !
Among them see, with looks serene and mild,
A few whose looks confess the tutor'd Child !
(Oh might my own much rather there be seen
A humble handmaid, than a worldly queen !)
Such was my *Lamden* lately, such he sung ;
So beat the faithful heart, so flow'd the tongue.
Ah me ! who shall the feeling loss retrieve ?
A friend like thee shall ever I receive ;
May I at last then trace that heav'nly way,
And reign with thee in realms of endless day !

.   .   .   .   .   .

Still let us praise Him, still revere His nod,
At once our Saviour, Comforter, and God.
And you His saints, who at His altar wait,
And know to praise, extol Him good and great.
Angels above and all that breathe below,
Each, as you can, His excellencies show.
Let yon bright orbs, which stud the azure skies,
Bless as they set, and bless Him as they rise :
Assist you meteors, that surprise the sight
With dazzling glories, and long trails of light.
To join them, vocal winds and waters deign,
And ev'ry honour of great Nature's reign.
Winter, which favouring us, its force restrains,
And at His word, unlocks its massy chains,
With future Spring, and Summer yet unseen,
Enrob'd in white, and that in living green,
As likewise yellow Autumn in the rear,
And sable Winter of th' ensuing year,
All times, all seasons to Eternity,
All beings praise Him, and may ever we.

JAMES NICHOLSON RICHARDSON.

J. N. RICHARDSON was born in 1846, and is the eldest son of the late John Grubb Richardson, the main founder of the well-known town of Bessbrook in North Ireland. He was educated at a private school, and afterwards at Grove House, Tottenham, then under the head-mastership of Thomas Hunton. While at Tottenham he made the acquaintance of Sir Joseph Pease's family, and remembers, gratefully, the kind interest taken in him during his youth by the late Jane Gurney Pease. After leaving school, he joined his father in his extensive linen industry, and was thus brought to know and sympathise with the thoughts and feelings of the working classes. In 1880, he entered Parliament as a moderate Liberal, being one of the members for the county of Armagh, in which is situated the town of Bessbrook.

During his Parliamentary career, he renewed his early friendship with W. E. Forster, whose confidence he enjoyed, and very much valued. After Lord Frederick Cavendish was murdered in 1882, he was offered the post of Junior Whip, but felt obliged to reluctantly decline it, in order to attend to his own and his father's business affairs. Owing to ill health, he did not seek re-election in 1885, but made a tour round the world, in order to get as far away as possible from business cares and anxieties. Since his return, much restored, he has continued to reside chiefly at Bessbrook, although not taking such an active part in business as formerly. In politics he is in Unionist.

His poems are, many of them, especially to those acquainted with his local allusions, extremely racy and clever. "The Quakri at Lurgan" was sold out at once, and all who are fortunate enough to possess a copy will understand how the good-humoured fun, and clever parody of the "Lays of Ancient Rome," caused laughter and mirth amongst the Quakri depicted in its pages.

"O'Neill, A Tale of Mourne," is a spirited poem of about thirty pages, published like the "Quakri" in pamphlet form. These are the only two published for sale, but through the kind courtesy of J. N. Richardson, I have been enabled to give a very beautiful short poem, more suitable than these longer ones for quotation.

LINES SENT TO LADY FREDERICK CAVENDISH,

On the occasion of the murder of her husband, May, 1882.

OH Lady, sorrowing o'er thy murdered lord,
  If Irish voice might break upon thy woe,
Thus would it say—"Tho' not with hand on sword,
  "And clad in scarlet he, when stricken low—
"Yet for these kingdoms was that life out-poured,
  "Whose beauty and whose wealth *thou best* didst know,
"As surely, as though shed in battle line—
"Mid Britain's hosts, at home or on the brine."

Not with war's lightnings in a red, right hand,
  Nor with war's thunders on a brow of gloom
Came he that morning to our Irish strand—
  But bearer of the olive branch, whose bloom
Too little flourished in the weary land—
  And in *such hour* he met the stroke of doom
Dealt by the dastard hand—oh dastard crime,
The last, the worst, the basest of our time—

And were it wondrous if with heart-strings torn,
    On high for vengeance thou aloud shouldst call?
Remembering the defiance ever borne
    Towards thy Saxon race—pens steeped in gall
Preaching a creed of hatred and of scorn—
    A creed of demons, if a creed at all—
Remembering this—say could we even blame
If thou shouldst ever hate the Irish name?

But like some melody from holier spheres
    Thy gentle voice breaks in upon the strife,
Like rainbow message shining through thy tears:
    "I would not have withheld my darling's life,
"If that my woe bring peace upon the years—
    "If that my loss may render rage less rife—"
Sure winter snows and summer suns may shine,
Or e'er we hear a Christlier prayer than thine!

And we who saw him borne to early grave,
    And heard at Edensor the church bells chime,
And marked the endless elms of Chatsworth wave
    O'er silent thousands, mourning for his prime—
Yea be it also ours to inly crave
    That God most high, from foul and savage crime,
By mystic means, should work some purpose fair,
And grant in very deed the widow's prayer

THOMAS CLIO RICKMAN.

THOMAS CLIO RICKMAN was the son of John and Elizabeth Rickman, and was born at the Cliff, Lewes, in 1761.

He became a bookseller in Upper Marylebone Street, London, but lived at one time in Leadenhall Street. He avowed himself an ardent disciple of his great friend, Tom Paine, both in religion and politics, and treasured up the table on which the latter had written many of his works, as a valuable relic. He was a frequent contributor of poetical pieces to various magazines, and published " Poetical Scraps " in two volumes in 1803.

He died in 1834, in the seventy-fourth year of his age, and was interred in the Friend's Burial Ground, Bunhill Fields.

ODE TO FORTUNE.

Written in a window at the Priory, St. Helen's, Isle of Wight.

This, dame fortune, let me crave,
Since I'm doomed to be thy slave ;   .   .   .
Sweet independence to enjoy,
And liberty that ne'er will cloy.

Give me ease, and give me health,
Give to others store of wealth ;
Let fair competence be mine,
And hang me, if I e'er repine.

To some peaceful, happy scene,
Where I may live with joy serene ;
Bear me from madness, and from folly,
From dulness, spleen, and melancholy.

Be mine some vicar's ancient seat,
Snug, and warm, and fair, and neat;
A study with good books well stor'd,
A parlour for my homely board.

Where in elbow chair he dos'd,
And his pamper'd bulk repos'd,
Casting dull learning's care aside,
With volumes of scholastic pride.

This grant me, fortune, and, if I,
To use thy blessings e'er deny,
Reject my vow, reject my prayer,
And let me feed with bards on air.

The Littleness of Human Wisdom.
An Ode.

Man measures earth, the air he weighs,
The spacious sky above surveys,
    The planetary sphere
Explores . . views suns on suns advance,
And worlds on worlds through heaven's expanse
    That roll in order there.

But how a single grass doth grow,
A cherry ripen, lily blow,
    To him is quite unknown;
Yet full of pride . . . temerity! . . .
Nature's grand scheme he would descry,
    So wondrous learned grown.

By laws his own, destroyeth worlds;
Or new ones into ether hurls;
    Pervades with piercing eye
All things in heaven, in air, on earth
What cause gives each effect its birth,
    Tho' plann'd by the Most High.

But how his feet obey his will,
At his command, move or stand still,
     He knows not, . . . yet would tell
(Such his presumptuous confidence)
The Almighty's place of residence;
     Where situated hell.

How God sees, acteth, and commands,
Past, present, future, understands;
     Yet ah! he doth not know,
Himself, how he the sense retains,
Of feeling pleasures, fears, or pains,
     Or doth exist and grow.

Go, wondrous creature! to be good
First learn; go give the hungry food,
     And clothe the naked poor:
Go cherish worth, . . . true merit prize,
Thy country's happiness devise;
     These, these, are in thy power.

This done, . . . of nature's secrets rare,
Take to the full thy allotted share:
     But what was pre-designed,
Too vast for thee, by heaven's high will,
Superior to all human skill,
     Leave to the eternal mind.

To whom these countless worlds belong,
Who made all right, thou judgest wrong,
     And over all presides;
Governs, directs the according whole,
Of beauty, order is the soul, . . .
     All to perfection guides.

RICHARD BALL RUTTER.

RICHARD BALL RUTTER is a nephew of William Ball, the poet, and was born at Bristol, in 1826. He married Anna Maria Clapham; and has published two volumes of poetry, "Scenes from the Pilgrim's Progress" (1882) and "Leaves from a Spiritual Diary." He has also written a great many fugitive pieces, hymns, etc., in magazines and papers, especially in the *Friends' Quarterly Examiner* and the *British Friend*.

His verse has the charm of perfect clearness and sincerity, and in some pieces, such as "A Prayer" (after Quarles), reaches a high level of quaint simplicity, and possesses that daintiness of touch which is so seldom met with in modern verse of its character. If R. Ball Rutter follows out this vein, instead of writing so much of a strictly didactic nature, he will yet give us, I believe, a book of verse, which will not only yield pleasure now, but will live in the music of the future.

His little fragment, "From Nature up to Nature's God," is almost perfect, and reminds one of some of Blake's delicate work; while his "Scenes from the Pilgrim's Progress" is full of a quiet serene charm, which is enhanced by the splendid production of the book; the beautiful paper, red-lined pages, and general richness of its outer presentment. "Leaves from a Spiritual Diary" is interesting from its evident truthfulness, though the workmanship is a very long way behind "The Prayer" (after Quarles). And this is the more to be regretted, as the subject would so admirably lend itself to the quaint and tender treatment of the poem referred to. A spiritual diary, treating of experiences which are common to most sensitive and devout spirits, might be made an exquisite work of art if done "after Quarles," or "after Herbert," and yet suffused with that modern thought which is so attractive in the ancient dress, if presented by genius.

A PRAYER

(AFTER QUARLES.)

AH, Lord!
How short a prayer may be,
Yet reach to thee !
Nor hath it far to go ;
And if it seem to rise, as incense, from below,
Yet is its first, invisible, silent flow,
Downward on me ;
From the Higher to the lower,
From the lower to the Higher,
In one eternal circle darts the Heavenly fire.

The joy to think
That every reaching forth to good that's given,
Is but a new and golden link
'Tween earth and heaven ;
That (whatsoe'er our spirit zone may be)
Love to thee, Lord ! means ever love from thee.

Nathless, would I begin
By telling all my sin,
Which yet cannot be told !
(How shall I separate new things from old ?)
Nor needs it now to unfold
The dismal story of a wasted prime ;
Better to use this richly dowered time,
In pressing straight
To Heaven's gate,
And handing in my cause to man's Great Advocate.

"We have an Advocate" with Thee,
Yea, one in Thee ;
Ah, wherefore should I fear Thou wilt not pardon me?
I fear my fear, I love my love ;—
Make fear grow less and love grow more ;
And hour by hour
Give growing power,
And calm where all was storm before.

"FROM NATURE UP TO NATURE'S GOD." :

AN EMBLEM.

"POOR little Child, poor little Child,
By a butterfly chase from home beguiled,
Trembling, lonely, and earth-defiled,
Poor little Child, poor little Child !
Listen to me ; no further roam,
I will lift you where you are lying ;
Cease your crying, your sobbing, your sighing,
I will carry you home !"

Now I ask, what made me kind to-day
To the poor little Child that had lost its way?

Ah, that gracious seed in me
Fell from no created tree !
Human love is from Love Divine ;
The pity in me was God's, not mine,
His from eternity.

A book may be torn, defaced, defiled,
And yet give a glimpse of its author's plan ;
If a man will pity a wandering child,
Will a God not pity a wandering man ?

JOHN SCOTT, OF AMWELL.

JOHN SCOTT was born in 1730, at the Grange Walk, Bermondsey, and was the son of Samuel and Martha Scott. His father was a draper, but retired to Amwell, a village in Hertfordshire, when John was about ten years old. The boy was sent for a short time to a day school at Ware, but did not stay long enough to gain much instruction. He had never been inoculated for small pox, and as both he and his parents seem to have had a morbid terror of this disease, he was kept away from school at the first hint of infection. He seems to have retained this fear for a considerable part of his life, as it is said, he lived for twenty years within twenty miles of London, and yet only visited the city once !

His family had neither many books nor much literary knowledge, but John Scott being passionately fond of reading, became acquainted with a neighbour, a bricklayer, named Frogley, who seems to have been a very remarkable man, and who, although uneducated, had a large acquaintance with good authors, and placed "Paradise Lost" in Scott's hands. This seems to have given the lad his first knowledge of poetry, and he cemented his friendship with Frogley by marrying his daughter, who, however, died in less than a year after her marriage to the intense grief of her young husband. He retired to the house of a friend at Cockfield, and after a time seems to have devoted himself to writing verse. His first productions were sent to the "Gentleman's Magazine," but when he was thirty, he published a small volume containing four elegies on the seasons, this little book was very favourably received. At considerable intervals appeared his poems, "The Garden"

"Amwell," "Collected Poems," and also "Critical Essays on the English Poets," and "Remarks on the Poems of Rowley." John Scott was an ardent patriot, full of public spirit, and enthusiasm, for what he considered right and just. He had an intimate acquaintance with the laws of his country, and although prevented by his Quakerism from becoming a magistrate, he acted as arbitrator in the disputes of his neighbours, and was most active in any schemes for local improvement. Ware and Hertford were indebted to him for the plan of making a good road between them, and he was most diligent in attending turnpike, land-tax, and navigation trust meetings. His prominent character and his verses gained him many eminent friends, amongst whom were Dr. Johnson, Sir W. Jones, Mrs. Montague, Lord Lyttelton, and many others.

Having in his thirty-sixth year submitted to inoculation, he went more frequently to London, and in 1770 married his second wife, Mary de Horne, at Ratcliff Meeting House ; they had one daughter, who was left an orphan at an early age, married a Mr. Hooper, but died without children.

John Scott himself died on the 12th December, 1783, in his house at Ratcliff, of a putrid fever, and was buried in the Friends' burial ground there. Amongst his works are the following—

Four Elegies	1760
Elegy to the memory of his wife	1768
Amwell, a descriptive Poem	1776
Four Moral Eclogues	1778
The Poetical Works of John Scott	1782

He also contributed many odes and other poems to various magazines.

John Scott was extremely fond of horticulture, and spent much time and thought in planting and building, and otherwise beautifying his place, Amwell House. In a paper which

16

appeared in the "Hertfordshire Illustrated Review," and from which many details of this sketch have been taken, we are told, "it was perhaps the intensely hot weather (1757) that gave him the idea of building the grotto, a most curious underground place of eight chambers dug out under a hill of solid chalk, and probably quite unique of its kind. The rooms are lined with shells and fossils, brought from many parts and ingeniously fitted together—a work requiring time, thought, and money—and he describes how he marched first, pickaxe in hand, to encourage his rustic assistants when the building was commenced. It still exists, and is well worth a visit. . . . he planted his grounds at Amwell House with great skill and taste, and there were some splendid trees there." Dr. Johnson who once visited him declared that "none but a poet could have made such a garden."

THE TEMPESTUOUS EVENING.

There's grandeur in this sounding storm,
That drives the hurrying clouds along,
That on each other seem to throng,
And mix in many a varied form ;
While bursting now and then between,
The moon's dim misty orb is seen,
And casts faint glimpses on the green.

Beneath the blasts the forests bend,
And thick the branchy ruin lies,
And wide the shower of foliage flies ;
The lake's black waves in tumult blend,
Revolving o'er and o'er and o'er,
And foaming on the rocky shore,
Whose caverns echo to their roar.

The sight sublime enwraps my thought,
And swift along the past it strays,
And much of strange event surveys,

What history's faithful tongue has taught,
Or fancy formed, whose plastic skill
The page with fabled change can fill,
Of ill to good, or good to ill.

But can my soul the scene enjoy,
That rends another's breast with pain?
O hapless he who, near the main,
Now sees its billowy rage destroy!
Beholds the foundering bark descend,
Nor knows but what its fate may end
The moments of his dearest friend!

ODE.

This scene how rich from Thames's side,
While evening suns their amber beam,
Spread o'er the glossy-surfaced tide,
And midst the masts and cordage gleam;
Blaze on the roofs with turrets crowned,
And gild green pastures stretched around,
And gild the slope of that high ground,
Whose cornfields bright the prospect bound.

The white sails glide along the shore,
Red streamers on the breezes play,
The boatmen ply the dashing oar,
And wide their various freight convey;
Some, Neptune's hardy thoughtless train,
And some, the careful sons of gain,
And some, the enamoured nymph and swain,
Listening to music's soothing strain.

But there, while these the sight allure,
Still fancy wings her flight away
To woods recluse, and vales obscure,
And streams that solitary stray,

To view the pinegrove on the hill,
The rocks that trickling springs distill,
The meads that quivering aspens fill,
Or alders crowding o'er the rill.

And where the trees unfold their bloom,
And where the banks their foliage bear;
And all effuse a rich perfume,
That hovers in the soft calm air;
The hedgerow path to wind along,
To hear the bleating, fleecy throng,
To hear the skylark's airy song,
And throstle's note so clear and strong.

But say, if there our steps were brought,
Would these their power to please retain;
Say, would not restless, roving thought
Turn back to busy scenes again;
O strange formation of the mind!
Still though the present fair we find,
Still towards the absent thus inclined,
Thus fixed on objects left behind!

SONNET TO BRITAIN.

Renowned Britannia! loved parental land!
Regard thy welfare with a watchful eye!
Whene'er the weight of want's afflicting hand
Wakes in thy vales the poor's persuasive cry—

When wealth enormous sets the oppressor high,
When bribes thy ductile senators' command,
And slaves in office freeman's rights withstand,
Then mourn, for then thy fate approacheth nigh!

Not from perfidious Gaul or haughty Spain,
Nor all the neighbouring nations of the main,
Though leagued in war tremendous round thy shore—
But from thyself thy ruin must proceed!
Nor boast thy power! for know it is decreed,
Thy freedom lost, thy power shall be no more!

LYDIA SHACKLETON.

LYDIA SHACKLETON was born at Ballytore, in 1828.

GOD KNOWS THE REST.

When sleep and childish weariness
    Upon her eyelids pressed,
She said but half her simple prayer,
    And then "God knows the rest,"
And laid adown her little head
    In slumber sweet and blest.

And doth God care for many words,
    With repetitions dry,
Or hearts submissive to His will,
    His name to glorify?
O little child! He knows our needs
    Better than thou or I

Our daily bread—His sheltering care
    Howe'er He deemeth best—
If bitter this, or dark that way,
    We bow to his behest,
And lay us down to sleep at last,
    Trusting "God knows the rest."

LOVELL SQUIRE.

LOVELL SQUIRE was the son of Lovell and Sarah Squire, and was born at Earith, in May 1809. He began his education at a day school in the village, and afterwards went to a boarding school at Godmanchester. In 1829 he went to York School as a teacher, and while there he did much to foster the study of Natural History among the scholars. In 1834 he left York, and went to Ashfield, near Falmouth, as a private tutor; afterwards opening a Friends' school at Kimberley. In 1836 he married Henrietta, daughter of William and Lucretia Crouch, and giving up his school some time later, became again a private tutor in Robert Barclay Fox's family and others. During this time he identified himself with all the scientific and philanthropic work going on in Falmouth: he was assistant secretary to the Polytechnic Institution, honorary secretary to the Dispensary and the Humane Society; Superintendent of the Meteorological Observatory, and one of the directors of the Cornwall Sailor's Home, and he learned Italian in order to read the Bible, in this Home, to Italian sailors.

He was recorded a minister in 1863, and published in 1876 a volume entitled "Day by Day," consisting of texts and original verses; he also published a collection of hymns, some of them his own composition. He died in March, 1892, at his residence at Chiswick.

STANZAS.

"To those who seek, O Lord,
 Thy purpose to fulfil,
And strive by prayer, in full accord
 With all Thy holy will,

Meekly to run their Christian race,—
To these Thou givest grace for grace.

O Grace Divine! No tongue
  In Eden's happy bower,
Hath all the mighty fulness sung
  Of Thine availing power,
By faith in Christ from Sin to Save,
And give the victory o'er the grave."

"Salute Apelles Approved in Christ."

"Approved in Christ!" and is this all the Bible says of thee?
Well, tis enough! would that of *us* such words might spoken be.
How sweet the blessed, holy thoughts, which cluster round a
    name,
So dear to an Apostle's heart, so little known to fame!
Thy friends, like thee, were firm in faith, and steadfast in their
    love,
They sought not the applause of men,—their record is above;
And, when our work on earth is done, be this our blessed
    reward,
To be, as Paul's Apelles was, "approved" of the Lord!

MATILDA STURGE.

MATILDA STURGE has kindly allowed me to copy the following autobiographical fragment, which gives a sketch of her life in her own words. But she does not tell us *how* useful that life has been, and is; how her active acute mind sets her in the forefront of all good causes, of all crusades against sin and suffering in her native city; how ready she has been, and is, to use pen or tongue (for she is an excellent speaker, humourous, racy, and convincing), either to help, or defend, what she believes to be right and true. Nor does she tell us anything of her excellent prose sketches, collected into a volume in 1885 under the title, "Brief Essays and Sketches;" but all readers of Friends' papers and magazines will remember the pleasure which the sight of her name at the foot of an article has given them, and will gladly turn to the selections we have been able to give of her poems.

"I was born in Bristol, and have resided in the neighbourhood of that city up to the present time. My history as to the outward, needs not to be told here. I was from childhood a great reader, and early conceived the idea of becoming an author; an ambition, however, which was laid aside for many years, and never more than partially fulfilled. I was fond of poetry, and as soon as I had gained some command of language, wrote occasional verses, chiefly imitative, though with here and there a thought of my own.

"My education, though good for the time of day, and tolerably wide in basis, left much to be desired as measured by the standard of the present time, and circumstances not under my control hindered me from spending much time in self-improvement, except in reading, for which opportunity was found, and which did much for my cultivation and development. The influence of my father, Jacob P. Sturge, who was a man of fine powers and great worth, and that of some wise and good friends, especially the late William Tanner, contributed much to the formation of my mind and character.

"After reaching middle life an opportunity occurred for further self-education. Lectures of the character of those now designated "University Extension" began to be given at Clifton, and I found in attending them and writing on the subjects proposed, a great mental stimulus, and the pleasure of being brought into communication with highly trained minds. In this way I also made the discovery that I possessed some powers of thought and expression not given to all who had had superior advantages. Ultimately I was led to devote these powers, such as they were, chiefly to religious objects connected with the Society of Friends, to which I belong. I have written for their periodicals, and have been engaged in a variety of work for objects of a religious and philanthropic kind. Much of this work has been exceedingly practical and prosaic, but still from time to time, the thoughts of quiet hours have found expression in poetry, some specimens of which are given here."

IN MEMORIAM.
WILLIAM TANNER, *ob.* 1866.

LET us give thanks that he hath fallen asleep,
Thanks for the finished course, the immortal prize;
Let us give thanks for him the while we weep,—
Such tender memories fill our hearts and eyes.

Let us give thanks that for a time we trod
Life's path beside him, that we marked him well
And felt how close his fellowship with God,
Who now hath called him with Himself to dwell.

That we have heard his words of holy cheer
And righteous warning ;—and more precious yet
His tones of sympathy which none could hear
Uncomforted, nor would again forget.

That while he dwelt on earth we learned to trace
His likeness to his Lord :—not only now
That death has hallowed each remembered grace
And shed a radiance o'er his pallid brow.

For all that he through heavenly aid hath been,
For all that gave him power to help and bless,
His loving wisdom and his joyous mien,
His manly strength and childlike tenderness

For the sweet converse that with him we shared,
Which made Heaven dearer, and yet earth more bright ;
For griefs he dreaded and hath now been spared,
And for his mansion in the world of light ;

Let us give thanks, nor mar the song of praise
With thought of murmuring, though the stroke that fell
Hath left a deeper shadow on our days,
Let us give thanks, we know that all is well.

"Weeping may tarry for the night, but joy cometh in the morning."
—Ps. xxx., 5 (R.V.)

NEVER so glad as when the heart is broken !
　　Never so joyful as when brought most low !
'Tis then the tender words of peace are spoken,
　　'Tis then that tears of gladness rise and flow.—
'Tis a hard lesson, hard and slowly taught,
　　That we are worthless still as in the past
That we who once our sins and follies brought,
　　Have little else to bring—from first to last.

'Tis a hard lesson, and we often wait
   In outer darkness, longing for the light,
Because we fear to enter through the gate,
   And still so poor, into His holy sight—
Wait on the threshold while He waits within,
   With such a welcome beaming from His face!
This is the privilege He died to win,
   To stretch to all the sceptre of His grace.

FREDERICK TAYLOR.

FREDERICK TAYLOR was born at Stratford, in Essex, in 1828, and was educated at Croydon school, and the Flounders' Institute, Ackworth. He conducted a private school at Brighton from 1858 to 1868, and from there removed to Sunderland, where he assisted the late Edward Backhouse in the Pottery Buildings Mission. He was an early contributor to the "Friend's Quarterly Examiner" and other magazines.

THE TOWERS OF INTELLECT.

THE towers, the lofty towers of Intellect !
    That frown majestic o'er Time's stormy sea,
And o'er Life's narrow valley looking down,
    Cast their long shadows to Eternity ;
Their lofty battlements, their solemn domes,
    Their stately spires, their glittering minarets,
Of Fame's illustrious line the eternal homes
    On which the Sun of glory never sets ;
These, waking from long lethargy to life,
    I saw, and yearned with most intense desire
Towards those proud towers, as in my bosom grew
    Exalted aims, and glowed the rising fire.
Then from thy voice, O Peace, I proudly turned,
    Thy bowers, Content, no more my footsteps stay,
For Fame's reluctant smile alone I burned,
    And longed to soar to those high courts away.
Then in the dark grove as I wandered lone
    With lofty visions and high musings stirred,
Thus at my side brake forth this solemn tone
    Sweeter by far than Summer's laureate bird.

"Youth, do yon towers of aspect most sublime,
    That to the starry cope of Heaven aspire,
And frown in grandeur o'er the sea of Time,
    Thy kindling soul arouse to high desire?
Attend whilst I the mysteries unfold
    Of those gigantic towers, so seeming fair,
Around whose base the fleecy clouds are rolled,
    But whose high summits scorn the fields of air.
Deep on the adamantine pillars vast
    Of night and gloom are their foundations laid,
In whose dark vaults that giant brood are cast
    Who dared the battlements of Heaven invade
With impious aspiration : there they groan,
    Wrung with fierce torments, and with massive chain
Sealed to the vast abyss, while forms unknown,
    Whom to describe in mortal speech were vain,
Glare with white eyeballs on the infernal crew,
    And o'er them flap their doleful humming wings ;
While screaming Horror rears her snaky crest
    And o'er the lost her baleful dirges sings.
There Darkness, throned amid the Furies, finds
    His dismal empire, and the vast vaults roar
With dashing waves, while storms and furious winds
    Howl ever on that undiscovered shore
Which, clothed in mists, spreads far into the deep,
    With huge rocks rising from the foaming pools,
On whose sharp cliffs, precipitous and steep,
    Rent sails, and broken oars, and stranded hulls,
Lie scattered far and near.   Oft thence resound
    The moans suppressed and the unuttered cry
Of shadowy ghosts that sweep the misty ground,
    Swift as the howling blast that cleaves the sky—
This call the Land of wild unhallowed Thought.
    But hence away : too long on scenes of dread

We linger ; on these realms of darkness wrought
   With massive beams those towers sublime are spread ;
There walk the wise, the good, the great of old,
   In sweet communion ;—at high festivals
And banquets of rich sense, with crowns of gold
   Upon their heads, they pace the marble halls,
Clothed in pure white : some chant a solemn strain
   To a high melody, with harps in hand
Warbling, or seek the lofty courts of Fame,
   And at her shrine with fuming censors stand,
Girt with the priestly robes ; when from her urn
   The fates of those who offer at her shrine
The goddess doth adjudge—when loftier burn
   Her incensed fires, and all her courts sublime
Are thronged with spirits from the rosy bowers
   Of Paradise : for these not rare attend
Her spacious courts, and hover o'er those towers
   In shining bands, and in the streets descend.
They love to gaze on deeds of holy love
   And high devotion, writ in words of gold
On silver tablets, whose reports above
   Have travelled, and in bowers of bliss are told.
So live the gods of intellect sublime :
   Their brows with fadeless laurel wreaths are bound,
And golden frontlets on their foreheads shine,
   Each with his several actions graven round.
No more may I the mysteries explain
   Of yonder towers : yet rightly mayst thou turn
With ardent hope those lofty heights to gain,
   And for high service in these temples burn.
Yet seek, o'er all, His smile, His praise, to whom
   Our noblest powers are due ; seek first to know
Him, to whose sacred feet all flesh must come,
   To whom the gods of intellect must bow."

PHILLIPS THOMPSON.

THIS eminent journalist, poet, and writer on social subjects, was born at Newcastle-on-Tyne in 1843. His father was a son of Thomas Thompson, of Liverpool, and his mother was a daughter of Thomas Robson, of Sunderland. He received his earliest education at Brookfield School, Wigton; but when he was thirteen the family went to Canada, and settled in Lindsey, Ontario. He studied for the Law, but drifted into journalism, at first as a reporter and correspondent; but afterwards as editor on the *Mail, Globe,* and several other Toronto papers. From 1876 to 1879 he was in Boston, engaged on *The Traveller.* In the winter of 1881-2 he travelled through Ireland as special correspondent of the Toronto *Globe* during the height of the Home Rule agitation. He travelled also through Maine, Pennsylvania, and Ohio to enquire into the working of Prohibition. Of late years he has devoted much time and attention to the Labour question, and written largely for the Labour and Social Reform Press. He considers himself a Socialist, believing if the people could be sufficiently educated to understand their true interests, and act unitedly, Socialism might be peaceably evolved from present conditions. In 1887, Philips Thompson published "The Politics of Labour," and, in 1892, appeared "The Labor Reform Songster," original and selected; the greater number of these songs are original, and were written and published, he says, to supply the want of suitable songs for singing at social gatherings, songs which should embody the spirit of the Labour Movement and the New Democracy. He has written much humourous verse, and contributed to a great many magazines and papers in America, but has not as yet collected his poems into volume form. He is also a successful lecturer. The poem called "Cheek," written about twenty years ago, has been reprinted very often, and will probably be familiar to most readers, but I quote it because it is a good example of Phillips Thompson's humourous vein.

THE PENSIVE MULE.

"Oh, pensive mule! they say thy heart
　　To sympathy is cold,
The stoic of the brutes thou art,
Unmoved by flagellations smart,
　　By kindness uncontrolled."

"They call thee unresponsive, mule,
　　To finer feelings dead ;
A stolid, automatic tool,
Whose breast no warm emotions rule,
　　Who ne'er a tear hast shed."

He turned, and winked his wicked eye,
　　And twitched his plenteous ear,
Then backing to a ditch hard by,
He bumped his back—his heels let fly,
　　And shed—a mule-teer.

CHEEK.

I've known men rise through talent, though such are exceptions
　　rare ;
And some by perseverance and industry and care ;
There are men who build up fortunes by saving a dollar a
　　week ;
But the best thing to make your way in the world is to travel
　　upon your cheek.

17

Now, here am I, in middle age, just able to keep alive,
By working away the lifelong day as hard as I can drive ;
Tom Wentworth takes things easy, and rolls in his carriage by ;
And cheek is the one sole reason why he is richer than I.

Why, Tom and I were schoolmates about thirty years ago,
I was reckoned one of the smartest, while at learning he was
    slow.
He didn't care for study,—played hookey half the week,—
But somehow always dodged the cane by the aid of con-
    summate cheek.

"Little boys," they used to tell me, "should always be seen,
    not heard."
When company came, I hung my head, and never could say a
    word ;
But Tom was a saucy, forward cuss, well able to take his part ;
So I got the name of being a fool, while every one thought him
    smart.

I grew up nervous and timid,—I never could blow or boast—
So people took it for granted that Tom must know the most.
Of what avail is learning—Arithmetic, Latin, or Greek—
If you haven't the talent to show it off for lack of the requisite
    cheek ?

Tom and I, as it happened, in love with the same girl fell.
I never could muster the courage my heart's desire to tell.
I think she liked me a little the best ; but, before I dared to
    speak,
Tom pressed his suit, and won her hand by steady, persistent
    cheek.

And then Tom struck for the city. He met with ups and
    downs ;
But always seemed to get ahead, in spite of fortune's frowns :

Like a cat, he'd always fall on his feet; was confident, bluff
    and bold;
And talked with the air of a millionaire in possession of wealth
    untold.

So Tom succeeded in business, and everything he'd touch,—
For people always help the man who passes as owning much,—
While I didn't have the advantage of either my brains or cash,
For want of the self-assurance and courage to make a dash.

If "modesty is a quality." as the ancient saying ran,
"Which highly adorns a woman," it oftentimes ruins a man;
And those who are shy and backward, and those who are
    humble and weak,
Will be elbowed aside, in the race of life, by the men who
    travel on cheek.

So Tom to-day is a millionaire, the flourishing merchant
    prince;
While, as for my hopes of success in life, I've given them up
    long since.
But the richest blessings of Heaven are promised the poor and
    meek,
And men can't crowd through the pearly gates by travelling on
    their cheek.

THE POWER OF THOUGHT.

FROM "THE LABOR REFORM SONGSTER."

Not by cannon, nor by sabre,
    Not by flags unfurled,
Shall we win the rights of labor,
    Shall we free the world.
Thought is stronger far than weapons,
    Who shall stay its course?
It spreads in onward-circling waves,
    And ever gathers force.

Hopes may fail us, clouds may lower,
　Comrades may betray,
Crushed beneath the heel of power
　Justice lies to-day.
But every strong and radiant soul,
　Whom once the truth makes free,
Shall send a deathless impulse forth
　To all eternity.

Words of insight, sympathetic,
　Flash from soul to soul,
Of the coming time prophetic,
　Freedom's distant goal.
Kindling with one aspiration,
　Hearts will feel their thrill,
And iron bands be ropes of sand
　Before the people's will.

Right shall rule whene'er we will it,
　All the rest is naught ;
" Every bullet has its billet,"
　So has every thought.
When the people wish for freedom,
　None can say them nay,
'Tis slavery of the darkened mind
　Alone which stops the way.

WILLIAM PHILLIPS THOMPSON.

W. P. THOMPSON was born in Liverpool, 1842. He was apprenticed to an engineering firm in Leeds, and while there wrote "Vera Paz." In 1868 he went to America, and in 1871, while engaged on a mineralogical survey in the southern states, wrote a number of short poems, most of which he published with "Vera Paz" on his return to England in 1872, in a small volume from which we give selections, but which is now out of print. Since then he has written some political squibs, and poems for various occasions, which have appeared either anonymously or under initials. His verses show great mastery over rhyme and rhythm, and are full of a quaint humour, which, while upholding everything noble and true, does not scruple to throw keen ridicule on sentimental fads and crotchets, whether religious or secular.

TAKING THINGS LITERALLY.

WITH frame of Nature's noblest mould,
  For hero deeds he seemed designed ;
O'er all his face ye well might trace
  The impress of a master mind ;
Yet in the paths of worldly fame
  John Dobson ne'er had sought to stray ;
With quiet zeal and heavenly flame,
  The Quaker preacher held his way.
Yet once he felt a great concern—
His heart within him seemed to burn
In christian love to travelling go

And preach the word round Buffalo.
There lived within that frontier town
A sad young rake named Sampson Brown.
It chanced they met ; said Sampson—" Friend,
Do you and your queer sect pretend
To *literal* take the old command—
If any man shall raise his hand,
And smite you on the cheek—that you,
Should meekly turn the other too ?"
" Yea," said the preacher : " Then take that,"
Said Brown ; and striking full and flat,
      He smote the Quaker's cheek.—
At once o'er all John Dobson's face
The crimson flush—of pain—took place.
      Yet calmly did he speak :—
" Young man," he said, " and hast thou read
Unto that sermon's end instead
      Of stopping at that verse ?"
" Yes," said the other : " Then," said John,
" Thou'st seen a trifle further on
      The words I now rehearse :—
' With whatsoever measure ye
To others mete, the same shall be
Measured to you again ;' and I
Obedience to this last shall try,
      Before I note the first."
Then down on Brown's devoted frame
A perfect hail of bruises came,
Until he feared—from out of flame
A being whom we will not name
      Had full upon him burst.
He screamed and roared—but all in vain,
Until in agonizing pain
He reasoned in a different vein,

And cried, "Stop! stop! you far out-strain
  The measure that is owing."
"I know," said John,—"but Scriptures say—
'Thou shalt unto thy neighbour pay
Full measure, heaped up every way,
  Pressed down and over-flowing;'
That is the measure I propose
To give to thee,—so now here goes!"
"But, oh!" cried he, "you've done that now."
"Yea," said the Quaker, "but I trow
Another text prevades my mind—
'That whatsoe'er thy hand shall find
To do,—that do with all thy might';
And scarcely half my power to smite
Has so far been bestowed on thee,
Therefore thy wish cannot yet be."
Then down again his pounding poured
Regardless how young Sampson roared,
Nor ever stopped his sinewy flail
Until his breath began to fail.
Then from the Quaker's loving heart
His duty's burden seemed to part,
From further work relieved,—he felt
Sufficient discipline was dealt.
Resting, he said, in accents bland—
"I now obey the first command,"
And full on Brown (distressed and weak)
He calmly turned "the other cheek."
He then remarked, "Misguided friend,
This counsel I to thee extend,
  Take it and be not vexed;—
With prayer and care the Scriptures read,
Upon the *whole* then found thy creed,
  Not *on a single text.*"

Wreck of the Grand Hotel.

A STRANGER rode into Jackson-town .
Weary and worn ; he asked a clown,
Who sat on a fence,—which he would say
To the Grand Hotel was the nearest way.
The loafer stared, then answered low,
In broken accents, sad and slow,
        "Gone is the Grand Hotel."

"Gone ! why you don't mean to say it has bust !
I thought that the owner had piles of 'dust !'
Or may be a fire has 'raked his pool ;'
Or he's leased the place for a boarding-school ?"
The loafer sighed, then answered,—" No,
I'll tell you as how it chanced to go,
        For gone is the Grand Hotel !

On Ramsay's creek, in Kentuck state,
I raised two powerful steers of late,
They ate—oh heavens ! how they did eat !
While all creation in *work* they beat.
I came to Jackson-town to trade,
And while I liquored my oxen staid
        To feed at the Grand Hotel.

I tied my steers to the stanchion ring
In front of the house, and bade them bring
An ocean of feed, for I had some fear
As seeing a field of clover near.
Alas, the villains ! they only brought
A single hay stack ! and that was nought
        To those steers at the Grand Hotel !

Meanwhile, as I liquored, we felt a shake,
The floor and the ceiling began to quake,
I rushed to the window, and saw with despair
My steers had eaten their hay-rick bare,

And were making tracks for the clover field,
Eating what fodder their way might yield,
    And dragging the Grand Hotel.

I screamed and shouted, ' Wo ! wo, Jack ! wo !
Wo, Buck !" but, alas ! it was all no go.
They tore along at a headlong rate
O'er stony ground with friction great,
Till all the bottom they wore away,
And the lower stories were gone that day
    From Jackson's Grand Hotel !

We made for the back, and reached the ground
As the building gave a tremendous bound ;
For the steers with the crashing had taken fright,
And were scudding along with all their might !
Their speed was quicker by far than the wind,
They left a telegram *miles* behind,
    As they dragged the Grand Hotel !

Not brick, nor iron, such work could stand !
The structure wore as it had been sand !
And the last that was seen of the durned old thing
Was my oxen dragging the stanchion ring
Three thousand miles from this wretched town ;
So I rather guess they have done me brown,
    And gone—with the Grand Hotel."

'Tis strange how human feelings flow
At simple truthful tales of woe ;
While scenes by harrowing fiction dressed
Draw forth a passing sigh at best.
O'ercome the stranger wept to hear,
And often since has he dropped a tear
    On the fate of the Grand Hotel.

JOHN TODHUNTER, M.D.

JOHN TODHUNTER was born at Sir John Rogerson's Quay, Dublin, in December, 1839. He was educated at the Friends' Schools of Mountmellick and York, graduated at Trinity College in 1866, and took the degree of M.D. in 1871, after walking the hospitals of Vienna and Paris.

For some years he practised as a doctor, in Dublin, but gradually made literature more and more his profession, and since 1874, he has resided chiefly in London. His first book "Laurella and other Poems" was published in 1876, though most of the pieces it contained had been written many years before. Its reception by the chief reviews was most cordial, the *Athenæum* and *Academy* amongst others, giving it high praise. His chief publications since "Laurella" have been :

Alcestis	1879
A Study of Shelley	1880
Forest Songs	1881
Rienzi	1881
Helena in Troas	1885
The Banshee	1888
A Sicilian Idyl	1890
The Poison Flower	1891
The Black Cat, performed but not published yet	
A Comedy of Sighs	,, ,,

Dr. Todhunter resigned his membership in the Society of Friends, some time ago. He is a strong poet; full of vigour and imagination, and yet with a delicate beauty of workmanship and touch, which render his poems delightful to read and remember, apart from their essential truth of thought and imagery. In the two poems "Lost" and "Found," he has caught the very spirit of Blake, and the strange mystical charm of that singer of dreams and visions, while "In a Gondola," suggested by Mendelssohn's 6th Lied; the languorous loveliness of the music, with its perpetual plashing of sleepy waters, and the rhythmic motion of the gondolier, are wrought into verse for us in this wonderful poem together with the glimpses of life, and the half sweet, half sad memories of dead lovers, which linger by the marble steps of the shadowy palaces, as the gondola and the poet glide by.

In quite another strain are the "Banshee" poems. Wild, despairing, strange, shadowy, are these ballads and laments. Brimful they seem of that Keltic atmosphere and spirit, wherein deep sorrow is ever and anon smitten across by wild gleams of joy, by visions of spiritual triumph which blot out the physical despair of the merely human. There is no fear of death in these strange wild poems, the Kelt is always strongly permeated by Browning's splendid line, "No work begun shall ever pause for death," and his weird despairing sorrow melts into triumph at the end, as the poet grows more and more the seer, and recognises that

> "Thy sorrows are the world's—
> Thy wrongs the world's."

and therefore that the world's Father must needs redress them.

[*From " The Banshee and other Poems."*]

AGHADOE.

I.

There's a glade in Aghadoe, Aghadoe, Aghadoe
There's a green and silent glade in Aghadoe,

Where we met, my love and I, love's fair planet in the sky,
'O'er that sweet and silent glade in Aghadoe.

II.

There's a glen in Aghadoe, Aghadoe, Aghadoe,
There's a deep and secret glen in Aghadoe,
Where I hid him from the eyes of the red-coats and their spies,
That year the trouble came to Aghadoe.

III.

O, my curse on one black heart in Aghadoe, Aghadoe,
On Shaun Dhuv, my mother's son, in Aghadoe!
When your throat fries in hell's drouth, salt the flame be in
    your mouth,
For the treachery you did in Aghadoe!

IV.

For they tracked me to that glen in Aghadoe, Aghadoe!
When the price was on his head in Aghadoe,
O'er the mountain, by the wood, where I stole to him with
    food,
Where in hiding lone he lay in Aghadoe.

V.

But they never took him living in Aghadoe, Aghadoe;
With the bullets in his heart in Aghadoe,
There he lay—that head my breast feels the warmth of, where
    'twould rest,
Gone to win the traitor's gold, from Aghadoe.

VII.

I walked to Mallow town from Aghadoe, Aghadoe,
Brought his head from the gaol's gate to Aghadoe,
Then I covered him with fern, and I piled on him the cairn,
Like an Irish king he sleeps in Aghadoe.

VII.

O, to creep into that cairn in Aghadoe, Aghadoe,
There to rest upon his breast in Aghadoe,
Sure your dog for you could die with no truer heart than I,
Your own love, cold on your cairn, in Agadoe.

A Dream of Egypt.

" *Where's my Serpent of Old Nile ?* "

Night sends forth many an eagle-wingëd dream
To soar through regions never known by day ;
And I by one of these was rapt away
To where the sun-burnt Nile, with opulent stream
Makes teem the desert sand.   My pomp supreme,
Enriched the noon, I spurned Earth's common clay ;
For I was Antony, and by me lay
That Snake whose sting was bliss.   Nations did seem
But camels for the burden of our joy ;
Kings were our slaves ; our wishes glowed in the air
And grew fruition ; night grew day, day night,
Lest the high bacchanal of our love should cloy ;
We reined the tiger, life, with flower-crowned hair,
Abashlessly abandoned to delight.

The Marseillaise.

What means this mighty chant, wherein the wail
Of some intolerable woe, grown strong
With sense of more intolerable wrong,
Swells to a stern victorious march—a gale
Of vengeful wrath ?   What mean the faces pale,
The fierce resolve, the ecstatic pangs along
Life's fiery ways, the demon thoughts which throng,
The gates of awe, when these wild notes assail
The sleeping of our souls ?   Hear we no more
Than the mad foam of revolution's leaven,

Than a roused people's throne-o'erwhelming tread?
Yes, 'tis man's spirit thundering on the shore
Of iron fate, the tramp of titans dread,
Sworn to dethrone the gods unjust from heaven.

QUATRAINS.*

* Most of these have appeared in the second " Book of the Rhymers' Club."

Creation.

Behind me lay life's endless avatars,
   Before me vague unfathomable dread,
    In wastes of space where Death himself was dead:
Then God went by me, silent, sowing stars.

Conscience (the Obverse).

Conscience is that fine critic of each thrill,
   Along the spirit's nerves, with instinct sane
    For life's fine art assaying joy and pain,
His loves and hates canons of good and ill.

Conscience (the Reverse).

Conscience is but a child who fears the rod
   Laid on by Mrs. Grundy or by God;
    But whose the stroke, or why the smite or spare,
The smarting child scarce guesses.   That is odd!

Morality.

Hating another's sins, I hate my own,
   Hating my own I grow the judge of men,
    Judging, I judge myself: with penance, then,
Harsh righteousness my sackcloth, I atone.

The Golden Key.

To love the right things rightly: this ensphere,
   Wisdom, religion, art; forges the key,
That opens Eden through the Gate of Tears,
   Where by life's river blooms the mystic tree.

IN A GONDOLA.

[Suggested by Mendelssohn's Andante in G. minor, Book I., Lied 6 of
the 'Lieder ohne Worte.'

I.

In Venice ! This night so delicious—its air
　　Full of moonlight, and passionate snatches of song,
　　And quick cries, and perfume of romances, which throng
To my brain, as I steal down this marble sea-stair,
　　　　And my gondola comes :
And I hear the slow, rhythmical sweep of the oar
　　Drawing near and more near—and the noise of the prow,
　　And the sharp, sudden splash of her stoppage—and now
I step in ; we are off o'er the street's heaving floor,
　　　　As my gondola glides—
Away past these palaces silent and dark,
　　Looming ghostly and grim o'er their bases, where clings
　　Rank sea-weed which gleams, flecked with light, as it
　　　　swings
　　To the plash of the waves, where they reach the tide-mark
On the porphyry blocks—with a song full of dole,
　　　　A forlorn barcarole,
　　　　As my gondola glides.

II.

And the wind seems to sigh through that lattice rust-gnawn,
　　A low dirge for the past : the sweet past when it played
　　In the pearl-braided hair of some beauty, who stayed
But one shrinking half-minute—her mantle close-drawn
O'er the swell of her bosom and cheeks passion-pale,
　　Ere her lover came by, and they kissed.　'They are clay
　　Those fire-hearted men with the regal pulse-play.'
'They are dust !' sighs the wind with its whisper of wail ;
'Those women snow-fair, flower-sweet, passion-pale !'

And the waves make reply with their song full of dole,
  Their fair barcarole,
   As my gondola glides.

III.

Dust—those lovers! But love ever lives, ever new,
  Still the same: so we shoot into bustle and light,
  And lamps from the festal casinos stream bright
On the ripples; and here's the Rialto in view;
And black gondolas, spirit-like, cross or slide past,
  And the gondoliers cry to each other: a song
  Far away, from sweet voices in tune, dies along
The waters moon-silvered. So on to the vast
  Shadowy span of an arch where the oar-echoes leap
  Through chill gloom from the marble; then moonlight
   once more,
  And laughter and strum of guitars from the shore,
And sonorous bass-music of bells booming deep
  From St. Mark's. Still those waves with their song full
   of dole,
   Their forlorn barcarole,
    As my gondola glides.

IV.

Here the night is voluptuous with odorous sighs
  From verandahs o'erstarred with dim jessamine flowers,
  Their still scent deep-stirred by the tremulous showers
Of a nightingale's notes as his song swells and dies—
   While my gondola glides.

V.

Dust—those lovers! who floated and dreamed long ago,
  Gazed, and languished, and loved, on these waters—
   where I
Float and dream and gaze up in the still summer sky,

Whence the great stars look down—as they did long ago :
Where the moon seems to dream with my dreaming—disc-hid
   In a gossamer veil of white cirrus—then breaks
   The dream spell with a pensive half-smile, as she wakes
To new splendour.   But lo ! while I mused, we have slid
From the open, the stir, down a lonely lane-way,
   Into hush and dark shadow ! fresh smells of the sea
   Come cool from beyond ; a faint lamp mistily
Hints fair shafts and quaint arches, in crumbling decay ;
And the waves still break in with their song full of dole,
      Their forlorn barcarole,
         As my gondola glides.

VI.

Then the silent lagune stretched away through the night,
   And the stars, and the fairy-like city behind,
   Domes and spires rising spectral and dim : till the mind
Becomes tranced in a vague, subtle maze of delight ;
   And I float in a dream, lose the present—or seem
   To have lived it before.   Then a sense of deep bliss,
   Just to breathe—to exist—in a night such as this ;
Just to feel what I feel, drowns all else.   But the gleam
Of the lights, as we turn to the city once more,
   And the music, and clangour of bells booming slow,
   And this consummate vision—St. Marks's ! the star-glow
For background—crowns all.   Then I step out on shore.
   The Piazzetta ! my life-dream accomplished at last,
         (As my gondola goes)   .
I am here : here alone with the ghost of the past !
But the waves still break in with their song full of dole,
      Their forlorn barcarole,
         As my gondola goes ;
And the pulse of the oar swept through silvery spray
Dies away in the gloom, dies away, dies away—
         Dies away—dies away—!

18

LOST.

I WANDERED from my mother's side
In the fragant paths of morn ;
Naked, weary, and forlorn,
I fainted in the hot noon-tide,

For I had met a maiden wild,
Singing of love and love's delight ;
And with her song she me beguiled,
And her soft arms and bosom white.

I followed fast, I followed far,
And ever her song flowed blithe and free ;
'Where Love's own flowery meadows are,
There shall our golden dwelling be !'

I followed far, I followed fast,
And oft she paused, and cried, 'O here !'
But where I came no flower would last,
And Joy lay cold upon his bier.

I wandered on, I wandered wide,
Alas ! she fleeted with the morn ;
Weary, weeping, and forlorn,
She left me in the fierce noontide.

FOUND.

NAKED, bleeding, and forlorn,
I wandered on the mountain side ;
To hide my wounds from shame and scorn,
I made a garden of my pride.

Till there came a tyrant grey,
He stript and chained me with disgrace,
And led me by the public way,
And sold me in the market-place.

To many masters was I bound,
  And many a grievous load I bore ;
But in the toil my flesh grew sound,
  And from my limbs the chains I tore.

I ran to seek my mother's cot,
  And I found Love singing there,
And round it many a pleasant plot,
  And shadowy streams and gardens fair.

Like virgin gold the thatch I see,
  Like virgin gold the doorway sweet ;
And in the blissful noon each tree
  A ladder for the angel's feet.

ARTHUR EDWIN TREGELLES.

A. E. TREGELLES is the only son of Edwin Octavius Tregelles, and Jenepher Tregelles (neé Fisher) and was born at Neath in 1835. He was brought up at Falmouth, and educated at the school conducted by Lovell Squire, himself a poet. In 1861, he started business as an ironfounder, and in 1867, he married his cousin, Janet M. Wright, of Darlington, who is also a poet of no little merit. In 1884, his health being delicate, he gave up business, and opened a school at his wife's native town, but has since left Darlington, and now resides at Falmouth. His dramas of English History, of which five have been published (both separately, and bound together in one volume), viz:—"Queen Elizabeth," "King James I." "King Charles I." "The Commonwealth," and "King Charles II," are interesting works. A. E. Tregelles has written two more, "James II.," and "William III.," but they have not yet appeared; I hope, however, the writer will receive sufficient encouragement to induce him to let these dramas shortly see the light. I quote a scene from "Queen Elizabeth" which will show the quality of his poetry, and presentment of the times and people treated of. He has also written a large number of fugitive pieces, which have not yet been collected into volume form.

From "QUEEN ELIZABETH."

Scene VI.

Queen Elizabeth *reclining on the floor on pillows, with attendant.*

ATTENDANT.

She sleeps, perchance the cordial she has taken
May do her heart some good. Oh queenly creature,

What a fair soul is prisoned in this body!
Ten days she's lain like this, alas the day!

                Queen E. (moans) Essex.

ATTENDANT.

    She calls on Essex, 'tis his death
Indeed, that troubles her, she cannot bring him
Back to this life, having once ta'en his head.
Ah weary soul! what can I do to aid thee?
I'll send for our Archbishop, his good counsel
May soothe her spirit.

            Enter Archbishop of Canterbury.

ARCHBISHOP.

How fares our gracious lady?

ATTENDANT.

Worse I fear, she moans and calls on Essex,
Methinks, your grace, it is his spirit haunts her.

ARCHBISHOP.

No spirit walks this earth, but by the sufferance
Of our good Lord in Heaven, and with the purpose
Of winning men's souls from their evil ways:
They do not walk for vengeance.
    (Kneels and prays)   Father in Heaven!
We pray Thee now for this our suffering Queen,
That Thou wouldst pardon all her past transgressions,
And if at times too hasty in her judgments,
For which we may not judge her, only Thou,
(Omniscient Father and all-seeing God),
That Thou wilt judge her very mercifully,
And through the blood of Thy most Holy Son,
Will wash away blood-guiltiness, and give her
An entrance in Thy pure and perfect kingdom
Of rest, and peace, and joy.

QUEEN E. (softly)

Amen.

After an interval, Queen Elizabeth dies.

ATTENDANT.

She's gone, and all the glory of this pale earth,
Is gone along with her.   She was a woman,
Of queenly presence, and of kingly power
To govern this round globe.   Our little England,
She has exalted to a state and place,
Above all other nations—Oh my God !
Grant her a fitting place, where she may praise Thee,
For ever, and for ever.

CHORUS.

Gone is England's glory
Quenched is England's might,
Her name's a household story,
A tower in the fight.
While roll the ocean surges,
While swell the British seas,
They do but sing sweet dirges,
Her spirit to appease.
When foemen come in battle,
Our children to oppress,
They'll need no other war-cry,
Than this, our good Queen Bess.

(*Exeunt omnes*).

ANNA LETITIA WARING.

THIS sweet singer of sacred melodies was born at Neath in 1823, and was the daughter of Elijah and Deborah Waring. Her hymns were first printed in 1850, and published in collective form under the title of " Hymns and Meditations." They have since gone into numerous editions. I am enabled to quote these beautiful compositions through the kind courtesy of Miss A. L. Waring, and the Society for Promoting Christian Knowledge, by whom Miss Waring's "Hymns and Meditations" are now published. A. L. Waring resigned her membership in the Society of Friends, and joined the Church of England, but her beautiful hymns are equally helpful and dear to all denominations; there is no sect in poetry, nor is there any in real religion, and these compositions are as much valued among the brethren she left, as among those she united with, and are almost universally known and read, as the numerous editions through which her " Hymns and Meditations " have passed, abundantly testify.

MY TIMES ARE IN THY HAND. Ps. xxxi, 15.

FATHER, I know that all my life
   Is portioned out for me,
And the changes that are sure to come,
   I do not fear to see ;
But I ask Thee for a present mind,
   Intent on pleasing Thee.

I ask Thee for a thoughtful love,
   Through constant watching wise,
To meet the glad with joyful smiles,
   And to wipe the weeping eyes ;

And a heart at leisure from itself
  To soothe and sympathise.

I would not have the restless will
  That hurries to and fro,
Seeking for some great thing to do,
  Or secret thing to know ;
I would be treated as a child,
  And guided where I go.

Wherever in the world I am,
  In whatsoe'er estate,
I have a fellowship with hearts
  To keep and cultivate,
And a work of lowly love to do
  For the Lord on whom I wait.

So I ask Thee for the daily strength,
  To none that ask denied,
And a mind to blend with outward life
  While keeping at Thy side ;
Content to fill a little space,
  If Thou be glorified.

And if some things I do not ask,
  In my cup of blessing be,
I would have my Spirit filled the more
  With grateful love to Thee—
More careful—not to serve Thee much,
  But to please Thee perfectly.

There are briers besetting every path,
  That call for patient care ;
There is a cross in every lot,
  And an earnest need for prayer ;
But a lowly heart that leans on Thee,
  Is happy anywhere.

In a service which Thy will appoints,
    There are no bonds for me,
For my inmost heart is taught "the truth"
    That makes Thy children "free;"
And a life of self-renouncing love
    Is a life of liberty.

"Arise, walk through the land, in the length of it, and in the breadth of
it: for I will give it unto thee."—Gen. xiii. 17.
"All things are yours . . . things present."—1 Cor. iii. 21, 22.

While toil and warfare urge us on our way,
    And heart is answering heart in signs of pain,
Have we no words of strengthening joy to say—
    No songs for those who suffer but to reign?

Oh for the faithful mind, the steadfast eye,
    To keep our Leader's glory full in sight,
And make our converse, even while we die,
    An interchange of triumph and delight!

Behold, the paths of life are ours—we see
    Our blest inheritance where'er we tread;
Sorrow and danger our security,
    And disappointment lifting up our head.

Kings unto God, we may not doubt our power,
    We may not languish when he says, "Be strong"—
We must move on through every adverse hour,
    And take possession as we pass along.

Yes, all is for us—nothing shall withstand
    Our faithful, valiant, persevering claim;
The rod of God's Anointed in our hand,
    And our assurance His unchanging name.

We need no haste where He has said, "Be still"—
    No peace where He has charged us to contend;
Only the fearless love to do His will,
    And to shew forth His honour to the end.

O ye that faint and die, arise and live!
  Sing, ye that all things have a charge to bless!
If He is faithful who hath sworn to give,
  Then be ye also faithful, and possess.

Take thy whole portion with thy Master's mind—
  Toil, hindrance, hardness, with His virtue take—
And think how short a time thy heart may find
  To labour or to suffer for His sake.

Count all the pains that speed thee to thy rest
  Among the riches of thy purchased right;
Yea, bind them in His name upon thy breast,
  As jewels for the Bride, the Lamb's delight.

And love shall teach us while on Him we lean,
  That, in the certainty of coming bliss,
We may be yearning for a world unseen,
  Yet wear our beautiful array in this.

Ours be a loyal love, for service tried,
  To shew, by deeds, and words, and looks that cheer,
How He can bless the scene on which He died,
  And fill His house with glory even here.

ROBERT SPENCE WATSON, LL.D.

D R. WATSON, poet, prose writer, traveller, lawyer, and orator, was born at Gateshead, in 1837, and is the son of Joseph Watson, who was a colleague of Bright and Cobden in the Anti-Corn Law League. He was educated at Dr. Bruce's school, Newcastle, and at York, and continued his studies at University College, London. He is a Fellow of the Royal Geographical Society; member of the Alpine Club; one of the founders of the National Liberal Club; honorary member of the Eighty Club; a Toynbee trustee, a Vice-President of the Liberation Society, and member of innumerable societies and useful bodies in his own town.

He was the first Christian who entered the sacred city of Wazan, and wrote an account of his journey, published by Macmillan, called "A Visit to Wazan." He went to France during the war as one of the Society of Friends' Commissioners to distribute relief to the starving peasantry, and was condemned to death during the struggle, but afterwards offered the Legion of Honour by the French Government, and as he declined this, was presented with a specially-struck gold medal.

He has written an excellent monograph on "Caedmon, the first English poet," "The History of English Rule and Policy in South Africa," "The Villages Round Metz," "A Visit to Wazan," "The Children's Xmas," written to the music of Myles Birket Foster, son of his cousin, Birket Foster, the artist, and two volumes of poems for private circulation, besides a large number of pamphlets, papers, and essays. His great oratorical power has made him widely known throughout the length and breadth of England, and it is said he has addressed more public meetings than almost any politician of the day.

GRACE DARLING.

WHERE King Ida's stately castle
    Watches o'er the Northern sea,
Lies a little island-cluster
    Where the surf breaks ceaselessly ;
Dreaded by the storm-tost sailor,
    Beautiful to you and me.

On those islands, where the light-house
    Long hath stormy seas defied,
On those islands holy Cuthbert
    Lived long years and meekly died ;
From these islands too our Fathers
    Came to preach the Crucified.

See, across the gloom of evening,
    Shining like a planet bright,
Gladdening the watchful seamen,
    Glows a clear and warning light ;
Hear it tell a thrilling story
    Of a gentle maiden's might.

'Twas a wild September evening,
    And the north-wind fiercely blew,
When the " Forfarshire " came drifting
    With a weary, hopeless crew,
And upon the Longstone striking
    With that warning light in view.

In the light-house dwelt a maiden,
    Stranger she to doubt or fear,
Little marvel that for ever
    All men hold Grace Darling dear !
When the bitter cry for life rose,
    Help they dreamed not of was near.

" Father," cried the dauntless maiden,
  " Hear you not the drowning call?
Heed not though the seas be raging,
  Launch our boat whate'er befal ! "
Seated in that boat a maiden
  And an old man, that was all.

To the rock through wind and tempest,
  Through the raging ocean's roar,
On that dread September morning
  Pulled that man and maiden o'er,—
Stormy sea and danger round them,
  Dying fellow-men before.

Sixty-three were in the steamer
  When she struck the fatal land,
All the night the raging billows
  Every hope of succour banned : .
How could man avail to save them ?
  One by one felt Death's stern hand.

But the nine who clung despairing
  All that wild and woeful night,
Heard a cry of help come ringing
  Through the air with morning light,—
Little marvel that the maiden
  Seemed to them an angel bright.

Saved them all !   The thrilling story
  Ran through England far and wide :
Whilst Grace Darling's fame and glory
  Were proclaimed on every side,
She lived humbly in her light-house,
  Humbly in her light-house died.

Come with me, my darling children,
  We will wander where she lies,
Gaze upon her simple head-stone
  Crumbling 'neath our angry skies ;
But her memory lives for ever,
  Such grand lesson never dies.

À TES PIEDS.

'À TES pieds, my love, I lie,
And gaze into the far blue sky :
That sky so blue, so far away,
Where summer cloudlets idly play,
That sky, this world so far above,
Seems to me emblem of our love.'

  'Our love ! and yet so far away :
  And still, my dearest, still you stay
    À mes pieds.'

'Yes, and would tarry there alway
Through Summer's shine and Winter's grey :
My love, my life, my all I lay
    À tes pieds.'

CHRISTMAS DAY.

THROUGH plains where sheep are cropping the grass,—
  Their shepherds keeping watch over them,—
Joseph and Mary wearily pass
  To David's city of Bethlehem.

In travail sore was the virgin mild,
  The crowded inn had no place for her,
She laid in manger her first-born child—
  The Son of God and the carpenter.

Since that strange birth in that far-off land
    Near nineteen centuries are gone :
To-day the world rings on every hand
    In praise of Jesus, the carpenter's son.

Hard was the scorn of his life to bear,
    Harder to bear must be the praise :
All call him Lord, and all raise the prayer,
    Yet no man doeth the things he says.

Has then that lone life been all in vain?
    His teaching void?   His death, too, sore?
Must Jesus be crucified again
    Ere we learn the lesson the angels bore?

Ah, brother, sister, it lies with each
    To live for his Lord through evil days—
Vain is our prayer and in vain we preach,
    If we will not do what our Master says.

NANTFIN BURN.

THE sun's bright rays burn fiercely in the cloudless sky—
    Not the shadow of a breeze
    As we plunge beneath the trees,
And up the bonnie burnie where the trouties lie.

The burden of great heat passes harmless by,
    Drawn to flecks of golden gleam
    Which dance gaily down the stream,
The wee bit bonnie burnie where the trouties lie.

Ah, must rare days of July so quickly fly?
    Must clouds spread the gloaming o'er?
    We shall, haply, never more
Scramble up yon bonnie burnie where the trouties lie.

CLOVELLY.

Is it a place, or is it a play,
Houses made to be put away,
Breakwater, inns, to be taken down
When *we* have passed to another town ?
Flowers bloom so gay in the break-neck street,
The sea lies so sheer beneath your feet ;
The boats look so small in the tiny bay,—
It must be a dream, or a passing play.

Masses of leaves wherever you look,
Rich autumn colour in every nook,
Bluest of skies and emerald seas,
The very cliffs are bowers of trees ;
Vines, grape-laden, climb up the wall,
Crimson creepers from chimnies fall,
Bright at night and brilliant at day,
It must be a dream or a passing play.

Yet each wee house has its tale of lives,
Working husbands and wearying wives,
Unconscious children whose woes are short,
Each little life with a future fraught.
And the gentle sea can be fierce and wild ;
And cliffs reck little of wife or child :
Under each roof-tree lurk care and strife :
It is bright and bitter as human life.

MISS DEBORAH WEBB.

DEBORAH WEBB was born in 1837. The following autobiographical sketch was not intended for publication, but was merely sent in answer to my request for biographical material to precede a selection of her poems; feeling however that her own graphic words give such a much better idea of the poet's personality than any of mine could do, I have begged permission to quote them just as they are :—

"We were all born in Dublin; Alfred, now a Nationalist M.P., Richard, the most vigorous of the family, but who died comparatively young, myself, and my sister Anne. Our parents, Richard D. and Hannah Webb, were much interested in literature, and in all reforms and good causes, especially that of the negro slave, and our house was a resort of various celebrities and philanthrophists, particularly of abolitionists and escaped slaves. At the ages of fourteen and sixteen my sister and I were sent to the London Bedford Square Ladies' College, which we continued to attend for two sessions, but the education of girls was, of course, not at that period so organized and ambitious as at present. Though residing in town, our family had always spent the summer more or less in the country. In 1859, my father took a place beautifully situated at the foot of the Dublin mountains—while continuing to carry on his printing business in town. Here he wrote, with much help in criticism and labour from my mother, a life of John Brown, who had been hanged for a raid in aid of some slaves. Here, in 1862, we lost our mother, after which the lovely country house seemed so sad

19

and lonely that we were glad to leave it in 1864 for a house in the suburbs. During our residence in the country my sister wrote her lines on the New Rock Mountain. In 1868, she met at a Scotch hydropathic establishment a Scotch gentleman, Donald Steel, whom she shortly afterwards married, going out with him to his tea plantation in India. Within a few months, as they were on a business voyage to Australia, cholera breaking out on the vessel, she was struck down. Her grave is in Ceylon Meantime my father and I were in the United States, America, having gone out with my brother Richard, whose home was in California. My father had long wished to visit his American friends and correspondents, and I, being in poor health, went on to some cousins in Ohio. Later I joined him in the east. Here we heard of my sister's death. The friend with whom we stayed (William Lloyd Garrison) being an ardent Spiritualist, I became much interested in the subject, and convinced of the fact of Spirit Communication, from which I derived much consolation. In 1872, my father died in our Dublin home. Soon after, I joined some friends in Italy, where I remained a year and eight months. Since then I have lived for fourteen years with my brother Alfred and his wife, and for the last eight years in my own snug little suburban home, which I am so fortunate as to have with a dear friend. Lately, going to Germany for three months, we remained there, chiefly in Hanover, for fifteen, which was a delightful experience.

"After our mother's death my sister and I had resigned our membership with Friends on various grounds. Though, in some respects, I always feel still to belong to them. I have never joined another religious body. I am deeply interested in the cause of equal rights, not only for my own sex and country, but for all humanity, and, being an optimist, I regard the obtainment of the same as only a question of time, for I hold with George Eliot that there is a kind of blasphemy in the expression, 'Too good to be true.'"

JOHN BROWN'S MARCH.

JOHN BROWN'S body lies mould'ring in the grave,
 It lies amidst the mountains of the Adirondack lone ;
A grey rock looms above it and the sighing grasses wave,
 But his soul is marching on.
   Glory, glory, hallelujah !
    He lives forever, though on earth his race is run ;
   Glory, glory, hallelujah !
    His soul is marching on.

They could not chain his spirit nor lay it below the sod ;
 They freed him from a prison here to mount in joy on high ;
"Though worms destroy this body, yet I shall behold my God,"
 Was his soul's exulting cry.
   Glory, glory, hallelujah !
    He lives forever, though on earth his race is run ;
   Glory, glory, hallelujah !
    His soul is marching on.

The torch by him left smould'ring shall give light in other hands ;
 His voice which now is silent shall be echoed o'er and o'er ;
Till slavery has ceased to be, and freedom in all lands
 Shall reign for evermore.
   Glory, glory, hallelujah !
    He lives forever, though on earth his race is run ;
   Glory, glory, hallelujah !
    His soul is marching on.

He failed, yet as a victor we will crown our hero brave ;
 Beneath Jehovah's banner was his duty nobly done,
And we grieve not that his body lies mould'ring in the grave,
 For his soul is marching on.
   Glory, glory, hallelujah !
    He lives forever, though on earth his race is run ;
   Glory, glory, hallelujah !
    His soul is marching on.

ROCKRUN, OHIO.

MORE than a thousand leagues of sea,
  More than a hundred leagues of land,
There stretch between that Western home and me,
  Yet on its porch I stand.

The quiet room, the pictured wall,
  Each well-known object on the floor,
'Neath clustering bitter-sweet, I see them all
  Unchanged for evermore.

'Tis eve ; through day's fierce breathless heat
  Only the fearless cricket chirred ;
But now, while welcome rain-drops pattering beat,
  The robin's note is heard.

Oh, robin ! sweetly thou dost sing
  Thy simple and unvaried lay.
What gives it such a charm, such power to bring
  Thoughts of a bygone day ?

Now down the fenced, familiar lane
  I wander in my waking dream.
I see Cuyahoga's calm expanse again,
  And Rockrun's rippling stream ;

The meadow path and woodland track,
  The rustic bridge and stately trees,
What memories I meet when venturing back
  To haunted spots like these !

Through changing seasons, every mood
  Of my own restless heart I've known
Deep in the shade of this Ohio wood,
  With Nature all alone.

Now each bare treetop seems a spire—
    The glen to a cathedral turns,
Among whose leafless aisles, an altar fire,
    The solemn sunset burns.

But fairyland the woods appear,
    When, under winter's magic hand,
Transformed to groves of shining crystal clear,
    And flashing diamond.

Now over crisp white fields I go.
    Fresh, keen, transparent as the air,
Heaven's cloudless blue and earth's pure sparkling snow
    Are wonderfully fair.

Within, old Rockrun's hearth beside,
    We scarcely marked Time's noiseless tread,
A few more months, and all are scattered wide :
    The living Past is dead.

Oh ! lay her tenderly away,
    For she is fixed as marble now ;
Shall she not have a resurrection day ?
    Strew violets o'er her brow.

ANNA LOUISA WESTCOMBE.

ANNA LOUISA WESTCOMBE is the youngest child of Samuel Thompson and Elizabeth Trusted Westcombe, and was born in December 1821, at Alcester, a little town on the borders of Warwickshire. Her father was descended from Thomas Lawson, the friend of George Fox, and her mother also was of old Quaker ancestry. A. L. Westcombe seems to have been an uncommon child; she had a passionate love for music and flowers, and would hold a book in her tiny fingers, making rhythmic murmurs and notions before she could speak, and the names of the flowers were the first words her baby lips uttered. It was no wonder then, that as the child grew, her inarticulate murmurs became musical verse, and her love of beauty in form and sound took tangible form in her poems.

In 1824 the family left Alcester and took a farm, where the young poet led a free and happy country life, until she was sent to school at Worcester; and her parents soon after removing to that place she has lived there ever since. When her school days were over she herself became a teacher in her sister's school at Worcester, where the other young poets, M. A. Binyon, and Hannah Bowden, were engaged in tuition. She has contributed verse to " The Olive Leaf" and many other magazines and papers, and in 1873 published her first book, " The Wasted Grain," composed of temperance verses, many of which had appeared as " Sudbury Leaflets." In 1880 she published " Leaves from the Banks of Severn," and in 1894, "Autumn Leaves from the Banks of Severn." Many of the poems in these volumes will be familiar to every reader, as they have been scattered far and wide in leaflet form,

this is especially the case with such as " Is it nothing to you?"
and " Lead not the Lambs astray."

I have quoted some not quite so well known, and which
are remarkable for their music and constant breath of flowers,
these poems show clearly that the child's love of beautiful
sound and form have grown with the woman's growth, and
supply the ever-present inspiration of her pen.

From the Mourner's Dream.

White-robed, in her little coffin
   Our only darling lay,
The flowers we had strewed above her
   Were fading like her away

.   .   .   .

But the watching, and the anguish,
   And the suffering were over now,
And peace that might never be broken
   Slept on her marble brow.

I felt that the hand of mercy
   Had laid her to rest at last,
And yet, as I gazed upon her,
   The stream of my grief flowed fast

For I knew that to-morrow morning
   I might look no more on that face,
And the dust that we loved so dearly
   Must be borne to its resting-place.

But He who comforts the mourner
   With more than a mother's love,
Sent me that night through the darkness
   A vision of light from above.

He has taken my garment of sadness,
  And clothed me with praise instead ;
  And now I rejoice for the *living*,
  Rather than weep for the *dead*.

FROM A MAY-DAY.

WHEN the sweet bells of the cowslip among the grass are
  springing,
 And through the opening elm leaves the breezes gently
  blow,
Like summer birds returning, across the blue sea winging,
 So back again to memory come the scenes of long ago.

Thoughts of a far-off springtime, when life was yet before us ;
 And if some passing sorrows within our pathway lay,
They were like the quivering shadows of the hazels bending
  o'er us,
 When we wandered through the copses on that bright
  May-day.

There was beauty all around us, for the flowers were freshly
  blooming,
 With the rose tints of the lychnis, and the hyacinth's deep
  blue,
And the starlight of the primrose, the shady banks illuming,
 And the violet and ground-ivy alike in azure hue.

There was gladness all around us, for the merry thrush was
  singing,
 In chorus with the blackbird, to the blackcap's roundelay ;
Among the distant orchards the cuckoo's note was ringing,
 When we wandered through the copses on that sweet May-
  day.

The woodpecker laughed loud, within the wood-depths hiding ;
  The nightingale had come to its summer home again ;
The small birds gaily sang, through the tangled thicket gliding—
  The redstart and the titmouse, the chaffinch and the wren.

The joyous lark was soaring above the cowslip meadow,
  Where the buttercups and daisies like gold and silver lay ;
No scorching in the sunshine, no gloom was in the shadow,
  When we wandered through the copses on that sweet May-
    day.

But since we trod those wood-paths, so blithesome and light-
    hearted,
  With all their cares and sorrows now fifty years have passed,
And they, who then were with me, have one by one departed
  Unto the better country, and I am left—the last.

Perhaps, in heavenly places, no kindred tie forgetting,
  They watch us in our journeyings, with angel-vision clear,
And say to one another, " Their sun is near its setting,
  The shadows are fast lengthening, and they will soon be
    here."

HANNAH MARIA WIGHAM.

HANNAH MARIA PEILE, afterwards Wigham, was born at Whitehaven, Cumberland, in 1828. She has lived since her marriage chiefly at Killiney, near Dublin. She is perhaps better known for her prose works than her poems, but many of the latter are very fine, although not so generally fascinating as her " Bag of Old Letters," and study of William Law.

FRAGMENT.

IN all around we see
Links of the chain that binds the soul of man
Unto his brother man.   No human eye
Can gaze undazzled where those links begin,
Nor trace them to their end.   Alone to Faith,
With her far eagle-gaze 'tis given to see
That the all-loving heart of Nature's God
And Man's Redeemer, is the burning clasp
That joins in one that all-embracing zone,
Round as the circle of eternity.

Yet everywhere
These links are scattered with a bounteous hand ;
They shine above us in the stars of night,
That tread with golden feet the courts of heaven,
Like angel-watchers o'er a sleeping world.
They look as brightly down upon us now,
When time and sin have furrowed earth's fair face,
As when the placid streams of Paradise
First mirror'd back with such effulgent glow,

Night's ebon beauty, and her jewell'd hair,
That, gazing long, she blushed herself away,
And gave her sceptre to the orient morn.

       And since those hours of holy innocence,
Through many an age the stars have kept their watch,
Seeming eternal in a world of change—
Untiring herald of our high descent
From Him, around whose throne the sons of God
And morning-stars together sang with joy,
When first our virgin earth sprang forth to light.
Oh, had man's ear been open to their voice,
His eye attentive to the wondrous page,
The illumined missal, where the golden stars
Inscribe in characters of liquid light,
Caught from the censers of the angel hosts,
Their holy teachings of the eternal truths,
How fair and bright had been his earthly lot !
In one high brotherhood of peace and joy,
Owning no chain save all-embracing love ;
The individual souls of men had shone,
Each in his sphere of far-extending light
Obedient to the universal law,—
None envying, none presuming, only them
Who burned most fervently with heavenly love
Crowned with a garland of the brightest beams
From heaven's own fountain of immortal light.
While from the spirits of the mighty whole,
As from the chords of some great instrument,
A stream of choral harmony had risen
And joined the harpings of angelic spheres.

Not less the flowers
Come missioned with a tale of love to man,
As one by one they meekly bend and write

Upon the pages of this furrowed earth
A hymn of praise, which " he who runs may read."
Each in the depth of its sweet chalice holds
As in a censer filled with frankincense,
Some message of the love of God to man,
And of His care over the meanest things.
In every age these silent messengers
Have borne from heart to heart the tale of love,
For man hath deem'd their silent eloquence
Of spirit-language, fittest far to breathe
The delicate thoughts that seem deformed and soiled,
Garbed in earth's common language.

The Brotherhood of Hills!
They, too, have lessons for the heart of man!
Who that hath marked the flying sunbeams chase,
The cloudshade o'er the steadfast mountain's brow,
Nor deem'd he saw an image of his life—
A fleeting shadow on the brow of time?
Amidst the wildering and incessant stir,
The dust and care of this our mortal life,
What joy to gaze upon their changeless forms,
Rising so solemly from earth to heaven!
To drink the waters of refreshment, poured
From the deep urns of Silence, who hath sat
Since the first dawning of Creation's morn,
Enthroned among the everlasting hills!
How fearlessly they lift their giant heads
Into the regions of the hurrying storm ;
Calm as when sunlight gilds their hoary locks
That so they may receive the tempest gift,
And send it forth in gushing rills and streams,
Gladdening the lands, and from the barren waste
Calling forth beauty in resplendent gleams—

An image of the true heart's mission here !
Thus stars and flowers, the mountains and the streams,
Yea, all the forms of this our outward world,
Have each their ministry and part to bear,
In teaching to the young immortal, man,
Some knowledge of his own mysterious soul,
And solemn truths that lie at Nature's heart.
This truth more beautiful than all beside,
That He, whose name is Love, and from whose heart,
As from a living and immortal root,
This whole fair universe hath budded forth,
Hath granted him the high and holy right
To call Him " Father."
       So that all things speak
God's Fatherhood, and the Brotherhood of man.

SONNET.

" Even such a shell the Universe itself,
  Is to the ear of Faith."
               — *Wordsworth.*

My little son sat joyous on my knee,
   And to his ear I held a twisted shell
" Now hearken dear " I whispered him "and tell
What has the pretty thing to say to thee,
Does it not talk about its native sea ? "
   A listening look upon the sweet face fell,
   A quiet came as of a holy spell ;
And then he answered low and reverently
I hear it say : " Father who art in Heaven."

Oh might it be, my heart has inly prayed,
That such a message from the mystic shell
Of Nature, unto questioning souls were given ;
That through the music by its windings made,
They too might hear : " Father who art in Heaven."

THOMAS WILKINSON.

THOMAS WILKINSON was born at Yanwath, in Westmoreland, April 29th, 1751; he lived upon a small estate of about forty acres, which he had inherited from his ancestors, on the banks of the river Eamont, which flowing out of Ullswater, forms for several miles the boundary between Cumberland and Westmoreland.

He describes his early education in a letter to a friend thus: "An old woman in the next village taught me to read, and a few weeks to write, and a few weeks to learn arithmetic, was what I got. My humble-minded father, without any views for my advancement in life, intended me to manage his estate, and having never gone a day to school himself, thought a little learning was sufficient for me." When he was thirty-four, Wilkinson's secluded country life was broken by a journey to London; he rode there on his pony to attend the yearly meeting of 1785. This journey was then considered so formidable that Wilkinson says; " My mother shed tears, and my sisters looked as long as I was in sight. At Kendal I met Elihu Robinson, whose friendship is very dear to me, and we rode on together."

In 1787, Wilkinson accompanied John Pemberton and David Ducat on a tour of religious service in the Highlands where they were well received by the family of the Duke of Argyle and others. During this journey he ascended Ben Lomond, the Cobbler, and Ben Nevis, and visited many places of interest on the way; he afterwards described them in his "Tours to the British Mountains." He gained the deep affection of his companions during his tour, and John

Pemberton bequeathed to him on leaving England, his saddle and bridle as a mark of friendship, and for the remainder of his life wrote frequently, sending Wilkinson presents of cocoanuts, hickory walnuts, etc.

In 1791, Wilkinson walked to London to attend the yearly meeting, performing the journey of 300 miles in eight days. Having become acquainted with Clarkson, he joined heartily with him in his efforts for the abolition of the Slave Trade, published an appeal, and assisted in getting up petitions on the subject. Clarkson at different times in his busy life, passed several months in Wilkinson's quiet home, and purchased some land a few miles from Yanwath, where he built a house, and lived for some few years, until his wife's delicate health obliged him to go further south. He afterwards wrote to introduce Charles Lloyd to his friend, and the young poet stayed with Wilkinson for some time to recruit his health both in mind and body. Mary Leadbeater of Ballitore, was one of Wilkinson's correspondents and to her he says: "I had lately a young poet seeing me who sprung originally from the next village. He has left the college, turned his back on all preferment, and settled down contentedly among our Lakes with his sister and his nurse. He is very sober, and very amiable, and writes in what he conceives to be the language of nature in opposition to the finery of our present poetry. He has published two volumes of poems, mostly of the same character. I transcribe thee a short piece as a specimen. His name is William Wordsworth." In another letter to her he says, " William Wordsworth has lately married 'an amiable person, a neighbour of ours ; but I am told, though one of the best poets in England, his sister used to write him his love-letters ! "

In 1806 Wordsworth stayed two days at Yanwath with Wilkinson ; indeed this quiet Quaker, living as he did in a distant and secluded part of England, met and knew many of

the most distinguished men of his time ; his letters mention
Southey, Wordsworth, Scott, Canning, Clarkson, Wilberforce,
Burke, Bernard Barton, Jacob Thompson the painter, and
others.

He continued to live his healthy out-door life, and to pursue
his literary occupations, until walking and riding over the Fells,
and reading and writing at home, became, through his growing
blindness increasingly difficult, and when nearly eighty years
old he was compelled to remain at home, or only visit those
households near his own dwelling ; but wherever he went, in
his old age as in his youth, he was always a welcome guest.
For the last few years of his life he became totally blind.
Joseph John Gurney visited Penrith in 1830, and records that
Thomas Wilkinson, though almost entirely blind, and very
infirm, was perfectly cheerful and bright. He died on the
13th of June, 1836, at the age of eighty-five. These
particulars have been gathered from Mary Carr's memoir of
her great uncle, published in the Friend's Quarterly Examiner,
and made use of by her kind permission. His chief poetical
works are :—" An appeal to England on behalf of the abused
Africans, 1780." "Emont Vale, a descriptive poem, 1860.'
He wrote also a great many fugitive pieces.

To My Thrushes, Blackbirds, etc.

(Some friends having found nine of their nests in my
garden and looked into the same, to the annoyance of the
inhabitants.)

> Ye finches and linnets, ye blackbirds and thrushes,
> Who dwell in my garden among the green bushes,
> Your company's sweet, and I'm happy to see
> You visit about from the juniper tree
> To the gooseberry bush ; but a recent intrusion
> Has thrown all your harmony into confusion !
> I pity you greatly. 'Twas very provoking

That while you sang sweetly to strangers a-walking,
They should rush on your privacy, little regarding
Your slumbering babes, and not caring a farthing
For your poor loving wives, who required kind attention,
A proceeding so rough is—unpleasant to mention !
Ye blackbirds and linnets, and finches and all,
No longer sit piping aloof when I call :
You know, my sweet birds, and it's known to your spouses,
I go not about, peeping into your houses ;
Your green sheltered houses as safe are from me
As if they were locked with a lock and key ;
How could I annoy you, when seeing your care
In collecting your mortar, your moss, and your hair !
How you tugged at your timbers, and toiled on the wing
While the winds were against you, your rafters to bring !
I once was a builder, nor have I forgot
How I laboured, like you, in erecting my cot ;
I thought, peradventure, like you, as I wrought,
Of a house of my own, and it might cross my thought
That a mate might sit by me and comfort my nest,
And there, in due time, that my chirpers might rest.
I have lived with you all without scolding or strife,
From the cushat and owl, to the wren and his wife ;
Round your mansions of moss you may warble all day,
From the apple-tree bough or the juniper spray,
Unmolested by me ; I partake of your joy,
Nor went about robbing your nests when a boy.
You've often amused a poor head full of care
With a bounce to the clouds or your tumbles in air ;
If you sing from the cedar I hear with delight.
And am ready to laugh when you bustle and fight ;
I scarce would forbid you the use of my trees
When you go with my cherries and pilfer my peas ;
With pleasure I see you display your light pinions,

And flutter and fly round your little dominions.
The whole of my garden is open and free,
Each tree shall be yours, and the boughs of each tree.

MARY, QUEEN OF SCOTS AT LOWTHER.

When good Sir Richard held these fair domains,
With pensive state along the silent plains,
From distant scenes a beauteous stranger came.
In meek distress appeared the lovely dame :
Her tender griefs seemed kindly felt by all ;
No sprightly airs resounded through the hall ;
The rural sports beneath the greenwood shade,
Were all suspended while the stranger stay'd.
While polished sense and wit's attractive light,
Prolonged the pleasure of the social night.
Her condescension spoke her high degree,
But more her sweet and serious dignity.
Such tempered grace the wond'ring menials saw,
Their Lord's attention touched their minds with awe ;
The fairest seat the honour'd stranger prest,
The first apartment lodged th' exalted guest.
Oft when the sun a mellow radiance threw,
Her pensive steps to silent shades withdrew ;
With lambs and flowers she breathed the balmy air,
And thus discoursed : " Ye simple wild flowers fair,
" That here unseen, far from the public eye,
" Unenvied live, and unmolested die ;
" Far happier you than the distinguished flower,
" That on the bosom flaunts its transient hour ;
" For soon its beauty fades, its fragrance flies—
" Then scorned and trodden in the dust it lies."
Now to the lambs she turns, that o'er the ground
With youthful speed in frolic circles bound :
Her sad presaging bosom seem'd to say,

"Sport, happy race ! your little hour away :
"A common lot perhaps our lives may close,
"But your blind innocence no sorrow knows."
At eventide her chamber oft she sought
And by the window lingered, lost in thought.
Far to the north she turned her wistful eyes,
That seemed to say "'Tis there my treasure lies."
At length these peaceful scenes she must forego,
And journey onward through untrodden woe.
Through folding doors her sorrowing host attends ;
But ere she down the winding stairs descends,
Low on her knees the pious mourner fell,
Prayed for her host, then took her last farewell :
The generous Richard turned to weep unseen,
While from his door went Mary, Scotland's Queen !

JAMES H. WILSON.

J. H. WILSON was born in 1853 at Newcastle-on-Tyne,
and was the third son of William and Sarah Wilson.
His mother seems to have been an uncommon woman, with a
passionate love of study in out-of-the-way fields. She was
steeped to the lips in the works and ideas of the Greek
philosophers and the early Christian writers, as well as the
fascinating literature of the Middle Ages. She had been
brought up in the quietest possible way among the restrictions
of a now obsolete Quakerism, and to the young Friend, who
during her girlhood had read scarcely anything save Quaker
books, the history of Popes and Jesuits, artists, poets, and
musicians, and other kindred subjects possessed a strange
fascination. James H. Wilson seems to have been her favourite
child ; she taught him from his earliest years long poems, Latin
hymns, and passages from the Greek philosophers, in order to
stimulate his imagination. His mother's lessons have borne
rich fruit in his poems as will be seen in those selected.

At the age of sixteen the youth left school, and entered his
father's office, where, with the exception of a few years spent in
London and other places, he has continued to work ever since.
During a part of this time he travelled for a London firm, and
his journeys led him through Northumberland and the Border
towns. He took long walks across this romantic tract of
country, and during these solitary wanderings first became
aware that he was a poet. After many happy careless years
with small earnings, but smaller needs, the young poet, free
from care or ambition as he thought, fell in love, and married
in 1886 Elizabeth Forsyth, and this free and joyous, but

materially unproductive life had to be abandoned. He returned to his father's office, and settled down to a quiet existence, full of work and literary activity, full too of the peaceful pleasures of home life. He published "Zalmoxis and other Poems" in 1892. This book was very well received by the critics, and contains much beautiful work. The Classical pieces seem to me peculiarly finely wrought, and the translations are excellently done. Some of the lyrics in "Clods of the Valley" sing themselves into one's memory, and are quite unforgetable; while behind the music of the words lies a shadow of subtle thought, sweet or sad, but beautiful always, and haunting one with a curious persistence. James H. Wilson will give us many another book I hope, justifying the fair promise of "Zalmoxis," which, however, even though it should always stand alone, clearly shows how well its author deserves the holy name of poet.

Orestes.

Bright and brighter! how it falls
That sweet sun on these grey walls.
How the storm-clouds and the gloom
For the blesséd light make room.
From my mind the darkness dies;
From my brain the madness flies;
Sister, raise my head awhile;
I will talk, and you shall smile.
Brighter still! it sends again
Summer memories through my brain;
When in tender days, we two
Laughed and played, as children do,
And the sunshine round us spread
Showed us pleasant paths to tread.
In the woods sweet sounds were heard;
In the woods dwelt every bird,

Up among the branches green,
Where the small brown nests were seen.

But the birds sang best of all
In one island, green and small.
In the stream that island stood,
Bright with flowers and thick with wood
And we said in childish joy
That charmed spot was famous Troy.
At the edge where willows grew,
Stood the sacred walls, we knew,
And the tall reeds round the coast
Were the countless Troian host.
We were valiant heroes then—
Children of the king of men ;
If we once that stream could ford,
Troy would tremble at our sword.
We would search each nook so green
We would reign there—king and queen—
And would sing such pleasant words
In the sunshine with the birds.

So we waded, I and you,
Naked-limbed the waters through,
But midway your courage died,
" Brother, bear me back !" you cried.
You forgot your greatness then—
Daughter of the king of men.
Sharply then I blamed your fear :
" Priam's sons your cries would hear.
How would Hector laugh for scorn,
And the chiefs in Ilium born ;
Our own heroes would deride,
Yea, the king, our father chide—

In his child dishonoured then,
Agamemnon, king of men."

Then you wept, because I chid ;
In your robe your face you hid :
(That small robe so white and fair,
Which in Argos children wear).

Ah, you smile ! that mimic Troy
Soon we reached with shouts of joy,
And we sang there pleasant words
In the sunshine with the birds.
When we told our fancies wild
To our mother—*how* she smiled !
Mother . . . mother . . . (I forgot)
Furies—hence ! approach me not.
Hideous hags, with snake-twined hair,
Get you gone—depart—forbear.
Dismal faces, mad with woe,
Sick with sorrow—let me go.
Savage scorpions, dread to name,
Tongues like swords, and eyes like flame.
Cursing mouths and scorching breath,
Hate and horror, blood and death !
Crawling monsters red with gore,
Writhing shapes, oh writhe no more.
Ravenous fangs ! that flesh is hot.
Hear it shriek ! oh, tear it not.
Shew no streaming wounds to me.
Close them. Hide them. Let them be.
If I sinned—if blood I spilt,
It was vengeance due to guilt.
His wronged ghost beset my path,
Filled my soul with sleepless wrath ;—

Then I did—oh what a deed!
But the gods that crime decreed.
Would such deed had ne'er been done!
No such mother! no such son!
Ah! you fade, as phantoms do;—
Gone . . . past . . . vanished . . . Sister? You?
Why, I thought that far away
You had fled, nor dared to stay.
Nay? you arms were round me? what?
And you spoke? I heard you not.
Called me "brother" soft and low?
Gentle girl, I did not know.
Fixed and stony, did you see
Glaring eyes which glared on me?
Pray the gods they come not back—
Foul and fierce, and filthy black.

Yes, my talk is wild indeed.
I was sick. 'Tis sleep I need.
If I sleep, I shall forget.
Lean your face down—closer yet.
Are those tears, which mark your cheek?
Nay, I know. You need not speak.
Though you fled not, when they came,
Though you stood here, all the same,
Yet you wept; I know you did.
In your robe your face you hid:
(That large robe, so queenly fair.
Which in Argos maidens wear).
Daughter of the king of men,
Weep not. All is well again.

Yes, I'm wearied. Sleep at last!
What good sleep brings! all seems past.

Wake me if he comes.—If who?
Why, the king. I thought you knew.
Far in Troy—but you forget ;
Such long years, and not come yet !
I can scarcely hear you now.
Yes, draw nearer. Stroke my brow.
Tell the watchman when the ships—
No tears needed ! kiss my lips !
If the king should come—the king—

.   .   .   .

Sister, *how* those birds do sing !
Walk beside me on the shore,
Children cross the stream no more.
Deep and wide the waters rush . . .
Let the birds sing . . . sister . . . hush.

How Long.

Love me not, dear, "till death us part,"
    Short union of a fragile life,
Keep me far longer in your heart,
    Closer than husband is to wife.

So when our souls have laid aside
    This home of flesh, these robes of clay,
The bridegroom still shall know his bride,
    And love her in that far-off day.

The Fairies' Glen at Melrose.

A morning in spring ! and the glory
    Of rivers which seawards run !
A joy in the glade and the woodland !
    The lifting of leaves to the sun !

And birds in the branches are singing
As gaily as ever they can :
And what do you want in our forest,
You lonely and sorrowful man ?

" I have wandered in shadow and tempest,
The skies have been clouded and grey :
Sing on, little birds, in the sunshine ;
The winter is past and away."

L' ENVOI.

DESERT so wild and grey—bare rocks—and wilderness places,
Here, O friends ! let me stray, though far from the sight of
your faces.
Whence were those bitter wails, those cries which awoke us
from slumber,
Tears from the darkness of jails, and sorrows which no man
can number?
These from the victims of hate, from the outcast sons of
oppression,—
Vengeance—the creed of the State ! and Law—the fierce Right
of Possession !
Lawgivers hard as the stone ! have ye joy of the wrecks ye are
making?
Flesh and blood like your own, but hearts that are broken and
breaking !

Onward the light crowd tread ; men are gay, and the feaster
carouses ;
Poets still dream of the dead, and embalm them, and build for
them houses.
Therefore I trampled my lute in the dust, and in silence I
ponder ;
Powerless to help, I am mute, and alone through the the wolds
I would wander.

What shall I find in the wilderness grey, save the dove and the
    swallow?

Shaken about by the wind, there are reeds for the mouth,
    smooth and hollow.

Each to his task! Ye are strong for the strife, and ye never
    did fear it.

I shall return with a song. Remember my words when ye
    hear it.

THOMAS HENRY WRIGHT.

THOMAS HENRY WRIGHT was born at Cork, in 1854. His father's family came originally from Plowland in Holderness, Yorkshire, where John Wright married in Henry IV.'s reign, Alice, daughter and co-heiress of John Ryther. Early in the 17th century the Wrights settled in Ireland. His mother was of German extraction. T. H. Wright was educated chiefly at a Friends' School, where the study of the Classics was discountenanced, and his acquaintance with Literature has been obtained by desultory but promiscuous reading. He left the Society of Friends in early life, and joined the Catholic Church. In 1886 he married Fanny Josephine Fisher, a member of the same communion, and like himself connected with Friends. They reside at present in Dublin. He has written many charming poems, some of which have appeared in the "Irish Monthly." I cannot help hoping that they will shortly be published in a collected form.

LOVE IN SILENCE.

"There was silence in heaven about the space of half-an-hour."

For one brief space within the heavenly choirs,
 The mighty wave of seraph harmonies
 Died on the shores of silence. Melodies
Of trailing sweetness sank upon the wires,
Like children that too great a pleasure tires.
 As evening stealeth on by slow degrees
 So stillness grew till not the faintest breeze
Of music trembled from th' angelic lyres.

Was there less love, when silence entered bliss
   And dropped like dew, upon the holy hill?
   Nay, doubly more!   Let thine ears drink their fill
Of lovers' vows; but, sweet, remember this;—
   I love more deeply that my lips are still,
Within the silence of the soul's abyss.

Lightning Source UK Ltd.
Milton Keynes UK
13 March 2010

151294UK00001B/41/P